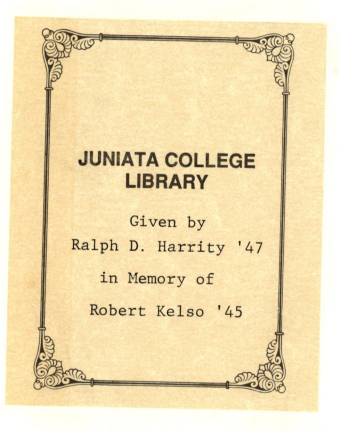

*Five Hundred Years of*

*Chinese Poetry,*

*1150–1650*

PRINCETON LIBRARY OF ASIAN TRANSLATIONS

# Five Hundred Years of Chinese Poetry, 1150–1650

The Chin, Yuan, and Ming Dynasties

YOSHIKAWA KŌJIRŌ

*Translated with a Preface by*
John Timothy Wixted

*Including an Afterword by*
William S. Atwell

PRINCETON UNIVERSITY PRESS

PRINCETON, NEW JERSEY

Copyright © 1989 by Princeton University Press
Published by Princeton University Press, 41 William Street,
Princeton, New Jersey 08540
In the United Kingdom: Princeton University Press, Guildford, Surrey

All Rights Reserved
English-language translation (and supplementary material) by arrangement with
the estate of the author.

This book has been composed in Linotron Galliard

Clothbound editions of Princeton University Press books are printed
on acid-free paper, and binding materials are chosen for strength and durability.
Paperbacks, although satisfactory for personal collections, are not usually suitable
for library rebinding

Printed in the United States of America by Princeton University Press,
Princeton, New Jersey

Translation of Kōjirō Yoshikawa, *Gen Min shi gaisetsu* (Chūgoku shijin senshū,
Series 2, Vol. 2) (Tokyo: Iwanami Shoten, 1963).

Library of Congress Cataloging-in-Publication Data
Yoshikawa, Kōjirō, 1904–
[Gen Min shi gaisetsu. English]
Five hundred years of Chinese poetry, 1150–1650 : the Chin, Yuan, and
Ming Dynasties / by Yoshikawa Kōjirō ; translated with a preface by
John Timothy Wixted.
p.  cm.
Translation of: Gen Min shi gaisetsu.
Includes index.
ISBN 0-691-06768-6
1. Chinese poetry—960–1644—History and criticism.  I. Wixted,
John Timothy. II. Title.
PL2322.5.Y6713 1989
895.1′14′09—dc19       88-37432

# Contents

PL
2322.5
.Y6713
1989

v

# Acknowledgments

I began work on the translation of this study in the late 1960s, as a doctoral candidate at Oxford University. While at the Research Institute for Humanistic Studies (Jimbun Kagaku Kenkyūjo) in Kyoto as a Research Associate from 1970 to 1972, I completed a draft translation of 80 percent of the work. I met twice monthly with the book's author, Yoshikawa Kōjirō, at the small office he had at the Haneda [Tōru] Kinenkan upon his retirement from the Literature Department of Kyoto University. We would go over a new installment of the translation and discuss any problems. In 1977, I revised the more than 150 classical Chinese verse translations that appear in the work. The author passed away in 1980. In 1987, after a decade of teaching, writing, and editing, I returned to the task of putting the work's modern Japanese text and classical Chinese poems into final English form. The help of numerous friends and colleagues over the years is most gratefully acknowledged as follows.

Burton Watson and Philip Williams kindly read the entire final draft of the manuscript and offered a variety of comments; among other talents, both have an excellent sense of the rhythms of English. William S. Atwell not only consented to critique the final manuscript and to write an Afterword to the work but also, during our graduate-student days together in Kyoto, read sections of the translation. William Hung went over most of the poem translations and offered numerous improvements and comments that proved invaluable. Andrew Plaks and Lin Shuen-fu served as readers for Princeton University Press, making thoughtful suggestions and corrections. Others at the Press were also helpful: Margaret Case, Beth Gianfagna, and especially Deborah Del Gais Muller. The following scholars kindly read one or more chapters of an early draft of part of the translation, making all manner of useful comment: David Hawkes, David R. Knechtges, Stephen Owen, and Robert M. Somers. Stephen Owen, in particular, took pains to offer detailed suggestions; Burton Watson and Sandra A. Wixted also made useful critical comments at this stage. Okagawa Nagao and Saegusa Kyōko thoughtfully clarified troublesome passages in Japanese. Paul Balaran and Paul D. Buell graciously corrected the romanization of Mongolian names. And Eugenia Y. Tu and Chou Ju-hsi helped clarify a residuum of puzzling passages in Chinese.

Necessary encouragement for the undertaking also came from Glen W. Baxter, Joshua Fogel, Mr. and Mrs. Takasuna Hiroo, and John F. and Julia L. Wixted. Yoshikawa Tadao, the author's son, kindly expedited copyright and other arrangements.

When doing final preparation of the manuscript, I availed myself of Charles O. Hucker's *A Dictionary of Official Titles in Imperial China* (Stanford: Stanford University Press, 1985) and Cheng Ch'ing-mao's Chinese-language translation of the work (see the Translator's Preface, note 7, for full citation).

Grant support for the project came from the Center for Chinese Studies of the University of Michigan, the Faculty Grant-in-Aid Program of Arizona State University, and Arizona State University's Mini-Grant Program. Part of the work was completed under a Language and Research Fellowship funded by the Committee on Scientific and Scholarly Cooperation with the United States (Academia Sinica, Taiwan).

# Translator's Preface

Yoshikawa Kōjirō wrote highly scholarly book-length studies on Yuan drama, on the poetry of Tu Fu, and on the *Shu ching*, or *Classic of Documents*. He also wrote popular works of scholarship on Chinese literature, especially T'ang poetry, that became best-sellers in Japan. In addition, he wrote articles that tend to fall somewhere between specialist pieces and popular ones, covering virtually every period of Chinese literature and most major literary figures. *Five Hundred Years of Chinese Poetry, 1150–1650* belongs to this last category. The second of a pair of introductory volumes to a series of books edited by the author and his Kyoto University colleague, Ogawa Tamaki, this book was designed for a broad readership, to whose more specialized interests it appealed. The series—devoted to traditional Chinese poetry of the Sung period and later—included ground-breaking volumes on individual authors who had scarcely been treated by earlier Chinese and Japanese scholars. Like the first introductory volume of the pair, the author's *An Introduction to Sung Poetry*,[1] this volume provided an overview of an entire period. It was both less specialized than the other volumes in the series and demanded more the perspective of a seasoned senior scholar.

Yoshikawa Kōjirō was such a scholar, and he wrote this study much in the tradition of Chinese *shih-hua*, or "causeries on poetry," which date back to the Sung dynasty. It is not that a *shih-hua* author would write a treatise on poetry or poetics to convince the reader through his argumentation that the views he was offering were correct. The words of a *shih-hua* generally have value because they are stated by the personality who is writing them: he is an important or interesting figure, usually one of wide learning.[2]

---

[1] See Introduction, n. 7, for complete citation.

[2] The author was such a figure, being the doyen of traditional Chinese studies in Japan and the most famous Japanese scholar of Chinese literature of the cen-

Such works were normally written in random or anecdotal fashion, sometimes with an almost stylized idiosyncracy. This study by Yoshikawa Kōjirō, although definitely in that tradition, is considerably more coherent in argument than most *shih-hua*.

Popular scholarly work has long garnered a large audience in Japan. Works of high quality by well-known modern scholars have circulated quite widely—for example, Nakane Chie's study of the structure of Japanese society or Ishida Eiichirō's work on comparative anthropology. In the 1950s and 1960s, publishers ventured to issue numerous multivolume series on Chinese literary and philosophical works to a public well-known for its avid book buying. Their issuance was prompted in part by interest in China, in Chinese culture, and in the Chinese background to Japanese culture. Such circumstances marked the appearance of the innovative series of volumes on major Sung and later Chinese poets for which the present work serves as an introduction.

The present study should be viewed as developing from these two strains: the Chinese *shih-hua* tradition of informal, anecdotal discussion of poetry, and the *haute vulgarisation* of scholarship in Japanese trade publishing at its best.

*Five Hundred Years of Chinese Poetry, 1150–1650* does not pretend to offer a comprehensive history of the poetry of the period. Nor does it present literary analysis of the poetic work it introduces—analysis as understood by students of New Criticism or later critical movements in the West. The volume is the only historical survey available, in any language, of Chinese poetry during the five-hundred-year period it treats.[3] As such, it offers something that might be likened to a tour of a wilderness area, one conducted by an especially experienced and intelligent guide who wants his charges both to learn from the experience and to enjoy it. Leading us into an uncharted region, the author points out its general fea-

---

tury. Moreover, what Yoshikawa Kōjirō has to say about poetry of the Chin, Yuan, and Ming dynasties—that it continues to be the most important literary genre over the period—carries special weight, as it is being said by one of the outstanding scholars of that period's fiction (specifically, its drama).

[3] There are survey histories of Yuan poetry, general surveys of the entire span of Chinese poetry and/or literature, and anthologies of Chinese poetry that include selections from the period.

tures, draws our attention to new and different phenomena, and pauses to introduce major items (and numerous minor ones), all the while taking pains to keep the entire amble interesting. In a word, this is old-fashioned literary history at its best.[4]

Yoshikawa Kōjirō's work also represents a balance of a different sort, one of literary style. Many (indeed, most) Japanese scholars of traditional China write works in turgid language, seldom straying from the use of learned Chinese compounds to write in a Japanese that can seem more intended to impress the reader with the author's earnest scholarliness than to communicate material clearly in what is supposed to be the author's native language. Such style is not unlike that of classical scholars or others in the West who write a very Greek or Latinate English or who, with little or no explanation, freely cite a host of technical terms that are virtually incomprehensible to the nonspecialist, intelligent reader.

By the same token, with the admirable intent of writing in a Japanese that contemporary readers can understand, a number of other Japanese sinologists have taken to writing in natural, modern Japanese. When done skillfully, the results can be admirable. What not infrequently happens, however, is that their writing becomes terribly prolix. Five characters in the line of an original Chinese poem, when translated, can become three lengthy lines of Japanese paraphrase; and much the same material may be rehashed in a footnote. Here and elsewhere in their work, what such authors really need is nothing so much as a good editing.

Yoshikawa Kōjirō belongs to neither of these categories. Writing in a particularly plain modern Japanese by sinological standards, he does not hesitate to insert the occasional *bon mot* in the form of an apt, but unusual (for modern readers) Chinese compound. Many of his sentences are quite short, being interspersed with longer ones; and occasionally there is the involved or convoluted sentence. The combination makes for fluid pacing. Clearly the author wanted his audience to enjoy what he has to say while

---

[4] It offers much the same pleasure that one can derive from reading Van Wyck Brooks, *The Flowering of New England, 1815–1865* (Boston: Houghton Mifflin Co., 1936; rpt. 1981), and other such titles.

reading it. He is never prolix; if anything, he errs in the opposite direction. In a word, he strikes a pleasing stylistic balance.[5]

Yoshikawa Kōjirō's renown among Japanese intellectuals in fields totally unrelated to his own stems largely from the informed readability of his writing. The famous twentieth-century *haiku* poet Nakamura Kusadao once told the translator how much he enjoyed reading Yoshikawa Kōjirō's work, mostly for the reasons just outlined.[6]

I suggest to those interested in checking the Japanese-language original of this study that they also consult Cheng Ch'ing-mao's fine Chinese-language translation of the work.[7] It is invaluable for its citation of the original Chinese for most prose excerpts in the work (which appear only in Japanese translation in the original). The Chinese version also occasionally includes supplemental passages that are cited from original sources (histories, biographies, and collected writings) to bolster the author's discussion of individual poets. Cheng Ch'ing-mao cites the original Chinese texts of the numerous poems that appear in the study, translating into modern Chinese only the author's appended notes on specific turns of phrase and poem lines or occasional paraphrasings of an entire poem. Otherwise, consistent with Chinese scholarly practice, there are no translations of the original poems into modern Chinese.

The Japanese original of the work is worth consulting for the "parsing" (*kundoku*) apparatus that is appended to all of the poems cited; this is the system of notation that has traditionally been used by Japanese to explicate classical Chinese. Generally, it is helpful to have such material in addition to the original Chinese poem-text, as the author frequently must indicate how he understands the use of words or phrases in an original poem; the notation may indicate whether a term is used as a verb, verb object, topic, or

---

[5] It is also true that the author wrote parts of this volume in haste. He skimped in clarifying some of its points and certainly developed others meagerly. And certain metaphors are overworked (toned down in translation), betraying the signs of perfunctory editing.

[6] Needless to say, I hope this translation creates an acceptable English-language analogue to the original.

[7] *Yuan Ming shih kai-shuo* (Taipei: Yu-shih wen-hua shih-yeh kung-ssu, 1986).

adverb and, if as a verb, whether it is construed as being passive, causative, or the like.

In making this translation, I had to commit myself in English in ways that neither Yoshikawa Kōjirō nor Cheng Ch'ing-mao was forced to do when treating the dozens of classical Chinese poems that are cited. English offers neither the option of simply indicating the constituent grammatical elements of a Chinese poem nor that of merely quoting the original poem without comment.

When I understand a line or passage in one of the poems in a way that clearly differs from the author's parsing or occasional paraphrasing of it into Japanese, I render the author's interpretation in the body of the text and offer my alternative in a footnote. Of course, in many instances, because of the nature of Japanese *kundoku* "construing" of Chinese texts, the author's interpretation of a poem is vague or opaque at best. It is worth noting, however, that on more than one occasion when I asked Yoshikawa Kōjirō which of two renderings of a passage he thought more correct, he shrugged his shoulders and said he did not know.[8]

Yoshikawa Kōjirō's study is useful for the parallels it draws between Chinese and Japanese literature, history, and thought, especially the influences of the one on the other. In order to keep the argument of the translation focused on Chinese poetry, however, I have removed most such material to the footnotes. It adds an interesting and important dimension to the work.[9]

I have not hesitated to rearrange material from the original in my translation so as to make it more consistent with the expectations of English-language readers. Most such adjustments are minor (e.g., placing the explication of a poem line immediately before the citation of that poem rather than after). One chapter in the original, however, has been divided in two, to form the Introduction and chapter 1 of the translation. This serves to make chapter

---

[8] This was an endearing quality of the man (and a rare one among famous scholars of Chinese literature, as many readers will appreciate).

[9] The only other book-length volume by the author translated into English (apart from the one noted on Sung poetry) treats similar issues: *Jinsai, Sorai, and Norinaga: Three Classical Philosophers of Mid-Tokugawa Japan*, trans. Kikuchi Yūji (Tokyo: Tōhō Gakkai, 1983).

1, which deals with the nature of Chinese poetry of the later imperial dynasties, consistent with *An Introduction to Sung Poetry*,
where the first chapter treats the nature of Sung poetry. Also, inasmuch as the discussion of Yuan Hao-wen in chapter 2 is hard to
follow as originally ordered, I have rearranged the author's treatment so that it falls more clearly into two segments: chronological
discussion of the poet's life and work, and general discussion of
his literary theory.

Virtually all that is included in the original work appears in the
translation, except for secondary names of poets or rulers (i.e., literary or posthumous names), dates needlessly repeated in terms of
reign periods (e.g., "1593 or Wan-li 22" is rendered simply as
"1593"), explication of poem lines clearly incorporated in the
translations, and a few redundant references by the author to his
own published work. The only important exception to this is the
abridged version of Ho Ching-ming's "Song of the Bright
Moon," which appears in chapter 7. The author cites the entire
poem, minus any commentary other than minimal *kundoku* annotation; as the poem is a long pastiche of allusions that make
little or no sense without lengthy explication, I decided that the
present excerpts adequately suggest the nature of the piece.

As for material that has been added to the original, most such
items are clearly identifiable by being enclosed in brackets in the
notes. Many minor explanatory points have been inserted in the
text (and occasionally in the author's notes) without such notation.

There is a small body of detail, however, that differs from the
original and is not so identified. It consists mostly of corrections
of minor misprints and errors in the original: incorrect dates,
poem titles incorrectly or incompletely cited, characters misprinted in the poems, and inadequate or misleading citation of
official titles. Some of these were pointed out to me personally by
the author. A few such corrections were noted by Japanese reviewers of the original book. Some are indicated by the author in the
three-page supplement and list of corrections that he appended to
the study, as reprinted in volume fifteen of his collected work.[10]
Several such items are rectified by Cheng Ch'ing-mao in his

---

[10] See Introduction, n. 1, for complete citation.

Chinese-language translation of the volume, and I corrected some in passing. It would be pedantic and cumbersome to list these in detail.

Citations in the translation have been kept to a minimum. They are mostly restricted to Western-language items, as specialists are presumed to know where to find relevant Chinese- and Japanese-language material. Moreover, with few exceptions, the notes refer only to *book-length* Western-language studies of *poets* treated in this survey. There are many books on the history of the period and a wealth of articles in English and other Western languages on many of the figures treated.

By the same token, I have indicated other Western-language translations only for those poems that are cited in their entirety.[11] There may be other renderings, complete or partial, of poems quoted here in excerpt form (sometimes only with a single couplet). Those that are pointed out are indicated simply as a courtesy to the reader. Except for some noted in chapters 2 and 3, most such translations were not in print during the long gestation period for the renderings in this volume.

Those who find the poetry of the period of interest might also wish to consult, in addition to the author's *An Introduction to Sung Poetry*, two recent anthologies directly related to the subject of this work: Jonathan Chaves, trans. and ed., *The Columbia Book of Later Chinese Poetry: Yüan, Ming, and Ch'ing Dynasties (1279–1911)* (New York: Columbia University Press, 1986), and Irving Yu-cheng Lo and William Schultz, eds., *Waiting for the Unicorn: Poems and Lyrics of China's Last Dynasty, 1644–1911* (Bloomington: Indiana University Press, 1986).[12] The first contains copious translations of the period's poetry, including works by several poets treated in this volume. The second discusses in its introduction some of the points brought up here in chapter 1 about Chinese poetry of the later imperial dynasties; also, the work can be read as a sequel to this volume, for it extends the author's treat-

---

[11] The only exception is in reference to the most famous poem by Kao Ch'i.

[12] Note also the published character text for the latter volume: Irving Yucheng Lo and William Schultz, eds., *Tan Lin Chi* (Bloomington: Indiana University Press, 1987).

ment of the Chin-through-Ming period into the subsequent
Ch'ing dynasty, as he himself had hoped to do. The following vol-
umes, which have articles on many of the figures treated in this
work, are also quite helpful: William H. Nienhauser, Jr., ed. and
comp., *The Indiana Companion to Traditional Chinese Literature*
(Bloomington: Indiana University Press, 1986), and L. Carring-
ton Goodrich and Fang Chaoying, eds., *Dictionary of Ming Biog-
raphy, 1368–1644* (New York: Columbia University Press, 1976).
Two additional works include entries on some of the figures
treated in the opening and closing chapters of Yoshikawa's study:
Herbert Franke, ed., *Sung Biographies*, 4 vols. (Wiesbaden: Franz
Steiner, 1976), and Arthur W. Hummel, ed., *Eminent Chinese of
the Ch'ing Period* (Washington, D.C.: U.S. Government Printing
Office, 1943–44; rpt. Taipei: Literature House, 1964).

Yoshikawa Kōjirō indicated to me that there was a contemporary
dimension to his study. He found much similarity between Chu
Yuan-chang, the Founder Emperor of the Ming dynasty, and Mao
Tse-tung. Various parallels are implicitly drawn between the two.
Chu and Mao were of similar origins; both brought the empire
under unified Chinese rule after domination by foreigners; like the
Founder Emperor, the Great Helmsman distrusted intellectuals
and suppressed them; and the two had similar policies for the
countryside and cities. (It is no accident that the author uses the
term "contradiction"—one strongly suggestive of Mao's famous
article, "On Contradiction"—to characterize the thinking that
prompted Chu Yuan-chang's policy of bolstering rural areas at the
expense of urban ones.) One might find additional similarities. I
cannot recall whether the author saw a parallel between Chou En-
lai and Liu Chi. Whatever the case, it is worth noting that this
volume was written at a time when uncritical enthusiasm among
Japanese intellectuals for Mao Tse-tung and the post-1949 China
of the time was especially high.

Dates are reported as they appear in the original work, that is, in
lunar-calendar terms. Birth and death dates of writers have been
added; poets' ages are given in Western count. Names (other than
Westernized ones) are given in Chinese and Japanese word order,
surname first.

In romanizing Chinese personal names, place names, and book titles, I have used the modified Wade-Giles system that is followed by the Council on East Asian Studies of Harvard University in most of its publications. That is to say, umlauts are used only in those syllables where it is critical to distinguish between renderings (e.g., *yü* as opposed to *yu*) and otherwise are dropped (from *yuan*, *hsu*, etc.).

For more information about Yoshikawa Kōjirō and his work, the reader is directed to the numerous Japanese-, Chinese-, and Western-language bibliographical and biographical entries for him that appear in the following: John Timothy Wixted, "Japanese Scholars of China: A Bibliographic Handbook," Unpublished manuscript.[13]

*Five Hundred Years of Chinese Poetry, 1150–1650* comprises slightly less than one-third of one volume—out of a total of twenty-eight volumes—in the complete collected edition of the author's work. Thus one can roughly calculate that the study represents slightly more than 1 percent of Yoshikawa Kōjirō's published work.

At the end of chapter 4, the author relates that Ku Ssu-li, the compiler of the *Yuan-shih hsuan*, or *Anthology of Yuan Poetry*, dreamed one night that dozens of men dressed in ancient court garb surrounded him and bowed, thanking him for his efforts in making their writing again available to the world. I venture to hope that Yoshikawa Kōjirō will approve of this translation and perhaps bow in my dreams.

TEMPE, ARIZONA

*June 1988*

[13] Western-language material on Yoshikawa Kōjirō includes J. P. Diény, "Yoshikawa Kōjirō (1904–1980)," *T'oung Pao* 67 (1981): 4–9; and "In Memoriam: Tributes to Kōjirō Yoshikawa, 1904–1980," Columbia University, May 8, 1980, a booklet of reminiscences of the author read at a memorial service for him (a copy of this comparatively rare item can be found in the Harvard-Yenching Library, cataloged as W2289.8/393).

*Five Hundred Years of*

*Chinese Poetry,*

*1150–1650*

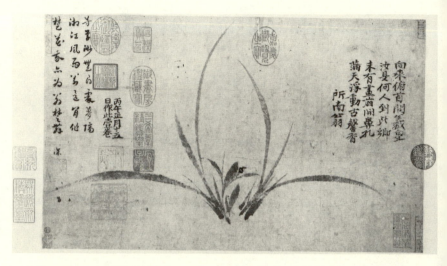

Cheng Ssu-hsiao, "Orchid," discussed on pp. 62–63, dated 1306. Handscroll, ink on paper, 25.7 × 42.4 cm. *Osaka Municipal Museum of Art, Abe Collection.*

# INTRODUCTION

Chinese poetry of the later imperial period—that is, of the Chin, Yuan, Ming, and Ching dynasties—has not received favorable treatment at the hands of literary historians in recent times. The standard view has been that the period's drama and vernacular fiction are what is important and that its poetry can either be slighted or ignored.

The literary history of this period is different from that of the preceding age. Earlier, that is, from Han times, passing through the Six Dynasties and T'ang periods, up to and including the Sung dynasty, poetry and nonfiction prose comprised the entire realm of letters in China. As for the small amount of fiction available, it consisted merely of "tales of the marvelous" (*ch'uan-ch'i*) by T'ang writers. In Yuan and later periods, however, fiction appeared in a virtual flood. Dramatic works, ushered in by thirteenth-century *tsa-chü* plays, were to flourish in the Ming and Ch'ing dynasties.[1] And in the late Yuan and early Ming period of the fourteenth cen-

---

[1] See my *Gen zatsugeki kenkyū* (Researches on Yuan Drama), 1948; reprinted in *Yoshikawa Kōjirō zenshū* (Collected Writings of Yoshikawa Kōjirō) (Tokyo: Chikuma Shobō, 1968–70, 20 vols.; 1973–75, 24 vols.; 1986–, 28 vols.), 14: 3–355. [Hereafter notes by the translator are enclosed in brackets.]

3

tury, the *Shui-hu chuan* and *San-kuo-chih yen-i* marked the formal beginning of Chinese vernacular fiction. In the Ming dynasty, the great vernacular novels *Hsi-yu chi* and *Chin p'ing mei* appeared. And China's most famous novel, the *Hung-lou meng*, was written during the Ch'ing period.[2] Thus fiction, in the form of the new literary genres of the period, and poetry and nonfiction prose in traditional literary forms, were all produced in great quantity over the later imperial period.

Only in the twentieth century did the task of systematically writing the literary history of China begin there or in Japan. In treating the period from Chin and Yuan times through the Ch'ing dynasty, Chinese and Japanese literary historians were interested only in the new literary genres, drama and vernacular fiction; the period's poetry and nonfiction prose were either deprecated or ignored.

One factor accounting for this was the introduction to Asia of the view that fiction, beginning with Homer, was central to the development of Western literature. It was felt that in East Asia as well, it was fiction that was of prime importance in literary study—an attitude in evidence in Japan by the late Meiji period (1868–1912), earlier than it appeared in China. As fiction had traditionally been looked down upon in premodern China, it absorbed scholars' interests earlier this century both because it was a new field of learning and because there was little written about its development. This helps explain scholarly emphasis in this area in recent decades.

There is a more important reason as well. In the early years after the establishment of the Chinese Republic in 1912, the Chinese-language reform movement took place—the so-called

---

[2] [The published English-language translations of these novels are titled as follows:

| | |
|---|---|
| *Shui-hu chuan* | *Water Margin*, *All Men Are Brothers*, and *Outlaws of the Marsh* |
| *San-kuo-chih yen-i* | *Romance of the Three Kingdoms* and *Three Kingdoms: China's Epic Drama* |
| *Hsi-yu chi* | *Journey to the West*, *Monkey*, and *The Journey to the West* |
| *Chin p'ing mei* | *Golden Lotus* and *Hsi Men and His Wives* |
| *Hung-lou meng* | *Dream of Red Mansions*, *The Story of the Stone*, and *The Dream of the Red Chamber*] |

Literary Revolution led by Hu Shih. It was successful in changing the official, public language from the literary (or classical) to the vernacular. Although laudable, it had the secondary effect of changing the criteria used for evaluating past literature. Poetry and nonfiction prose of premodern times were written in the literary language; but the nonfiction literature that newly emerged over the period being discussed here, in the form of drama, vernacular fiction, and the like, was new also in that it used the spoken language for expression. Literary scholars earlier this century misconstrued this fact and held that the difference between the two types of expression, literary and spoken, also determined their literary value. As a result, because poetry of the later imperial dynasties is written in the literary language, it was slighted, ignored, or scorned; and for the sole reason that the spoken language is used in drama, vernacular fiction, and other fiction forms, they received undeservedly high praise.[3]

With more of a basis in fact, some scholars have argued that because the poetry of the later imperial dynasties made conscious use of literary models, it was always dull; and because drama and vernacular fiction were new literary forms, they were always vigorous. Another view that has been current is that poetry, by virtue of its ancient heritage, always served to defend a conservative, "feudal" tradition; and that drama and vernacular fiction, by way of contrast, were written in conscious opposition to tradition.

I consider such views but a temporary deflection on the way toward achieving a proper understanding of the history of later Chinese literature. For authors of the Chin, Yuan, Ming, and Ch'ing dynasties, as for those of preceding periods, it was poetry and nonfiction prose that formed the heart of Chinese writing. It is to these literary forms, and especially to poetry, that one must look for their most serious expression of feeling. In contrast, since drama and vernacular fiction were considered second- or third-rate literature until the Literary Revolution of this century, it was rare for anything serious to be written in these genres.[4] Novels or

---

[3] For more about the relationship between Chinese written and spoken language I refer the reader to my work, *Kambun no hanashi* (On Chinese Texts), 1962; reprinted in *Yoshikawa Kōjirō zenshū*, 2: 56–202.

[4] I might assure the reader in passing, I am no novice when it comes to Chinese drama and vernacular fiction.

stories written with a self-awareness of the value of fiction, like the *Tale of Genji* in Japan, scarcely existed in China prior to the appearance of Lu Hsun, who was active in the first part of this century.

In view of this, I feel poetry should be given prime importance in the study of the literature of the later imperial dynasties. Put another way, proper understanding of the period's literature is impossible if one excludes its poetry. Since the judgment of literary value by the sole criterion of the kind of language it uses, either literary or colloquial, was a hasty (and largely political) decision made earlier this century, I think the time has come that it be reconsidered. Also, to base a work's literary value on whether it is (a) fiction or (b) poetry or nonfiction is to display shallow judgment based on half-understood Western literary history. Even if the literary forte of the West since the time of Homer has been fiction, East Asia can justly stress poetry and nonfiction, especially poetry, as its special skill—one in which the West has been comparatively lacking.

It is important for social history as well that leaders of poetry in the later imperial period were townsmen.[5] Examination of the relationship between this stratum of society and the poetry of the time can provide a more correct understanding of the history of drama and vernacular fiction, the only writing literary historians until now have treated as being "townsman literature."

It appears in most cases that it was only after having first attained proficiency in writing poetry that townsmen poured their remaining energy into the writing of fiction. If such was the case, the two were in a complementary rather than a contradictory relationship. The fact that the rise and decline of poetry and the rise and decline of drama and vernacular fiction largely trace parallel lines is probably the best proof of this, as is well illustrated by the situation in Ming times.[6] Thus, if there were "feudal characteristics" in poetry, they were present also in drama and vernacular

---

[5] An understanding of the history and value of the period's Chinese literature would probably also provide important hints for considering the same problems in Japanese *waka* and *haiku* poetry. Were they, in fact, "secondary arts" or not?

[6] Of course, the two did not invariably trace parallel lines. *Tsa-chü* rose in the Yuan dynasty while poetry was in decline and vice versa. But even granting this, while studying the one area one cannot ignore the circumstances operative in the other, nonparallel area.

fiction; conversely, if there was an awareness of "opposition to tradition" in drama and vernacular fiction, it was also present in poetry. Study of the history of the period's poetry is important not only in its own right; it is also important for the history of the period's drama and vernacular fiction.

It appears that scholars are gradually correcting the earlier skewing of the period's literary history. A desire to redress the balance has been operative in recent literary histories by Chinese; but I feel it has not been strong enough. Besides, the impetus to advocate poetry and nonfiction prose as the special province of East Asian literature has been lacking.

Written with these considerations in mind, my book is only an exploratory effort, not a comprehensive study. What makes the undertaking especially difficult is the immensity of the material at hand. Such was already the case for the Sung period, treated in my earlier work, *An Introduction to Sung Poetry*.[7] I pointed out there how the total number of poets included in the *Sung-shih chi-shih*, or *Notes on Sung Poetry*, 3,812, was nearly twice the number included in the *Ch'üan T'ang-shih*, or *Complete Poems of the T'ang Dynasty*, more than 2,200; and how the great poets of the Sung were all voluminous writers. Yet these tendencies accelerated in the later imperial dynasties, both because a broad stratum of townsmen became poets and because the fecundity of Sung poetry was continued. The compilation of a complete record of the poems of one of the periods here under study, in the form of the *Complete Poems of the T'ang Dynasty*, has appeared only with the *Ch'üan Chin-shih*, or *Complete Poems of the Chin Dynasty*. A *Complete Poems of the Yuan Dynasty* is the collection most likely next to appear. As for a *Complete Poems of the Ming Dynasty* or *Complete Poems of the Ch'ing Dynasty*, there is little possibility of their appearing, even at some time in the future.

The flow of Chinese poetry is like a great river. I am already sixty years old and have scarcely read 1 percent of the giant stream. Work must be carried on by younger scholars.

---

[7] *Sōshi gaisetsu*, 1952; reprinted in *Yoshikawa Kōjirō zenshū*, 13: 3–196. [Translated into English by Burton Watson, *An Introduction to Sung Poetry* (Cambridge, Mass.: Harvard University Press, 1967); also translated into Chinese by Cheng Ch'ing-mao, *Sung-shih kai-shuo* (Taipei: Lien-ching ch'u-pan shih-yeh kung-ssu, 1977). Page citations hereafter refer to the English version.]

# Chapter 1

# CHINESE POETRY OF THE
# LATER IMPERIAL DYNASTIES

I hope to outline in this volume and in a subsequent one the history of Chinese poetry from Chin and Yuan times, through the Ming period, up to the end of the Ch'ing dynasty—that is, from the mid-twelfth century until our own. This volume treats roughly the first half of this period, until the end of the Ming dynasty.[1] It marks a continuation of my earlier study of Sung period poetry.[2]

What is meant by "poetry" here is the term *shih* in its narrow sense in Chinese. That is to say, it refers to poems in the three genres of poetry that took final shape in T'ang times: "old-style poems" (*ku-shih*), "regulated verse" (*lü-shih*), and "quatrains" (*chüeh-chü*).[3] It is my intention to outline briefly how such writing continued the earlier poetic tradition and in what ways it devel-

[1] [No draft of a complementary volume treating the poetry of the Ch'ing dynasty was completed by the time of the author's death in 1980.]

[2] *An Introduction to Sung Poetry*; see Introduction, n. 7.

[3] For discussion of these poetic forms, see Ogawa Tamaki, *Tōshi gaisetsu* (An Outline of T'ang Poetry) (Tokyo: Iwanami Shoten, 1968), pp. 94–121. They comprise what is called *kanshi* in Japanese.

oped over the nearly eight-hundred-year span of the Chin, Yuan, Ming, and Ch'ing dynasties.

Heir to the tradition of earlier ages, poetry was the most important literary form of the Chinese people. Over the period under consideration, it continued to display uninterrupted development through a staggering number of poets and poems. Its development gives the lie to the overly rash estimation of "Oriental stagnation" and reflects the continued material and spiritual development of Chinese civilization. Poetry was a literary form having an ancient tradition, and the writing of poetry carried with it a consciousness of being the guardian of tradition. But at the same time poetry was also the literary form that expressed most faithfully both the new emotions springing up spontaneously from within the people over succeeding ages and their reactions to new realities they were daily confronting.

Yet the poems of what is here called the later imperial dynasties were written under circumstances that differed from earlier times in two ways. First, poetry became a literary form in the production of which a broad stratum of people participated. Most leaders in the world of poetry were ordinary townsmen rather than officials. In the history of earlier Chinese poetry poets, until the end of T'ang times or even until the end of the Northern Sung, were as a rule "specialists" in poetry; at the same time, they were either government officials or were striving to become such. Han Yü and Po Chü-i in T'ang times, as well as Ou-yang Hsiu, Wang An-shih, and Su Shih in the Northern Sung, besides being poets representative of their respective periods, were ministry-level officials in their time; and China's most famous poets, Li Po and Tu Fu, sought rank in government and failed. This situation began to change in the thirteenth century, from the final years of the Southern Sung onward. In the last chapter of my previous volume on Sung poetry, I noted that poems of the late Southern Sung were written not by officials but by townsmen. This marked the beginning of a future trend; with each later dynasty, the situation became more pronounced. In Yuan times, the Mongol regime restricted the participation of Chinese in government, which served to turn the energies of a still greater number of townsmen in the direction of poetry. Again in Ming times, because the structure of government was such that men of townsman origins more readily came into their own, the phenomenon of a broad stratum of people participating in the writing of poetry became even more pronounced. And the pattern carried over into the subsequent Ch'ing period.

Of course, officials of the time also wrote poems. Indeed, the writing of poetry was a necessary prerequisite for qualification as an official. But officials of the later imperial dynasties were degree holders (at least *hsiu-ts'ai*, or "flourishing talents," i.e., preliminary graduates) who came from the ranks of townsmen and obtained government position after having participated in the public government-service examination. A distinguishing characteristic of Sung and later Chinese society was the disappearance of the aristocratic order. This characteristic was special not only to this period in China, it also distinguished China from the rest of the contemporary world. Although the system of inheriting position by birth existed to some degree through T'ang times, it had disappeared by the Sung. The officials of later dynasties were ordinary townsmen who gained their position in government not through family status but by individual ability.[4] As a result, their lives were never completely cut off, either physically or psychologically, from the lives of ordinary townsmen. This being the case, officials of townsman origins frequently became the leaders of townsman poetry,[5] which in turn helped stimulate a further increase in the number of townsman poets. Over this nearly eight-hundred-year period there quietly unfolded a situation in which thousands to tens of thousands of poets, or at least people having minimal ability to write verse, became conscious of themselves as writers of poetry.[6] The area of highest density for this was in the provinces of the lower Yangtze Delta, namely in Kiangsu, Chekiang, and Anhwei, as well as in Kiangsi. But with variation of density it prevailed throughout the empire.

What has been discussed above is the first and main feature differentiating poetry of this period from earlier Chinese poetry.

---

[4] Su Shih offers an early example in the Sung period. It is possible that until his grandfather's generation his ancestors were cloth merchants.

[5] The Earlier and Later Seven Masters of the Ming, discussed in chap. 7, serve as cases in point.

[6] Just as in Japan today the number of *waka* and *haiku* writers reaches several tens of thousands, such a situation took hold quite early in China.

As it is something I feel scholars until now have insufficiently stressed, it should be pointed out first as the most important feature of the age.

The second difference between the poetry of the later imperial dynasties and earlier verse is the growing use of past poetry as a model to be followed in the writing of one's own verse.[7] From the Yuan dynasty on, this tendency became much more pronounced. Such a development was perhaps inevitable, given the spread of poetry writing and the increase in the number of poets. Generally speaking, over the period under discussion it was T'ang poetry that served most as the literary model to be followed. In T'ang times the three genres of poetry, old-style verse, regulated verse, and the quatrain, had become fully established. It was natural that, in terms of both diction and emotional content, T'ang poetry was often looked back upon as a model. Respect for T'ang poetry rose from the end of the Sung on into the Yuan dynasty. And in Ming times, especially in the sixteenth century during the time of the so-called Old Phraseology (*Ku-wen-tz'u*) movement, T'ang poetry became the model to be emulated to the exclusion of all others. In cases where it was felt that the imitation of T'ang poetry, with its emphasis on the lyrical, was not adequate to treating realities that were daily growing more complicated, the more discursive and rationalistic poetry of the Sung became the secondary model to be followed;[8] and even from among T'ang poets, writers whose style was closer to Sung poetry, like Po Chü-i, were added as models. It is not until quite late, in the final years of the Ch'ing dynasty, that the exclusive use of Sung poetic models first developed.[9]

These two distinguishing features of Chinese poetry of the later imperial dynasties—the increased number of poets and the

---

[7] Earlier poets, of course, stood indebted to their predecessors. Even Tu Fu had spoken of the models for his poetry: "Thoroughly verse yourselves in the principle behind the *Wen hsuan* (Literary Selections)"; "Cut yourselves free from false style! Come close to the *Shih ching* (Classic of Songs); / Then will the many masters be your guide."

[8] See *An Introduction to Sung Poetry*, chap. 1, "The Nature of Sung Poetry."

[9] The situation in Japan is analagous. *Waka* poetry writing long had either the *Man'yōshū* (A Collection of Myriad Leaves) or the *Kokinshū* (A Collection of Poetry Ancient and Modern) as a model. It was only in the late Edo (1603–1867) and early Meiji periods that the *Man'yōshū* became the exclusive *waka* model.

use of poetic models—were either new to the history of poetry or were much more in evidence than before. Each had its good and bad effects on the writing of the age.

As a bad feature of the new milieu, the use of literary models often produced insipid, weak, carelessly written, vapid, or lifeless poems that merely imitated the external features of their models. The increase in the number of poets and their fecundity made this all the more likely.

Yet there were good features as well. The increase in the number of poets afforded greater occasion for the emergence of reflective, discerning writers. For such poets literary models worked in a positive way as something that heightened poetic intensity. Especially important is the fact that a large number of townsmen took part, as poets of some ability, in the production of literature. They formed a newly ascendant social stratum (comprising a different percentage in each dynasty) that sought to express its vitality first of all in poetry. It was they who first sensitively absorbed the new realities taking shape around them and gave expression to them. In addition, the Neo-Confucianism that Chu Hsi and others had established in Sung times became the philosophy of life for the townsmen of the period. This philosophy taught people broadly of their responsibility as members of society, "In the rise and fall of the Empire, the common man shares responsibility." This awareness is often found operative in the poems of individual townsmen.[10] In short, the main feature of the poetry of the period is that it was an expression of the state of mind of successive generations of a new social stratum.

As a result of the mixture of these good and bad features, the poetry of the later imperial dynasties can be judged, on the whole, to have had a healthy development and to have continued to comprise, as poetry had before, the heart of Chinese literature.[11]

Here again, two points should be kept in mind. First, although T'ang poetry served as a literary model, the despair and excess of sorrow that were often evident in T'ang poems were not,

---

[10] Rare was the treatment throughout a poem merely an insouciant one of "flowers and birds, wind and moon," of the sort found in much late Six Dynasties poetry.

[11] Unlike late *waka* in Japan, the writing of this period in China was not filled with dull, lifeless poems.

for the most part, carried on in later dynasties. The self-awareness ordinary townsmen had of being a newly ascendant stratum in society acted as a restraint to such a tendency. In my previous volume on Sung poetry, I discussed in some detail the fact that the poetry of Su Shih early broke with the sorrow and despair that had been nearly universal in the poetry that preceded him. Of townsman origins himself, Su Shih was the forerunner of poetry in the later dynasties.

Second, the poems of the period that excelled were not the ones that were simple expressions of feeling; these frequently could not avoid being repetitions of the poems they were modeled upon. Rather, the poems that excelled were descriptive of, or written in reaction to, new realities. Stated simply, theme is more interesting in the poetry of the period than expression; what is being written about is more compelling than how it is written. There already was such a tendency in Sung poetry, and it continued and became more general in later periods.[12]

There was an additional new factor that, more than any other, contributed to poetic intensity: the former submissiveness of non-Chinese peoples toward the Chinese with whom they came in contact disappeared, and serious clashes between Chinese and non-Chinese frequently took place. In the thirteenth century, the destruction of the Chin and Southern Sung dynasties by the Mongols; in the seventeenth century, the overthrow of the Ming regime by the Manchus; and in the nineteenth and twentieth centuries, the oppression of the Ch'ing dynasty by the West—each of these occasioned a most intense poetry in the form of poems of reaction or resistance by Chinese.

This volume will emphasize the process by which poetry over the first five hundred years of the later imperial period became the literature of a broad stratum of society. Because this has been touched upon little by earlier scholars, I will lay particular stress on it. Also, in light of the fact that poetry of the time was largely modeled on earlier poetic writing, I will describe what those

---

[12] This direction in the writing of poetry, which appeared in Japanese *waka* only in the late Edo period with Hiraga Motoyoshi (1800–1865), Tachibana Akemi (1812–1868), and Ōkuma Kotomichi (1798–1868), was early in evidence in Chinese poetry.

models were and how they changed over time. Finally, I will at-
tach importance to the fact that this was a period of discord pro-
ducing an intense poetry of reaction or resistance. Such was al-
ready the case during the period under discussion in the following
chapter.

# Chapter 2

## CHIN DYNASTY POETRY: REACTION TO THE MONGOL INCURSION, 1150–1250

### The Mongol Storm

The most important event in thirteenth-century Chinese history, indeed of world history of the time, was the series of foreign conquests carried out by Mongol tribes under the leadership of Chinggis-qan (Genghis Khan) and his successors,[1] which swept the world like a violent storm. China, being situated next to the Mongol homeland, was of course affected. To the east, the Mongols reached Japan, where they were referred to as *Genkō*, or "Yuan bandits"; to the west, they swept over the western fringes of Asia, pressing on as far as Eastern Europe. The Chin dynasty,

---

[1] [The Chinese-style posthumous titles accorded the early Mongol rulers reflect their place in the establishment of the Yuan dynasty:

| Name | Posthumous Title | English Equivalent |
|------|------------------|--------------------|
| Chinggis | T'ai-tsu | Ultimate Paterfamilias |
| Ögödei | Ta-tsung | Great Patriarch |
| Güyük | Ting-tsung | Establishing Patriarch |
| Möngke | Hsien-tsung | Exemplifying Patriarch |
| Qubilai | Shih-tsu | Generational Paterfamilias (Dynasty Founder)] |

which had been established by Jurchen tribes in North China, fell
victim to the Mongols in the first half of the thirteenth century,
and its demise gave rise to Yuan Hao-wen's poetic laments. Mean-
while to the south, the Southern Sung dynasty was temporarily
beyond the reach of Mongol depredations, and poetry by ordinary
townsmen prospered there amid a regional peace. But forty years
later, during the latter half of the thirteenth century, the onslaught
extended south and destroyed the Southern Sung, bringing all of
China under Mongol domain. Such were the circumstances under
which poems of resistance by Wen T'ien-hsiang and others were
written.

Poetry written in reaction to the Mongol incursions is the
main subject of this and the following chapter. This chapter will
discuss it as it appeared in the first half of the thirteenth century in
North China after the fall of the Chin dynasty. In terms of actual
time, it coincides with the period of the Southern Sung treated in
the final chapter of my earlier volume, *An Introduction to Sung
Poetry*.

It was at the beginning of the century, in 1206, that Chinggis,
or Temüjin, was installed as qan (khan).[2] First he set his sights on
the Chin, which occupied the territory stretching from Manchuria
across North China. No more than nine years later, in 1215, he
forced the capitulation of the Chin capital of Peking (called
Chung-tu, or Central Capital) and seized the area north of the
Yellow River. The Chin dynasty, transferring its capital south of
the Yellow River to Pien-ching, or present-day Kaifeng, gained a
temporary lease on life because the Mongols turned their attention
west and swept on to Europe. Under Chinggis-qan's son, Ögödei,
they again turned eastward and destroyed the Chin dynasty,
bringing all of North China under Mongol control. The year was
1234.

The Mongol onslaught was violent in the true sense of the
word. Those towns that requested submission when first encircled
by Mongol troops would be passed over. But those that prior to
surrender had attempted even slight resistance had their entire
populations slaughtered, the only exception being made for those

[2] [Note the study by Paul Ratchnevsky, *Činggis-khan: Sein Leben und Wirken*
(Wiesbaden: Franz Steiner, 1983).]

with special skills, such as carpenters and actors. For town after town forced into surrender within the Chin domain, the rule was strictly enforced.

This is given concrete illustration in "Hsiao-tzu T'ien-chün mu-piao," or "A Tomb Inscription for the Filial Son, Mr. T'ien," which was written for T'ien Hsi by his friend, the Yuan poet Liu Yin (who is discussed in chapter 3). On the seventeenth day of the twelfth lunar month, 1213, the city of Pao-ting in Hopei surrendered to the Mongols and all of its inhabitants were driven outside the city walls. T'ien Hsi and his father were among their number. In the evening the command was given to kill all old people. Soldiers lined them up in a row and carried out the order with gusto. There were ten to twenty men ahead of T'ien Hsi's father. Taking advantage of its being dusk, T'ien Hsi stood in his father's place, putting his hands to the ground and stretching out his head. Receiving two knife blows, he passed out and, when he came to, it was midnight. Two days later a second command was issued. This time the slaughter was to be carried out with no regard to age. As an artisan, T'ien Hsi was exempted from execution and taken in custody to nearby An-su. There, upon learning of his father's death, he returned to search for the body, escaping notice by the Mongol army. Fording rivers by night, he temporarily buried the father's remains in his mother's grave.

Lines like the following, which appear in Yuan Hao-wen's poetry, are no poetic exaggeration.

> Tenderly, wild vines enwrap bones of the slain;
> Why does the setting sun cast light on empty city walls?

The Chin dynasty's lease on life was gradually running out. In 1231 the strategic area of Feng-hsiang in Shensi province, called Ch'i-yang, fell into Mongol hands. It was then that the above couplet from one of three seven-character regulated verses titled by the latter place name was written. Note also:

> The vicious struggle of the dragon and snake daily intensifies;
> Soon shields and lances will extinguish all life.

These lines were recorded by Yuan Hao-wen the following year, while witnessing the imminent fall of the Chin dynasty capital of Kaifeng after months of siege.

The Mongol invasion was not only a threat to human life. It also signaled the extinction of civilization, for the Mongols were the non-Chinese people who least respected Chinese civilization. At least such was true of them at the time under discussion. In this they were different from northern tribes or peoples previously invading China, who had respected Chinese institutions after entering the empire.[3]

The invasion of China by northern tribes by no means began with the Mongols. The Chin dynasty itself, which fell prey to Mongol encroachments after lasting roughly one hundred years, had non-Chinese monarchs. At the beginning of the twelfth century, the Chin dynasty was established when Jurchen tribes from Manchuria seized the Sung capital of Kaifeng and the northern half of Sung territory. Thus, the Chin leadership was referred to contemptuously by its Southern Sung rivals as "Hu," "Lu," "Ch'iang," "Jung," or "I-ti"—terms for barbarian tribes—or with epithets like "dog-sheep," "dog-pigs," or "animals." The Southern Sung poet Lu Yu (1125–1210) was full of hatred and vengefulness toward the Chin. The following is from a seven-character old-style poem he wrote in 1177, entitled "Autumn Sentiments":

> On the Central Plain, days and months follow the Tartar calendar;[4]
> In Peking, the old chieftain dons royal yellow.
> The splendid Yellow and warm Lo rivers, what places are these?
> Should they long remain the homeland of fur-clad barbarians?

The "old chieftain" in Peking (or Yu-chou, as it is called in the original) is the Chin ruler, Emperor Shih-tsung. He is depicted as arrogating imperial status, both by wearing yellow robes and by ordering the days with a barbarian calendar—specifically, by using the reign-period title Ta-ting, or Great Pacification (1161–1189). The implied answer to the rhetorical question about the rivers— what places are these?—is that they flow through the heartland of Chinese civilization and are, from Lu Yu's point of view, part of

---

[3] Scholars feel that the reason Mongols acted differently from other northern tribal groups may partly be because, before coming into contact with Chinese civilization, they had contact with the cultures of Central Asia in the Western-Regions area.

[4] [Use of the word "Tartar" in English to describe the calendar of a Jurchen ruler of Chin period China conveys roughly the same pejorative imprecision as the term "Hu" in the Chinese original.]

"our" Southern Sung domain; hence the disgrace that they are under barbarian occupation.

But the Chin empire with its Jurchen monarchs was not the cultural wasteland Lu Yu implies. Rather, of the states set up in China by tribal peoples from the north, the Chin was the most receptive to Chinese culture. Although the dynasty's monarchs, nobility, and a minority of its officials were Jurchen, the majority of officeholders were Han Chinese.[5] A sign of respect for Chinese civilization is found in the way the dynasty faithfully carried out the public examination system, the pride of Chinese civilization. A special feature of the Chin system is the importance given to "poetry" (*shih-fu*) as an examination topic, a rubric encompassing literature. While the Southern Sung dynasty emphasized "Ch'eng studies," that is, the moral-ethical philosophy of the brothers Ch'eng Hao and Ch'eng I, the Chin dynasty propounded "Su studies," namely, the academic tradition of Su Shih that attached special importance to training in literature.

Jurchen monarchs were skilled at writing Chinese. Although the Jurchen scripts that had been developed were declared for official use, this was done only out of pro forma ethnic consideration and had little consequence in fact. The third and fourth Chin rulers, Ho-la, or Emperor Hsi-tsung (r. 1135–1149), and Ti-ku-nai, the monarch Hai-ling Wang (r. 1149–1161, whose Chinese name was Wan-yen Liang), were both skilled at writing Chinese. The following seven-character quatrain is said to have been written by Hai-ling Wang at the time when the Chin army, in an attempt to take over the Southern Sung (whose Wu Range is referred to), had pushed as far as the northern banks of the Yangtze.

> For thousands of miles, axle widths and written script were once
>     standard;
> How can the south remain a separate realm?
> Camping a million soldiers by West Lake,
> I will stand my horse on First Peak of Wu Range.

[5] [Cf. the following: "The Chinese, who at first only constituted 28 percent of the ruling stratum, became increasingly important with the lapse of time. But the Chinese percentage never exceeded 50." Tao Jing-shen, *The Jurchen in Twelfth-Century China: A Study of Sinicization* (Seattle: University of Washington Press, 1976), p. 54. Note the table on the same page.]

Other Chin emperors were also men of culture in Chinese terms. After Hai-ling Wang was assassinated in his camp north of the Yangtze River, Wu-lu, the Emperor Shih-tsung, reigned for nearly thirty years from 1161 to 1189. Along with Emperor Hsiao-tsung of the Southern Sung, whose rule extended over almost the same period (1163–1189), Shih-tsung was considered an enlightened ruler, notwithstanding Lu Yu's reference to him as a barbarian "old chieftain." He was a Confucian monarch even to the extent of being called a "miniature Yao and Shun of the barbarians," Yao and Shun being legendary early Chinese sage-emperors. Shih-tsung's son, the crown prince Hu-t'u-wa, although dying young, was skilled at painting bamboo. And Hu-t'u-wa's son, Ma-ta-ko, the Emperor Chang-tsung (r. 1189–1208), was the most Chinese-style man of culture among Chin monarchs.[6] The official compilation for the period, the *Chin shih*, or *History of the Chin Dynasty*, records that Chin rulers from Hai-ling Wang onward would sometimes personally screen the papers of examination candidates.

Even if the Chin dynasty was not the equal of the Southern Sung in producing great poets and philosophers of the caliber of Lu Yu and Chu Hsi, it was, given the atmosphere described above, a land of considerable culture. The scornful way men of the Southern Sung referred to those of the Chin as "Hu-lu barbarians" and "dog-sheep" reflects a hostility in part owing to the fact that there was a virtual iron curtain between the two states, each side poorly understanding the circumstances of the other. According to the treaties that existed between them, apart from the payment of an indemnity to the Chin by the Southern Sung, the sole window of communication between the two was the exchange of envoys to dispatch New Year's greetings and news of births, marriages, and deaths in the two royal houses. In 1170, when Fan Ch'eng-ta, the Southern Sung poet who was a contemporary of Lu Yu, went to the Chin capital of Peking as an envoy of the Southern Sung emperor, the Jurchen official who received him did not know several

---

[6] The rumor is recorded in the *Kuei-hsin tsa-shih* (A Kuei-hsin Miscellany) by the Southern Sung writer Chou Mi (1232–1298) that Chang-tsung was the grandson of the last emperor of the Northern Sung, Hui-tsung, who died captive in Chin territory. [Kuei-hsin was the name of the street in Hangchow where Chou Mi lived.]

quite simple Chinese characters. Fan Ch'eng-ta ridicules this in a seven-character quatrain inserted among his poems giving an account of the journey. That this description does not give a full picture of the state of affairs under the Chin was probably beyond the comprehension of an envoy sternly restricted to a hostel for foreigners.

Although the Southern Sung capital of Hangchow—at the time, the greatest metropolis in the world—was especially extravagant, the sumptuous living that accompanies civilization was also present in the Chin capitals, first in Chung-tu, or Peking, then in Pien-ching, or Kaifeng.[7] The young Yuan Hao-wen, who in the following seven-character quatrain refers to himself as wearing the "long gown" of a student, describes the bustling activity on the fifteenth of the first month, the day of the lantern festival, in the new Chin capital of Kaifeng. The city was thriving beyond what one might expect, given the imminent Mongol threat.

> Beautiful women in splendid dress everywhere one looks;
> In the lantern light of the six thoroughfares, children tumultuous.
> How did I end up among them in my long gown,
> A subject of laughter and talk by passersby?

Yet the Mongols pressed on unremittingly. It was not long before Kaifeng, after a siege of nearly a year, fell. And the last Chin monarch, Ning-chia-su, the Emperor Ai-tsung (r. 1223–1234), who had fled Kaifeng in the hope of staging a comeback, committed suicide in a village on the Honan border, thus confirming the end of the dynasty. As noted before, this final event occurred in 1234.

Chinese culture and its splendor were suddenly in eclipse. The Chin dynasty had maintained unimpaired both traditional Chinese respect for literature and learning and the mechanism that insured that literature and learning were reflected in government, the examination system. But such niceties were beyond the understanding of the Mongols. Cultural activity ceased and the examination system was abolished. This not only robbed educated men

---

[7] Kaifeng was a far more flourishing city than Kyoto and Kamakura, its counterparts in Japan of the time. It was during this period that the *Shin kokinshū* (A New Collection of Poems Ancient and Modern) was compiled (1205) and Minamoto no Sanetomo was killed (1219).

of their access to special privilege; it also threatened their mode of existence, even their very lives.

It was under these circumstances that the poetry of Yuan Hao-wen, the foremost poet of the century, was written. But before discussing his writing, I would first like to touch on the Chin dynasty poetic tradition that predates him. With its Chinese-style culture, the Chin formed an important one-hundred-year link in the Chinese poetic tradition. Yuan Hao-wen was always to attach importance to it, both because it nurtured his own poetry and because it offered proof of the cultural achievement of his native dynasty. After the fall of the Chin, Yuan painstakingly edited a comprehensive collection of the dynasty's poetry, the *Chung-chou chi*. By first touching on this work, we will also be paying respect to Yuan Hao-wen.

## Twelfth-Century Chin Dynasty Poetry prior to Yuan Hao-wen: The *Chung-chou chi*

The collection of Chin dynasty poetry compiled by Yuan Hao-wen, the *Chung-chou chi*, or *Anthology of the Heartland*, contains 1,982 poems by nearly two hundred poets.[8] They represent the approximate one-hundred-year span of the dynasty from 1127, when the Sung dynasty was forced south and Chin rulers became masters of North China, until 1234, when the Chin dynasty was destroyed by the Mongols. The title *Chung-chou chi* embodies Yuan Hao-wen's pride in the Chin territory of North China as being the center and true heir of Chinese civilization.

In the short biographies that preface the poems of those included in the anthology, Yuan Hao-wen often inserts his views concerning the history of Chin dynasty poetry. According to these sketches, Chin poetry at the time of the establishment of the dynasty was first composed by officials taken prisoner from the Sung

---

[8] [The author here follows Kuo Yuan-yü (cf. n. 12 below). According to an actual count by Chan Hok-lam, however, the *Chung-chou chi* contains 2,062 poems by 249 poets (excluding the two Chin emperors cited in the preface). *The Historiography of the Chin Dynasty: Three Studies* (Wiesbaden: Franz Steiner, 1970), pp. 74 and 110, n. 19.]

who served the newly established dynasty against their will. Yü-wen Hsu-chung and Wu Chi were such figures.

Yü-wen Hsu-chung (d. 1146), while serving as an envoy of the Sung, was interned and coerced into becoming a Recipient of Edicts in the Han-lin Academy under the Chin. The following seven-character regulated verse, entitled "1129, Recording My Thoughts," was written while under detention.

> Leaving my native land in haste, a year has passed;
> Being of no help to state or self, I am equally at a loss.
> Unconvincing in my counsels then,
> Now, deep in sorrow, unworthy of pity.
> Life and death are determined before birth,
> But right and wrong remain for later telling.
> This lonely courtier has none of the bitterness that drowned Ch'ü
>     Yuan in the Hsiang—
> Only forlorn gazing at an unfamiliar San Han sky.

The phrase "San Han," which normally refers to Korea, is used here to include the early Chin capital in Manchuria. Unlike Ch'ü Yuan, who drowned himself because his sovereign would not listen to his counsel, Yü-wen Hsu-chung's grief is not owing to any lack of sagacity on the part of his ruler, the Sung emperor; rather, it has been caused by the violence of the Chin dynasty.

Wu Chi (d. 1142) was the son-in-law of Su Shih's friend, Mi Fei. He came to the Chin as a Sung legate, was put under house arrest, and became an Edict Attendant in the Han-lin Academy. His poem, "On a Painting of the Hsiao and Hsiang Streams," is a seven-character quatrain in which he contrasts his former life under the Sung, one of southern boats on southern streams, with his present circumstances under the Chin, on a northern horse in a grim landscape.

> On springtime waters of the Southland, greener than wine,
> Wanderers ply back and forth, boats for their home.
> Suddenly seeing this painting, it seems but a dream,
> For now, on saddled horse I age in windswept sands.

The following is a poem from the same series, also prompted by a painting of the south. Wu Chi would know that the city on the

Ch'ien-t'ang River, Hangchow, had become the new capital of his old homeland, the Southern Sung.

> To garden rear, scattered trees stand tall, entering the clouds;
> Great gusts coming from hundreds of miles rage in the night.
> The scene brings to mind a temple on the Ch'ien-t'ang River,
> Where from pine windows and bamboo pavilions, I would gaze
>     at autumn swells.

During the reign of Hai-ling Wang in the mid-twelfth century, the leading figure in the emperor's secretariat, the Han-lin Academy, was a former Sung official, Ts'ai Sung-nien (1107–1159). Yuan Hao-wen recounts how, in the latter half of the century during the reigns of Wu-lu, the Emperor Shih-tsung, and of Ma-ta-ko, the Emperor Chang-tsung, those who became the leading figures in the Han-lin Academy and the world of poetry were men of letters born and raised solely under the Chin who had qualified as Presented Scholars (*chin-shih*) through the examination system. In rapid succession, there appeared Ts'ai Sung-nien's son, Ts'ai Kuei (d. 1174); T'ang Huai-yin (1134–1211), who had been a classmate of the Southern Sung "song-poetry" (*tz'u*) writer, Hsin Ch'i-chi, when the latter was in the north; and Yuan Hao-wen's own mentor, Chao Ping-wen (1159–1232). Of course, these writers are not to be compared with the great Southern Sung poets, Lu Yu, Fan Ch'eng-ta, and Yang Wan-li. What is noteworthy, however, is that natural features of the north beyond the purview of writers in the south often entered into their poetry. For example, in the following old-style poem by Liu Ying (d. 1180), entitled "Vast the Sands," the subject is presumably a journey in desolate Manchuria.

> Vast the sands,
> Limitless the grass,
> Mountains to the south, mountains to the north, face one another;
> My journey takes me between their ranges.
> This traveler gazes up and, seeing no birds in flight,
> Realizes how few the trees are on the frontier.
> Vast the sands,
> Limitless the grass,
> If only I could mount the west wind and travel home.

Servant, don't complain of thin clothing;[9]
With hardly more myself, I worry that you may take a chill.

In the thirteenth century, activity in poetic circles became pro-
portionately more lively as the fortunes of the dynasty declined.
This occurred during the twenty-year so-called Southern Transfer
period from 1214 to 1234—that is, from the time the Chin capital
was forced by the Mongol takeover of the region north of the
Yellow River to move to Kaifeng, until the fall of the dynasty.
Southern Sung writers at the time were modeling their poetry on
T'ang and especially late T'ang models, and Chin writers as well
were imitating poetry of the late T'ang. But whereas the poetry by
ordinary townsmen of the Southern Sung was modeled on minor
verse by late T'ang writers dealing with minor themes, such as
poems by Yao Ho and Chia Tao, the model followed by Chin
writers was poetry of the "pure art" representative, Li Shang-yin.
This was probably owing to the fact that Chin poetry was centered
around the Han-lin Academy. According to Yuan Hao-wen, two
poets in particular were major figures in the academy, his
teacher Chao Ping-wen and Yang Yun-i (1170–1228). The col-
lected complete prose and poetry of Chao Ping-wen, the *Fu-shui
wen-chi*, or *Fu-Stream Literary Collection*, is extant, the complete
editions of other Chin authors' writings having rarely survived. In
Chao's work, in addition to seven-character regulated verse in the
style of Li Shang-yin, there are several poems patterned after Su
Shih's poetic series in which the same rhyme words are used in
exactly the same order as in poems by T'ao Ch'ien; this practice is
probably a manifestation of "Su studies" under the Chin. Chao
Ping-wen's skill as a poet does not measure up to Yuan Hao-wen's
commendation of him. Only a few of his poems descriptive of nat-
ural features of the north excite any interest. The following is a
seven-character quatrain entitled "Returning Home at Dusk."

> Enjoying watching a lone bird enter the folds of clouds,
> I scarcely noticed signs of rain looming in the green wood.
> I cross a broken-down bridge, the sandy path black;
> Suddenly, a flash of lightning reveals a village.

[9] The "servant" would refer to the poet's carriage driver.

A poem by his disciple Yuan Hao-wen on the same theme is both more animated and profound.[10]

Notwithstanding Yuan Hao-wen's assertive pride in *Chung-chou chi* authors, Chin dynasty poets prior to Yuan himself, who was truly outstanding, were all minor. Yuan Hao-wen considers their strong point to be their "limpid strength" (*ch'ing-ching*). True, poems by these writers are limpid and strong if compared with those of contemporary Southern Sung authors. Yet it seems that when a *Chung-chou chi* poem is limpid, it lacks strength; and when it has strength, it lacks limpidity. Rarely does one find both. Because it has the interest that attaches to the verse of minor poets, the *Chung-chou chi* has sometimes found the favor of widely learned critics. In the seventeenth century, the late Ming and early Ch'ing critic Ch'ien Ch'ien-i drew readers' attention to the long-forgotten *Chung-chou chi*, using the collection as a model for his own anthology of Ming poetry, the *Lieh-ch'ao shih-chi*, or *Poetry Collection of Successive Reigns*. But Ch'ien's endorsement of poetry in the Chin anthology received an immediate dissent from his disciple, Wang Shyh-chen.[11] And although the *Ch'üan Chin-shih*, or *Complete Poems of the Chin Dynasty*, with 5,544 entries compiled during the Ch'ing dynasty by Kuo Yuan-yü,[12] supplements the 1,982 poems in Yuan Hao-wen's *Chung-chou chi*, the *Ch'üan Chin-shih* has not become a poetry classic.[13]

Under the Southern Sung dynasty, the early twelfth century

---

[10] See p. 33 below.

[11] [Here and elsewhere in this volume, the romanization "Wang Shyh-chen" is used to distinguish this Ch'ing dynasty poet-critic (1634–1711) from "Wang Shih-chen," the Ming poet (1526–1590) treated in chap. 7. The two have different characters for their names, which would normally both be romanized as "Wang Shih-chen."]

[12] [The number cited is the one given in the work's preface by its compiler, Kuo Yuan-yü; but Chan Hok-lam finds 5,624 poems by 361 poets. *The Historiography of the Chin Dynasty*, pp. 92 and 118, n. 82.]

[13] In Japan the *Chung-chou chi* was early reprinted, first in the so-called Yoshino period of division between the Northern and Southern Courts (1336–1392), and then repeatedly in Gozan editions. Although read by Zen priests of the Muromachi period (1338–1573), the work was later long forgotten. Not until 1806, amid the troubled atmosphere of the late Edo period, did it again gain some measure of attention; that was the date the *Chin-shih hsuan* (Selected Poems of the Chin Dynasty), edited by the Ch'ing writer Ku K'uei-kuang, was reprinted with a preface by Kameda Hōsai (1752–1826).

marked the first flourishing of poetry by ordinary townsmen. In the north, however, which for some reason lagged behind, it was Han-lin Academy officials rather than townsmen who were at the center of poetic activity. But signs of participation by the latter were not completely lacking. Hsin Yuan (d. 1231), who was engaged in farming in Fu-ch'ang prefecture, Honan, styled himself Chi-nan shih-lao, or the Old Poet of Chi-nan. In the *Chung-chou chi*, Yuan Hao-wen commended him together with Li Fen and Li Hsien-fu as one of Three Friends Who Understand Each Other (*San chih-chi*). According to the short biography of him in the anthology, until the age of twenty-five Hsin Yuan did not know any Chinese characters. To illustrate what sort of poetry he wrote, I here offer, from the approximately twenty poems by him that are extant, a seven-character quatrain entitled "My Garden in the Hills."

> Year's end, too lazy to tend my hillside garden,
> Yet I worry that orchids will wither and chrysanthemums shrivel.
> Green, green, a few nameless weeds
> Vie to grow in the patch warmed by the setting sun.

When the *Chung-chou chi*, after being laboriously compiled by Yuan Hao-wen as the cultural record of his by-then-defunct native dynasty, was published under the auspices of a friend, Yuan boasted that the poetry of his Chin fatherland was not at all inferior to that of the Southern Sung. The assertion appears in the first of a series of five seven-character quatrains appended to the work as a postface.

> Ts'ao Chih and Liu Chen of Yeh are truly heroic in spirit;
> East of the River, the Hsieh family's poetic rhythm is superb.
> But judging by poetic beauty or substance,
> Southern poets are not likely to win the brocade robe.[14]

The third-century poets from North China, Ts'ao Chih and Liu Chen, are used here to represent the heroic spirit Yuan says abounded among Chin poets of the north. By contrast, "the Hsieh

[14] A brocade robe was awarded in T'ang times by Empress Wu (r. 690–705) to the winner of a poetry-writing competition. The term *Wu-nung* in the final line of the original refers to southerners from the Soochow area of South China. [Cf. the translation of the poem by Chan Hok-lam, *The Historiography of the Chin*, p. 71.]

family" from "east of the River" refers to the early fifth-century Southern Dynasties writer Hsieh Ling-yun and his poet-relatives, whose superlative flair is meant to stand for Southern Sung poetry. Although, Yuan Hao-wen argues, the strong points of Chin and Southern Sung poetry differ, judged by external elegance or internal content, the prize for poetic quality should be awarded to his homeland of the north.

Although Yuan Hao-wen's boast does not hold true for poetry in the *Chung-chou chi*, which contains Chin dynasty poetry prior to his own, it certainly holds true for Yuan Hao-wen himself. The one hundred years of Chin poetry prior to Yuan Hao-wen serve as a prelude to that great writer, who appeared at a time when fortune dictated the demise of his dynasty. He was the foremost Chinese poet of the thirteenth century, north or south; his Southern Sung contemporaries, the minor poets of the Chiang-hu, or River and Lake School, were no match for him. Although much the same sorrow over the loss of homeland that Yuan Hao-wen put into verse over the first half of the century came also to be expressed by Southern Sung poets experiencing the same fate during the latter half of the century, their poetic ability did not measure up to his. Yuan Hao-wen was not only the foremost literary figure of the thirteenth century, he is one of the great Chinese poets of all time.

## Yuan Hao-wen
## (1190–1257)

Yuan Hao-wen was a native of Hsin-chou, situated slightly north of T'ai-yuan in Shansi.[15] This area, close to the northern reaches of what was traditionally considered China proper, corresponded with the former geographical region of Ping-chou. As he describes in the ballad, "Song of the Ping-chou Youth," the natural features of his native region were such that "The north wind, stirring the earth, rises; / At sky's edge, floating clouds teem." In one of his

---

[15] [Note the study by John Timothy Wixted, *Poems on Poetry: Literary Criticism by Yuan Hao-wen (1190–1257)* (Wiesbaden: Franz Steiner, 1982) (Calligraphy by Eugenia Y. Tu).]

old-style poems Yuan also describes an autumn scene in his native Hsin-chou.

> Once the frosty air has invaded,
> Blurred autumn hills turn deserted.
> Climbing high, I look down on misty trees—
> Falling yellows among red and green.

Yuan Hao-wen occasionally uses extremely simple and straightforward expressions in his poetry, which may well be a manifestation of northern Chinese temperament. By way of example, there is his seven-character quatrain entitled "Upon Hearing a Song, Remembering Old Friends in the Capital."

> Out front, someone is singing the "Lü-yao ts'ui";
> Towards far-off Liang-yuan, my mind again turns.
> I recall once at the Tu family pavilion,
> Hearing the same strains with Hsin-chih and Ch'in-yung.[16]

To take too seriously such generalizations about geography and temperament can result in a pointless determinism.[17] But in the case of Yuan Hao-wen, there probably is a relationship between the nature of his poetry and the natural environment where he was born and grew up.

The central characteristic of Yuan Hao-wen's poetry is its depth and gravity. Although Yuan was a man of intense feeling with a poet's temperament that reacted sensitively to external stimuli, he disliked giving hasty expression to his keenly felt reactions. He would painstakingly scrutinize the stimuli to which he was responding, examining every aspect of a subject. For this reason, there are exceptionally few meaningless or empty phrases in

---

[16] The Tu family referred to is that of Tu Shan-fu. Hsin-chih is the courtesy name of Ma Ko, and Ch'in-yung that of Li Hsien-fu. All three were poet-friends of Yuan Hao-wen. He inserts their first names directly into the poem, along with the name of a folk ballad. Except for the ornate reference to the Chin capital of Kaifeng as "Liang-yuan," the poem employs no allusions.

[17] In historical compilations that date from the early T'ang—the *Sui shu* (History of the Sui Dynasty) and *Pei shih* (History of the Northern Dynasties)—the difference in temperament between North and South China is represented as follows when comparing the Confucianism of the two regions: "Southerners are concise; they extract the essence. But study in the north is florid; they exhaust the branches and foliage."

his poetry. The product of mature deliberation, his expressions were carefully polished, which further intensified their depth and gravity. In this respect Yuan Hao-wen may well be the foremost Chinese poet from Tu Fu to the present.

The year of Yuan Hao-wen's birth, 1190, nearly coincides with the first year in the reign of the most cultured of the Chin monarchs, Ma-ta-ko, or Emperor Chang-tsung (r. 1189–1208). The rumor that Chang-tsung was a grandson of Emperor Hui-tsung of the Sung has no apparent basis in fact.[18] Like Hui-tsung, this "barbarian" monarch was expert at painting, calligraphy, and music; yet Chang-tsung was unlike him in that he did not experience the virtual demise of his dynasty. Centered around this man of refinement, not only did Chin dynasty culture reach its zenith, the prestige of the dynasty also seemed at its highest. Southern Sung leaders broke their treaty with the Chin and were defeated in the hostilities that followed; as a condition for peace the decapitated head of the Southern Sung prime minister, Han T'o-chou, was sent to the Chin capital of Peking. This occurred in the last year of Chang-tsung's reign, in 1208, when Yuan Hao-wen was eighteen years old.

While Chinese remained yet unaware, the Mongol storm was fast approaching. At the time when the decapitated head of Han T'o-chou was delivered from the south, Chinggis had already become qan in the north. Three years after the death of the childless Emperor Chang-tsung, during the Ta-an, or Great Peace, reign period (1208–1212) of his uncle Wei-shao Wang (r. 1208–1213), the Chin were soon under attack. Wei-shao Wang was assassinated, and when the elder brother of Chang-tsung, Wu-tu-pu, the Emperor Hsuan-tsung (r. 1213–1223), ascended the throne, the range of Mongol attack widened, extending to the person of young Yuan Hao-wen himself.

In the third month of 1214, Yuan Hao-wen's native place of Hsin-chou in Shansi surrendered to the Mongols, and his older brother Yuan Hao-ku fell victim in the ensuing massacre.[19] During the eighth month of the same year, the Chin capital was moved

---

[18] [See n. 6 above.]

[19] In the epitaph written by Yuan Hao-wen, he describes his unfortunate brother as having been on bad terms with his (own) wife after failing the examinations.

to Kaifeng. The following year, the Central Capital of Peking capitulated and the area north of the Yellow River fell into Mongol hands. The Yuan family fled south to San-hsiang prefecture in Honan. Yuan Hao-wen's famous series, "Thirty Quatrains on Poetry," discussed below, dates from this time.

Yuan Hao-wen became a Presented Scholar in 1221 at the age of thirty-one, achieving success in examinations presided over by Chao Ping-wen. From an earlier time, when he had been highly praised for his poetry by Chao Ping-wen—"From Tu Fu until now, there has been nothing to compare with such writing"—Yuan had been a special favorite of the man thirty years his senior. Consequently, Chao was criticized for having personal bias when Yuan passed the examination.

The atmosphere of the Chin dynasty poetic world of the time, which favored using the poetry of the late T'ang "pure art" poet, Li Shang-yin, as a model, also affected Yuan Hao-wen.[20] It is illustrated by the following seven-character regulated verse, "Wild Chrysanthemums," which was written by Yuan at Chao Ping-wen's request.

> A thousand years now, since the Ch'ai-sang poet died;[21]
> Delicate chrysanthemums, multicolored, still turn orblike.
> As we all enjoy how they vividly reflect autumn's colors,
> Can we let them lie, jumbled in scattered mist?
> Barren the field borders, broken the dikes—after a fresh frost;
> Butterflies lean, crickets chilly—before evening's shadow.
> Lest flowering spring laugh at tardy autumn,
> I have written this to set forth the latter's subtle charm.[22]

The makings of a poet with a discerning eye appear in this poem, in which Yuan Hao-wen finds "subtle charm" in wild chrysanthemums flourishing out-of-season. Although the poem may be little more than an exercise in elegant writing, in Yuan's case training in

[20] As for Yuan Hao-wen's personal life at the time, according to an item in his prose writings he spent much of his time drinking in the carpe diem atmosphere that prevailed after the transfer of the Chin capital to Kaifeng.

[21] The "Ch'ai-sang poet" refers to T'ao Ch'ien of the fifth century, who wrote poems about chrysanthemums and once resided in Ch'ai-sang.

[22] [Throughout the poem and especially in the last couplet Yuan Hao-wen is being deferentially complimentary toward Chao Ping-wen, implicitly likening him to aging wild chrysanthemums.]

such writing proved an effective process, for the poems of his later years lend that much more weight to carefully thought-out expressions using apt diction rich in implication.

About the time he was forty, Yuan Hao-wen served in a series of posts in southern Honan as a local official. He was governor of three prefectures—Nei-hsiang, Nan-yang, and Chen-p'ing—all in southwest Honan. Nei-hsiang was then alive with literati refugees, and Tu Shan-fu and Ma Ko in particular were his good poet-friends.

It was from about this time that Yuan Hao-wen's characteristic poetic discernment began to come into its own. It is illustrated by the following seven-character regulated verse entitled "Relating Events in the Nei-hsiang Prefectural Hall." The scene is the governor's residence late at night, after the secretaries have left the office.

> Clerks gone, past midnight in the public hall,
> My heart is heavy with a hundred cares smoldering.
> Re tax levies, nothing of note on my promotion record;
> And no one wants to contribute grain for war expenses.
> Hungry rats surround my bed, as if to complain;
> Startled ravens crying at the moon are more than I can bear.
> Unable to take to sea in a tiny boat,
> I feel ashamed before my Ch'ung-ling ancestor.[23]

Yuan Chieh, an ancestor of Yuan Hao-wen, was a T'ang dynasty local official in Ch'ung-ling, Hupei; his "Ch'ung-ling Song" expresses the idea of abandoning public office and putting out to sea in a small boat. Yuan Hao-wen reproaches himself for not having the same sentiment.

There are two notable features about the above poem. First, the theme of a government office at night had scarcely appeared as poetic subject matter prior to this time. A poem written a short time before this by the Southern Sung writer, Lu Yu, is the only instance I know of. Yuan Hao-wen's discerning eye, like that of Tu Fu before him, often encompassed new poetic material. Second, in terms of diction, the expression "a hundred cares smoldering" was quite new. Taken individually, the words in the phrase

---

[23] [The rendering "I reproach myself as did my ancestor in his 'Ch'ung-ling Song' " may be preferable.]

were common enough; but joined together, they were experienced as something fresh and new. The ability to give life to hackneyed phrases, a talent Yuan Hao-wen often displayed, came from his discernment and mature powers of reflection.

Turning to nature, the poet's keen eye made discoveries there as well. The following, dating from about the same time as the last poem, is a seven-character regulated verse entitled "At Registrar Chang's Thatched Retreat, Written about a Storm."

> Feebly frogs croak, telling of rain's approach;
> Suddenly, silver arrows flit about mountains on all sides.
> Great waves of the Yangtze nearly overflowing,
> High Heaven and deep Earth seem enclosed in a hunt.[24]
> Wind and clouds for hundreds of miles unfold an awesome sight;
> My hair stands in fright at the lingering intensity.
> A long rainbow appearing, forest light astir,
> In silence the deserted village seems as nothing in the setting glow.

The above is a splendid example of poetic modeling: the croaking of frogs, "silver arrows" of rain darting here and there, a curtain of water covering heaven and earth, and then a suspended rainbow and quiet sunset that make these all seem unreal. It is fair to say that Yuan Hao-wen uncovered secrets of nature that poets before him had overlooked. The word "astir" in "forest light astir" is an instance of the poet's bringing life to a hackneyed word, like "smoldering" in "a hundred cares smoldering" mentioned before.

When at the age of forty-one Yuan Hao-wen began serving as an official at the capital, the Chin dynasty was on the verge of collapse. His poems written over the next three years are literary masterpieces that deal in a profound and mature way with this most trying state of affairs. One series of three seven-character regulated verses, entitled "Ch'i-yang," was written when that strategic area of Feng-hsiang in Shensi province fell to the Mongols. Various poems were written during the ten-month period beginning in spring of the following year, while Kaifeng was under siege by the Mongols. And there is the series of five seven-character regulated verses, entitled "An Account of What Happened in the Twelfth Month of 1232, After the Imperial Carriage Went on Tour to the East," which was written after seeing off Emperor

---

[24] [A barricade hunt of the kind that narrows into a dead end.]

Ai-tsung, who fled the besieged capital at the time indicated.[25] The
final couplet of one of the poems in this last series is particularly
noteworthy.

> Oh autumn wind! No need to buffet my white hair;
> The ocean in turbulent flow, I am truly needed.[26]

I would paraphrase these lines as follows. "Autumn wind, don't
blast my grey-white hair! The waters of the ocean deep, that place
of great repose between Heaven and Earth since time immemo-
rial, are stirring up violent waves. From ancient times, Chinese
civilization has never been extinguished. But with the Mongol
storm, that is precisely what it now confronts. Here in the middle
stand I, whirlpool waves pouring directly in upon me. Yet for pre-
cisely this reason, my survival is all the more important. I may be
helpless to carry out political resistance. But let my eyes unflinch-
ingly open wide to bear the witness of a poet who truly sees. Let
that be my duty!"

As a result of a coup d'état by General Ts'ui Li, the siege of
Kaifeng ended in the second month of the following year, 1233,
with the city's surrender to the Mongols. Yuan Hao-wen was
coerced into composing a stele inscription lauding Ts'ui Li's vir-
tue, for which he was criticized in the official biography of him
written after his death. But later scholars in the Ch'ing dynasty
who wrote "chronological biographies" (*nien-p'u*) of Yuan Hao-
wen—Ling T'ing-kan, Weng Fang-kang, and Shih Kuo-ch'i—all
plead in the poet's defense.

As part of their postsurrender policy, Mongol troops ordered
the forced resettlement of men of the "three teachings" (*san
chiao*)—Buddhism, Confucianism, and Taoism—as well as physi-
cians and artisans. Being a "man of Confucian teaching," Yuan

[25] [I.e., January 1233.]

[26] [The expression "the ocean in turbulent flow," given its original context in the
*Ku-liang chuan chu* (Commmentary on the Ku-liang chuan) by Fan Ning (339–
401), carries the implication that the speaker making the allusion—perhaps faced
with the death of an earlier master or leader and certainly confronted with a world
in turmoil—will carry on the earlier tradition. The couplet might be better ren-
dered as follows (reading *yao* as *shua*):

> Oh autumn wind! No need to buffet my white hair;
> The ocean in turbulent flow is making sport of me.]

Hao-wen was evacuated from Kaifeng on the twenty-ninth day of the fourth month, 1233; crossing north of the Yellow River on the third day of the following month, he was interned at Liao-ch'eng in Shantung.[27] What he witnessed along the way appears in many of his poems. Also, a letter addressed to the Yuan prime minister, Yeh-lü Ch'u-ts'ai, dated a week before Yuan's removal from Kaifeng, appears in Yuan Hao-wen's collected writings. The letter lists the names of over fifty Chin literary figures, including Yuan himself, and requests that they receive appropriate treatment as preservers of Chinese culture. He states, "The rites and music of court, the documents of state, all reside in these men."

The following five-character regulated verse, one of two entitled "Twelfth Month, Sixth Day,"[28] was written by Yuan Hao-wen while under house arrest in Liao-ch'eng.

> The empire still full of arms,
> At this edge of the world, the year again renewed.
> The dragon has shifted, leaving fish and turtles lost;
> The sun eclipsed, unicorns are fighting.
> Brambles amid grasses, these desolate hills are snowy;
> In my old garden, mist and flowers mark the spring.
> Here in Liao-ch'eng, a moon out tonight,
> I feel disconsolate still away from home.

It was about this time that Emperor Ai-tsung, who had fled Kaifeng in hopes of mounting a counteroffensive, committed suicide in Ts'ai-chou, Honan. The destruction of the Chin was complete. The somber news reached Yuan Hao-wen while he was in confinement and perhaps gave rise to the phrases above, "the dragon has shifted" and "the sun [is] eclipsed."

Yuan Hao-wen wrote as many as several dozen poems about apricot blossoms. When long northern winters come to an end and mountains are decked with countless flowers, the most enchanting flowers of all are apricot blossoms.

> Yet unopened, what does an apricot blossom resemble?
> A suckling babe's natural flush, with deep red lips.
> Now crying, now laughing—artless and silly;

---

[27] [I.e., June 8 and June 12, 1233.]
[28] [I.e., December 27, 1234.]

We have here a hundred babes portrayed, though unreal.[29]
Half opened, what does an apricot blossom resemble?
The marriageable maid next door to the east.
The balmy season warms her, stirring thoughts of love;
Silent, as if about to speak, from time to time she gently knits her
   brow.

The above excerpt is taken from a long poem written in the apricot
garden of a certain Chi Tzu-cheng while Yuan Hao-wen was in-
terned in Liao-ch'eng. The poet may have seen himself reflected
in blossoms that, only half-opened, are likened to a maid who
holds herself back with a frown when her emotions are stirred. By
the same token Yuan Hao-wen was a poet of great passion who,
while giving expression to his emotions, kept them in check only
with considerable effort.

Yuan Hao-wen's house arrest was lifted after two years. His
poetic eye remained ever discerning, but all that it now encom-
passed was the desolate natural scenery distinctive of North
China. Not only was the civilization that the Chin dynasty had
managed to maintain completely stifled, even the fundamental ele-
ments of government had become unclear. For several decades,
North China remained in a kind of suspended state.

Mongols extracted pledges of loyalty from their subjects by
slaughtering those who refused allegiance. They entrusted great
responsibility to certain Chinese who, having the force of arms of
powerful provincial lords, received their mandate from Mongols
unpracticed in civil administration. Such Chinese leaders included
the so-called Four Myriarchs (*Ssu wan-hu*), each in charge of
10,000 households: Yen Shih of Tung-p'ing in Shantung, Chang
Jou of Pao-ting in Hopei, Shih T'ien-tse of Chen-ting in Hopei,
and Tung Chün of Hao-ch'eng in Hopei.

These military men were among many throughout North
China who became patrons of the cultural figures of the former
Chin dynasty, Yuan Hao-wen and his colleagues. Those who were
particularly solicitous of the poet were Yen Shih and his son; the
local military commander under them, Chao T'ien-hsi; and Chang
Jou. The remainder of Yuan Hao-wen's life was spent going back

---

[29] [The array of blossoms is likened to the dozens of babies that were depicted
in paintings given to couples at their marriage, in hopes of numerous offspring.]

and forth between their residences and the study he built on Book-reading Mountain (Tu-shu shan) in his native Hsin-chou.

Two tasks remained for Yuan Hao-wen: to leave behind a record of the culture of his defunct Chin fatherland and to leave behind a record of its government. The cultural record was achieved through his editing of the *Chung-chou chi*, which has been handed down to us. As for the record of government, Yuan set about writing such a work in the form of a history. At the age of forty-nine (fifty by Chinese count), he built a study near his native Hsin-chou and called it Yeh-shih t'ing, or Unofficial-History Pavilion. The following poem, a five-character regulated verse entitled "New Year's Day, 1239," was written just prior to settling in.

> At fifty, one is not really old,
> Yet my appearance keeps worsening.
> As the hair on my head grows thinner,
> So too the image in the mirror changes.
> My unofficial history just outlined,
> Yet undetermined is the site of my retreat.
> It would not do, riding my gaunt horse,
> To reenter the world's red dust.

Yuan's efforts compiling the history are referred to in his other poems.[30] More than a century later the official *Chin shih*, or *History of the Chin Dynasty*, was completed. Its outstanding quality can be attributed to the extensive use made of material drafted by Yuan Hao-wen.

Astride his gaunt horse, Yuan Hao-wen traveled throughout North China for the remainder of his life, gathering historical materials. In a five-character regulated verse entitled "Eleventh Month, 1255, En Route to Chen-chou," which was written at the age of sixty-five, Yuan Hao-wen speaks of traveling to the Chen-ting area of Hopei. In the empty landscape, a long bridge takes shape like a vision.

> The village quiet, happy the call of birds;
> Mountains low-lying, images of geese in the distance.
> Shadows on the plain sporadically turn bright,
> As cold rain lightly descends.

---

[30] For example, "In Imitation of (Su Shih's Series,) 'Poems on Moving to the Eastern Slope'" [Poems #071–078; see n. 32 below].

Traveling afar, first the heart grows weary;
Feeling chilled, wine quickly wears off.
In the red dust, forgetful of north or south,
I make out, indistinct in the distance, a long bridge.

Poetry about mountain climbing, which is seldom found in the writings of other Chinese poets, also characterizes Yuan Hao-wen's work. As these poems are long pieces, none will be presented here. I will only offer the opening line from an old-style poem entitled "An Excursion to Hsuan Spring in Ch'eng-t'ien," "The poet's love of mountains is a love that penetrates the bones."

During his later years, Yuan Hao-wen had an audience with the future qan, Qubilai (Khubilai), at K'ai-p'ing in present-day Inner Mongolia. It was while the latter was prince over Chinese settlements in the area. It appears that Yuan to a certain extent placed his hopes on this leader, for Qubilai had the best understanding of Chinese culture among members of the Mongol aristocracy. Yuan Hao-wen, Chang Te-hui (the friend through whom the audience was arranged), and others requested that Qubilai accept the title "Grand Patriarch of Confucian Teaching"—an appellation he is said to have accepted with pleasure.[31]

Yuan Hao-wen died in 1257 at the age of sixty-seven, twenty-three years after the fall of the Chin dynasty. His extant poems number more than thirteen hundred.[32] Although for a period (through the Ming dynasty) Yuan's poetry was forgotten, with the rediscovery of both it and the *Chung-chou chi* by Ch'ien Ch'ien-i in the early Ch'ing, Yuan Hao-wen's reputation was reestablished. It has since remained unshaken.[33]

[31] The title is "Ju-chiao ta tsung-shih"; its opening two-character phrase, "Ju-chiao," or "Confucian teaching," is rarely used in China, although common in Japan (read as *Jukyō*).

[32] [For a poem-by-poem listing of Yuan Hao-wen's corpus of 1,366 *shih* poems that includes information on Western-language translations (including partial translations of poems), see John Timothy Wixted, "A Finding List for Chinese, Japanese, and Western-Language Annotation and Translation of Yüan Hao-wen's Poetry," *Bulletin of Sung-Yüan Studies* 17 (1981): 140–85. (Note the publisher's printing correction in vol. 18 [1986]: 3.) The Yuan Hao-wen poems treated in this chapter are as follows (parentheses indicate partial translations): (#462), (#473), #797, #1103, (#315), (#095), #968, #415, #440, #450, (#475), #346, (#238), #352, #400, (#264), #137, #081.]

[33] In Japan as well, from the late Edo period on, Yuan Hao-wen has had many admirers.

Yuan Hao-wen was a discerning critic of earlier poetry.[34] His comments were often expressed through his own poems, the most famous example being the early work, "Thirty Quatrains on Poetry." This poetic series reflects the resolve of a young man of twenty-seven to investigate poets and schools of poetry, ancient and modern, from Han and Wei times to the present, and to distinguish between what was "true and false" in them so as to promote correct poetry for both study and emulation. In that series and in later writings, Yuan's efforts as a critic were directed toward determining correct poetic models. As mentioned in chapter 1, Chinese poetry from the thirteenth century onward was marked by strong consciousness of the need to set proper literary models to be followed. Similar efforts were carried out by later poets and critics, but Yuan Hao-wen was the forerunner of the practice.

Yuan Hao-wen, being in the tradition of Chin dynasty "Su studies," comments on Su Shih, whom he much respected.[35] But he most esteemed T'ao Ch'ien, the poet Su Shih admired. He especially loved the way that T'ao Ch'ien's poetry, dispensing with useless embellishment, contains something of substance in every line. The following is a five-character old-style poem by Yuan Hao-wen, prompted by praise of T'ao Ch'ien in a poem by Yuan's friend Chao I-lu, whose literary name was Yü-hsuan.

> Yü-hsuan is endowed with poetic discernment;
> In discussing letters, he values what is natural.
> He has doubts about poets nowadays,
> Who exhaust their years embellishing and touching up.
> Just look among T'ao Ch'ien's works,
> At his poems on drinking wine and returning to the fields.[36]
> That old man did not write poetry—
> He wrote truly what was in his heart.

[34] [For translation and discussion of the critical writings by Yuan Hao-wen referred to in the following section, as well as of the *Chung-chou chi* postface poem cited earlier, see Wixted, *Poems on Poetry*.]

[35] Only the prefaces remain from separate studies that Yuan Hao-wen did of Su Shih and Tu Fu—*Tung-p'o shih-ya* (The Elegance of Su Shih's Poetry) and *Tu-shih hsueh* (A Study of Tu Fu's Poetry)—which date from a few years after "Thirty Quatrains on Poetry."

[36] [These are probably the most famous poems in T'ao Ch'ien's corpus. Among available translations, see James Robert Hightower, *The Poetry of T'ao Ch'ien* (Oxford: Oxford University Press, 1970), pp. 124–57 and 50–56.]

The natural is to the artificial
As mutually exclusive as true and false.
Thus we know that fashionable adornment,
Rouge and tint, struggle fruitlessly to gain affection.
Bare simplicity is sufficient for enjoyment;
Do not be attracted by empty show.

The essentials of poetry, in terms of content and expression, are here said to be truth and naturalness. The "bare simplicity" that they engender is something to be enjoyed. And by "bare simplicity" what is advocated is poetic expression fully developed through mature reflection, not Taoist or Buddhist "emptiness" or "vacuity" of the sort often associated with T'ao Ch'ien.

The need for mature or "pained reflection" is elaborated in a five-character old-style poem entitled "With Chang Hung-lueh, Court Attendant, Discussing Literature." The addressee in the title, the son of the myriarch Chang Jou, wished to study literature, so Yuan Hao-wen presented the following poem to him.

Writing issues from pained reflection;
But who writes with pained reflection?
Even if there were one of pained reflection,
In all the world, how many would recognize him?
Skillful prose and skillful poetry
Are very like the chess of a champion master;
Though a grand master may respond casually,
There is a knack to his every move.
Unless one looks on, move by move,
It will be the same as peeking at the sky through a tube.
A text has to be written character by character;
It should also be read character by character.
Mulling over places where there is an aftertaste,
A hundred readings will not suffice.
If, by effort, one achieves full comprehension,
Its language will become like next of kin.
It was only allowed the ancient musicians Kuang and K'uei,
Hearing plucked strings, to discern proper music.
Men of today, going through texts,
Sweep over ten lines at a glance.
A stopped-up nose cannot distinguish fragrant from foul;
Bad eyesight confuses red and green.
If the tiniest part is overlooked,
The perceived object could be as disparate as Ch'u and Shu.

No wonder that at the foot of Ching Mountain,
One often hears the weeping of the maimed one.

In ancient times Pien Ho is said to have discovered on Ching Mountain a singularly precious but unpolished jade, which he offered to the court. Not only was it rejected, it was considered a hoax, so Pien Ho's feet were cut off in punishment. He was later heard to lament, not that his feet were cut off, but that true jade was taken to be ordinary stone. By implication the poet is saying that true writing is seldom appreciated by the world.

Yuan Hao-wen argues that the reason for valuing truth, naturalness, and mature reflection in the writing of poetry is that literature must be an expression of sincerity. This opinion appears in the preface he wrote to the collected poems of his friend, Yang Hung-tao, entitled the *Hsiao-heng chi*, or *Modest-Enjoyment Collection*: "T'ang poetry surpassed poetry that came after the *Shih ching* (Classic of Songs) in that it was concerned with what is basic. What is it that is basic? The answer is sincerity." Citing the *Chung yung*, or *Doctrine of the Mean*, Yuan also states in the preface, "Unless there is sincerity, there is no substance." In other words, if writing is not true or sincere, it has nothing of content.

It is not surprising that, T'ao Ch'ien aside, the poet most admired by Yuan Hao-wen was Tu Fu. Tu Fu esteemed sincerity of expression and truthfulness of content. Various short quotes from Tu Fu's work are cited by Yuan Hao-wen in the preface he wrote to the collected poems of his friend, Yang P'eng, to support his argument that what is fundamental in poetry is the expression of true sentiment.[37]

As a final word of summary, one can say that Yuan Hao-wen's own poetry is consonant with the aims expounded in his poetic theory.

The *Ho-Fen chu-lao shih-chi*, or *Poetry Anthology of Elders from the Yellow and Fen Rivers*—a pamphlet edited by Fang Ch'i (dates uncertain) containing verse by surviving Chin dynasty officials—was written under the same conditions that Yuan Hao-wen faced during his later years. Setting that work aside, however, I will touch

---

[37] [The Tu Fu quotations, here omitted (as they make little sense out of context), are included in the translation of the preface by Wixted, *Poems on Poetry*, pp. 244–46.]

instead on the Chinese poetry of a figure in the Mongol camp. I refer to the high official under both Chinggis- and Ögö-dei-qan, Yeh-lü Ch'u-ts'ai.

## Yeh-lü Ch'u-ts'ai
## (1190–1244)

The family of Yeh-lü Ch'u-ts'ai, whose surname Yeh-lü is also given as I-la, was by origin Khitan. His father, Yeh-lü Lü (or I-la Lü), had been a personal attendant of the Chin emperor Shih-tsung. An admirer of Su Shih, it is recounted that Yeh-lü Lü discredited references to Su Shih in popular oral performances of the time as being fabrications.[38]

Yeh-lü Ch'u-ts'ai was born the son of this important Chin minister in 1190, the year of Yuan Hao-wen's birth.[39] In 1214, when Peking fell, he was an administrative official at the capital and surrendered to the Mongols. He later joined Chinggis-qan on his campaigns to the west.

After the death of Chinggis, Yeh-lü Ch'u-ts'ai gained the trust of Ögödei-qan, becoming one of his top advisers. Many features of Yeh-lü's leadership are enumerated in the "spirit-way stele" (shen-tao pei) written for him upon his death by Sung Tzu-chen (1187–1266). Countering the view held by some Mongols that all Chinese should be slaughtered and their land turned into pasture, Yeh-lü argued that the Mongol regime would profit from revenues generated by work performed by Chinese. By convincing Ögödei not to eliminate the populace of Kaifeng when that city fell in 1233, he saved 1,470,000 lives. Yeh-lü worked to preserve Chinese culture by setting up an Editorial Bureau in Peking and a Bureau of Literature in P'ing-yang, Shansi. Moderating the excessive views of Quduqu, he established a more appropriate tax sys-

---

[38] See my *Gen zatsugeki kenkyū*, as reprinted in *Yoshikawa Kōjirō zenshū*, 14: 206–7.

[39] [Yeh-lü Ch'u-ts'ai's dates of birth and death as given above (1190–1244) are the traditional ones, which the author follows. The dates 1189–1243 are probably more accurate. See Igor de Rachewiltz, "Yeh-lü Ch'u-ts'ai (1189–1243): Buddhist Idealist and Confucian Statesman," in *Confucian Personalities*, eds. Arthur F. Wright and Denis Twitchett (Stanford: Stanford University Press, 1962), pp. 119 and 362, n. 18, where de Rachewiltz draws on a study by Ch'en Yuan.]

tem for Chinese land. Also, he regulated usurious interest rates charged by Uighurs and quashed plans to recruit virgins for the Mongol court. When Ögödei, angered because a Chinese taxation-bureau chief was guilty of improprieties, said, "You tell me Confucius's teachings are to be implemented and that Confucians are all good, so how is it I end up with this sort?" Yeh-lü acted as an apologist, arguing that only a few Chinese officials were bad. And it was to Ögödei, who was fond of alcohol, that Yeh-lü showed the stopper of a wine cask, saying, "Soaked in wine, even iron ends up like this." Such are the items in Sung Tzu-chen's memorial for Yeh-lü Ch'u-ts'ai. It concludes, "If you had not appeared when you did, where would mankind be now?"

Yeh-lü Ch'u-ts'ai's poetic corpus, the *Chan-jan chü-shih chi*, or *Collection of the Lay Believer of Settled Quietude*, is one of few such collections from the period to survive. The scenes and products of far-western regions appear in his poetry. For example, the following seven-character regulated verse, the third in a series of five entitled "Feelings on a Spring Outing in Ho-chung," describes Ho-chung, or Samarkand.

> In the border region of Ho-chung, as spring draws to a close,
> The dense luxuriance of garden and wood seals crumbling walls.
> Above the mountains to the east, skies blue on blue after the
>   passing of rain;
> In West Park flowers falling, riotous layers of blue-green.
> Bluish olive branches have begun forming fruit,
> Green grape-thickets already enwrap dragons.[40]
> Amid idleness, fragrance ended, spring is on the wane;
> Languid beneath the leaves, a spent butterfly flutters slightly.

Yeh-lü Ch'u-ts'ai's collected poems, which could serve as a useful source for historians and geographers, have yet to be seriously studied. His prose work, the *Hsi-yu lu*, or *Record of a Journey to the West*,[41] after being long buried in the Japanese palace collection, was brought to light earlier this century by Kanda Kiichirō and is prized by scholars in Central Asian studies.

---

[40] [Presumably the twisting and turning of grape thickets give the appearance of dragons.]

[41] [Translated by Igor de Rachewiltz, "The *Hsi-yu lu* by Yeh-lü Ch'u-ts'ai," *Monumenta Serica* 21 (1962): 1–128.]

# Chapter 3

## SOUTHERN SUNG LOYALIST POETRY, 1250–1300

### The Fall of the Southern Sung

While North China was falling victim to Mongol advances in the early thirteenth century, to the south the Southern Sung remained untouched. The dynasty's capital of Hangchow prospered and, along with it, the poetry of its urban populace. A prevailing ignorance of outside affairs bred a kind of indifference and seems even to have helped bring about a flourishing of townsman literature.[1]

During the reign of Ögödei-qan (r. 1229–1241), son of Chinggis-qan (Genghis Khan) and second in the ruling line, Mongol cavalry were occasionally spotted along Southern Sung borders. However, events were soon to remove the Mongols and their threat from the minds of southerners. First, Ögödei suddenly redoubled his determination to conquer to the west rather than to the south. Also, after his death in 1241, the internal unity of the Mongols weakened.

---

[1] The circumstances are similar to those in Japan during the late Edo period: abroad, the West was making serious incursions into India and China, while at home, much the same sort of situation and attitude prevailed as during the later years of the Southern Sung.

The lull that these events brought to the south was intermittently broken. In 1258, for example, Möngke-qan (r. 1251–1259) and his younger brother Qubilai (Khubilai) led an army that was to cut Southern Sung territory in two.[2] Upon Möngke's death this plan collapsed and a false lull resumed. The Southern Sung prime minister at the time, Chia Ssu-tao, held peace discussions with Qubilai at the front and purposely carried back to his sovereign false reports about the disgraceful terms of settlement.[3] Thus was the capital city of Hangchow able to remain in an undisturbed state of peace.

When the century passed the three-quarter mark, the day of reckoning finally came. It was Chinggis's grandson, Qubilai, who finally defeated and annexed the Southern Sung. Qubilai-qan (r. 1260–1294) viewed himself as being above all else the ruler of China.[4] Both in this and in the way he paid unstinting respect to Chinese culture, he differed from preceding Mongol rulers, who had considered themselves rulers of an empire in which China was merely a part. In recording dates, earlier Mongol rulers had used such names as the Year of the Rat or the Year of the Cow. Symbolically, Qubilai departed from this when he became qan in 1260. He employed Chinese-style names for his reign periods: Chung-t'ung, or Central Unification (1260–1264), and Chih-yuan, or Achieving a Beginning (1264–1294). In the fifth year of his reign Qubilai established the Great Capital (Ta-tu), or Qan-balïq, on a site encompassed by modern metropolitan Peking (to the north of Yen-ching). Three years later, in 1267, he named the

---

[2] [Note the study by Thomas T. Allsen, *Mongol Imperialism: The Politics of the Grand Qan Möngke in China, Russia, and the Islamic Lands, 1251–1259* (Berkeley: University of California Press, 1987).]

[3] [For an evaluation of Chia Ssu-tao's role that differs from this received one, see Herbert Franke, "Chia Ssu-tao (1213–1275): A 'Bad Last Minister'?" in *Confucian Personalities*, pp. 217–34. For the historical background to Sung loyalist poetry, see Jennifer Wei-yen Jay-Preston, "Loyalist Personalities and Activities in the Sung to Yüan Transition, ca. 1273–1300," Unpublished Ph.D. dissertation, Australian National University, 1983 (revised version forthcoming in the Occasional Papers series, Program in East Asian Studies, Western Washington University); and Paul D. Buell, "The Sung Resistance Movement, 1276–1279: An Episode in Chinese Regional History," *Annals of the Chinese Historical Society of the Pacific Northwest* 3 (1985–86): 138–86.]

[4] [Note the study by Morris Rossabi, *Khubilai Khan: His Life and Times* (Berkeley: University of California Press, 1988).]

new dynasty the Yuan. Unlike the earlier Han and T'ang dynasties, which took their names from the native regions of their ruling families, the name Yuan was consciously based on a passage in the *I ching*, or *Classic of Change*, where it suggests a "new beginning." It was about this time also that Qubilai engaged the Neo-Confucian scholar, Hsu Heng, as Chancellor of the National Academy. Hsu was the first of many Chinese men of letters brought to the Yuan court.

Qubilai, China's unifying emperor, could not read Chinese. Nor was his respect for Chinese civilization without limit. He was cool to the examination system, steadfastly refusing to allow its reinstatement. Yet he listened to lectures on Confucian doctrine translated for him into Mongolian. And he seemed especially pleased with the practical Neo-Confucianism advocated by Hsu Heng, which stressed the ordering of the individual self so that there might be equanimity in the family; this in turn would lead to the state's being properly ruled and to peace prevailing in the world. With Qubilai's accession to the throne, the threat to Chinese civilization posed by the Mongol invasions diminished considerably.

Given his aspiration to unify all of China, Qubilai was determined to be successful in the undertaking. Immediately upon becoming qan in 1260, he gave priority to establishing contact with the Southern Sung, so as to prepare the way for unification. He sent Hao Ching (1222–1275), a disciple of Yuan Hao-wen, as his State Envoy to the South.[5] The prime minister of the Southern Sung at the time, Chia Ssu-tao, afraid the truth about his dishonorable conduct in earlier negotiations with Qubilai might leak out, detained Hao in the small city of Chen-chou on the banks of the Yangtze, a house arrest that was to last some fifteen years. The following poem from this period by Hao Ching, "Springtime Reflections at New Hostel," mentions a tally, the insignia of his charge as legate.

> Tarrying here, no one to talk with,
> In melancholy thought I go my rounds under the eaves.
> A nocturnal chill tinges the moon in the river;

---

[5] [Note the study by Dietlinde Amann Schlegel, *Hao Ching (1222–1275): Ein chinesischer Berater des Kaisers Kublai Khan* (Bamberg: K. Urlaub, 1968).]

Spring trees darkly give off mist.
Though inept at my own welfare, I still grip firm the tally;
My road at dead end, I would like explanation from Heaven.
It takes supreme effort, steel wound round one's finger,
Despite countless twists to maintain an ever firmer will.

Using the stratagem of Su Wu, the Former Han figure who, while a captive of Hsiung-nu tribesmen, communicated with the Han emperor by fastening letters to the feet of wild geese, Hao allegedly kept Qubilai informed of his activities by using birds flying north.

In order to help overcome the tedium of confinement, Hao Ching, like Su Shih in Sung times, took to writing a complete set of poems employing the same rhyme words in the same order as those found in the poetry of T'ao Ch'ien. This clearly reflects how, as a disciple of Yüan Hao-wen, he was part of the Chin dynasty tradition of "Su studies."

One reason for Qubilai's dispatching an army in 1274 to conquer the south was Hao Ching's continued confinement there. Along the Yangtze town after town fell to the Mongols. The commander in chief, General Bayan, had received orders not to kill indiscriminately. Two years later, in 1276, his conquering army entered the Sung capital of Hangchow.

The Sung court had virtually disappeared. All officials with the least bit of ability had fled, leaving only the helpless behind. The two empress dowagers, the mother and grandmother of the six-year-old Sung emperor, Kung-tsung, were in a state of utter confusion. At Kao-t'ing Hill on the outskirts of the capital, the Mongols, now in the heart of Chiang-nan, or the Southland, presented a demand for immediate surrender.

*Ping-tzu* year, first month, thirteenth day[6]—
Timbrels beating, drums pounding, they descend upon Chiang-nan.
On Kao-t'ing Hill, blue smoke rising,
Our ministers gape at one another as if soused.[7]

Thus did the courtier Wang Yüan-liang record the painful event. The poem, a seven-character quatrain, is the first of a series of

---

[6] [I.e., January 30, 1276.]

[7] [Cf. the translation by Watson, "Translator's Preface," *An Introduction to Sung Poetry*, p. v.]

ninety-eight written by Wang entitled "Songs of Hu-chou." The
third reads:

> In the audience hall, crowds of courtiers dumbly silent,
> General Bayan presses for surrender papers.
> Their Three Majesties together behind pearl blinds,
> Ten thousand cavalry, curly-bearded, surround the palace steps.[8]

Only one man of courage among the courtiers remained in the
city. The widowed empresses were to make him prime minister,
charging him with carrying out negotiations with the Mongols.
Thus did Wen T'ien-hsiang, as the Southern Sung was about to
fall, emerge as the outstanding figure in the Chinese resistance
movement against the Mongols. He also was to become China's
model poet of resistance.

## Wen T'ien-hsiang
## (1236–1283)

Like many other Sung poets, Wen T'ien-hsiang was born in
Kiangsi; in fact, he came from the same county-district of Lu-ling
in Chi-chou as did Ou-yang Hsiu.[9] At the age of twenty, in 1256,
Wen was First-Place Graduate in the metropolitan examinations.
He was highly praised by his examiner, the widely learned Wang
Ying-lin, who wrote on the examination paper known to him only
by number that the writer displayed "loyalty steadfast as iron and
stone."

As a youth, Wen T'ien-hsiang enjoyed the carefree, leisurely
existence of a pampered son living in a great family in times of
peace. Even after becoming an official, he spent much of his time
amid the quiet calm of his resort, Wen shan, or Literary Mount,
on a peak south of his native town. Lines like the following appear
in his work dating from this period:

---

[8] [Cf. the translation by Watson, ibid., p. v.]

[9] [Note the studies by Horst Huber, "Wen T'ien-hsiang (1236–1283): Vorstu-
fen zum Verständnis seines Lebens," Unpublished Ph.D. dissertation, Universität
München, 1983, and William Andress Brown, *Wen T'ien-hsiang: A Biographical
Study of a Sung Patriot* (San Francisco: Chinese Materials Center Publications,
1986).]

> Living amid mountains, startled that the dynasty is already the
>   Eastern Chin,[10]
> On my mat, I write many a poem in the late T'ang style.

Here he was influenced by the late Sung fashion of imitating the minor poems of the late T'ang.

Wen T'ien-hsiang was forty years old when the Sung dynasty fell. From that time on, his life—as fully recorded in his anthologies of verse—was a series of traumas. Wen's first anthology, the *Chih-nan lu*, or *Southward-Pointer Record*,[11] commences at the time when, as prime minister, he was sent by the Sung empress dowagers to negotiate with the Mongol forces outside Hangchow. He rode unaccompanied into General Bayan's camp outside the city walls and proceeded to deliver a lecture on great events past and present in Chinese history. From the expressions on their faces as they listened to his words being translated, Wen could tell the Mongol generals were impressed.

> Proud and dignified, I ride out alone to the barbarian camp—
> Successes and failures, past and present, I lay out directly.
> Northerners, staring, style me "a real man,"
> As if to say one still remains in the South.[12]

The Mongols were in fact so impressed that they refused to let Wen T'ien-hsiang return. They sent him off by boat to Peking, in escort with other captive Sung officials.

Together with his trusted subordinates, Wen T'ien-hsiang planned an escape. After arriving by boat at Chen-chiang in Kiangsu they managed a successful break, but ran into trouble in the nearby Sung loyalist enclaves of Chen-chou and Yangchow,

---

[10] [A reference to T'ao Ch'ien's "Peach-Blossom Spring," where, after happening upon a utopian enclave out of the past, a man returns to his Eastern Chin home. The Eastern Chin, like Wen T'ien-hsiang's Southern Sung dynasty, was a period when the north was occupied by non-Chinese "barbarians."]

[11] [A "southward pointer" is a compass, used here metaphorically in the sense of the poet's having his direction or bearings, of following the set and proper course ordained by the natural order. Wen T'ien-hsiang also suggests his constancy in being ever oriented to the south—here, the Southern Sung. Moreover, the compass points south—that is, imperially—with its "back" to the north.]

[12] The fact that the character ending line one does not rhyme with those ending lines two and four, as is customary with poems in the quatrain genre, probably reflects the hasty circumstances of its composition.

where all suspected him of having become a Mongol spy. Denied city entry, with enemies to the front and rear, he managed despite extreme hardship to get to the Kiangsu seacoast.

Poems in the *Chih-nan lu* relate each of these events. The following is a five-character regulated verse written upon reaching the coast. Leaving the "Imperial City" of Hangchow, the party had reached the Hai-men, or Gateway to the Sea, district of Kiangsu, hiding in thickets by day and traveling on foot by night.

> Amid bitter weeping, I left the Imperial City,
> And came in disguise to this Gateway to the Sea.
> Long have I not heard the crow of cocks,
> And lately, too, there've been lice to squeeze.
> Many a white hair has probably sprung up,
> While few blue-kerchiefed followers remain.
> Yet as long as I am allowed to live,
> I will do my utmost to be worthy of Heaven and Earth.

The group set out by sea from the Kiangsu coast for Foochow in Fukien. A government in exile was being set up there by Emperor Kung-tsung's younger brother, Chao Li, the Prince of I. Wen T'ien-hsiang's first poetic record of events, the *Chih-nan lu*, comes to an end after he passes Wen-chou on the Chekiang coast, Foochow still the goal.

After having helped install the Prince of I as emperor in Fukien, Wen T'ien-hsiang rushed off to his home region in Kiangsi to lead anti-Mongol guerilla activity in the area's districts. However, dissension continued in the Fukien court; Wen was given a new title, Duke of Hsin, and kept at a polite distance. The child-emperor Tuan-tsung died in 1278, two years after his installation. The reign of his younger brother began with a new reign-period title, Hsiang-hsing, or Auspicious Rise (1278–1279). At the end of the same year Wen T'ien-hsiang was taken captive by the Yuan general Chang Hung-fan at Ch'ao-yang in Kwangtung. Wen took poison, hoping to kill himself, but the attempt proved unsuccessful. No poems date from this two- to three-year period.

Wen T'ien-hsiang's second poetic anthology, the *Chih-nan hou-lu*, or *Southward-Pointer Later Record*, records events from spring of the following year, 1279, when, tracked down and cornered on the Kwangtung sea, the Sung leadership was fighting its last battle. Wen T'ien-hsiang witnessed events aboard the ship of his captor, Chang Hung-fan. When requested to write a letter advising the Sung forces to surrender, Wen remained silent, simply showing the general the following poem. His brave words—which incorporate place names fortuitously at hand, Shore of Shame and Estrangement Sea—are an attempt to overcome the feeling of despair on the occasion.

> Hardship, my lot since passing the single-classic exam;
> Shields and daggers in futile struggle four years now.
> Native hills and streams shattered, like wind-buffeted catkins,
> Life floats haplessly as duckweed beaten by rain.
> At Shore of Shame, I speak of shame;
> On Estrangement Sea, lament estrangement.
> From of old, who among men has escaped death?
> Leave a heroic heart shining in the pages of history![13]

Chang Hung-fan, the brother of Chang Hung-lueh (the poetic follower of Yuan Hao-wen mentioned previously), was a man of considerable literary accomplishment. When showed the above poem, he remarked, "A fine man and a fine poem," and continued to press the pursuit of the Sung emperor's boat.

On the sixth day of the second month, 1279,[14] while Wen T'ien-hsiang looked on helplessly, the tutor of the young Sung emperor, Lu Hsiu-fu, and other Sung loyalists hurled themselves into the sea rather than surrender to the Yuan.[15] The event inspired many of Wen T'ien-hsiang's longer poems. Here is a shorter example, a five-character regulated verse in which he puts a brave face on despair.

> Since calamity came to the Southern Sea,
> Men die, strewn like tangles of flax.
> Putrid waves pound my heart to bits;
> Whirlwinds blast my hair white.
> Each hill and each stream,
> Neither home nor country!
> Yet, with the will of a thousand years,
> My life is without end.

[13] [Cf. the translation by Brown, *Wen T'ien-hsiang*, p. 155, n. 354.]
[14] [I.e., February 28.]
[15] This is reminiscent of the famous episode acted out in Japan by the Heike clan at Dannoura in 1185.

From the Kwangtung southern extremity of the empire Wen T'ien-hsiang, as the foremost captive of the Mongols, was sent under escort to Peking far in the north. He composed one poem after another en route and, while passing through his hometown district of Lu-ling in Kiangsi, tried unsuccessfully to commit suicide by fasting. In Peking, Wen T'ien-hsiang was treated most graciously by Qubilai and the Yuan court. Even when repeatedly urged to give allegiance to the new dynasty by Sung officials and by Kung-tsung, the former Sung child-emperor who had capitulated, Wen refused. Thereafter he was removed to the damp, mud-walled prison of the Yuan quartermaster general.

It was during the third year of his captivity in Peking that Wen T'ien-hsiang wrote his most famous and representative work, "Song of the Upright Spirit."[16] The "spirit" informing his uprightness, a concept put forward in Sung Neo-Confucianism, might best be translated as "energy." Wen T'ien-hsiang's preface to the poem, in which he describes his life since being taken prisoner by the Mongols, helps the reader understand his work.

> I am captive in the northern court, placed in a dark mud room eight feet wide and two rods deep that has been hollowed out of the ground. It has a single doorway, low and small, and unpainted windows, short and narrow.
>
> On a summer day like today, I am enshrouded in various energies. When puddles of water converge from all sides, setting my chair afloat, this is the "energy of water." When muck half dries and is covered with bubbles of steam, this is the "energy of earth." When the weather clears and in the fierce heat no breeze can pass through, this is the "energy of the sun." When cooking fires kindled under the eaves add to the cruel heat, this is the "energy of fire." When stores turn rotten and are left to decay, their staleness oppressive, this is the "energy of rice." When one is thrown in with others, rank-smelling and dirty,[17] this is the "energy of men." And when assorted foulnesses come forth—from outdoor privies, dead corpses, and rotting rats—this is the "energy of filth."

[16] [Cf. the translations of the poem cited by Brown, *Wen T'ien-hsiang*, p. 2, n. 5; in addition, there is one by John Turner, *A Golden Treasury of Chinese Poetry* (Hong Kong: Chinese University of Hong Kong, 1976), pp. 280–87.]

[17] Probably a reference to the Mongols.

Faced with several such energies at once, few would not fall ill. But weak as I am, I have lived under these conditions for two years. You might wonder, what has sustained me? I scarcely know myself. Mencius once said that he "nourished his floodlike spirit-energy." Those energies mentioned above number seven; mine is but one. Yet in fighting seven with one, I am not at all concerned—especially since this "floodlike spirit-energy" is none other than "the upright spirit of heaven and earth." Thus it is that I have written the following "Song of the Upright Spirit."

After the preface comes Wen T'ien-hsiang's poem proper, presented here with short explications of the historical incidents to which it alludes.

Heaven and Earth are infused with an Upright Spirit
That gives varied shape to a stream of manifestations:
On earth below, the great river and sacred peaks,
In heaven above, the sun and stars.
In man, it is a greatness of spirit,
Overflowing, that fills the firmament.
The imperial way, meeting with tranquility,
Offers a genial age of enlightened rule.
Yet when the age ends in impasse, steadfastness appears
In one example after another in history's annals.
The spirit is found—
   In the bamboo slips of the Grand Astrologer of Ch'i,

> The historian of the Spring and Autumn period who was executed for recording on bamboo slips that Ts'ui Chu had assassinated his sovereign. The two younger brothers who succeeded him faced the same circumstance and met the same fate.

In the brush of Tung Hu of the State of Chin,

> Who in the Spring and Autumn period assigned responsibility for his lord's murder to Chao Tun, who would not prosecute those in his clan who had killed the leader (with whom Chao had had a falling out).

In the hammer of Chang Liang,

> Who tried without success to assassinate the harsh First Emperor of the Ch'in dynasty.

And in the pennant of Su Wu.

> Who, remaining loyal to his sovereign while held captive by Hsiung-nu barbarians, never parted with this emblem of his charge as a legate.

Among its manifestations, one finds—
The head of General Yen Yen,

> The Three Kingdoms general who, upon defeat, declared, "You have
> rudely wrested away our land. The land may have generals with severed
> heads, but it has no generals with heads that bow in allegiance."

The blood of the court chamberlain, Chi Shao,

> The Chin minister who died defending his sovereign from attack. The
> ruler directed his ministers not to wash away the blood of Chi that had
> spattered his robes.

The teeth of the Sui-yang defender, Chang Hsun,

> The T'ang soldier whose mouth was pried open by the sword blade of one
> of An Lu-shan's soldiers after defeat. Most of his teeth had been gnashed
> away in fury at the rebels.

And the tongue of the Ch'ang-shan defender, Yen Kao-ch'ing.

> The T'ang official whose tongue was cut out for cursing the victorious
> rebel leader, An Lu-shan.

It appears in—
The one with the Liao-tung cap,
Whose purity was sharper than ice or snow,

> The black beretlike cap of Kuan Ning, the scholar who at the end of the
> Han sought refuge in Liao-tung (present-day Manchuria), preferring to
> lead an unsullied life there to serving the Wei emperor, Ts'ao Ts'ao.

Chu-ko Liang's memorial on his expedition,
Of a heroism that brings tears to the gods,

> The rousing third-century "Ch'u-shih piao," or "Memorial on Setting Off
> with My Troops," which Chu-ko Liang submitted to the throne upon de-
> parting to attack the state of Wei.

The beating of the boat paddle
In stouthearted avowal to swallow the Chieh,

> The paddle Tsu T'i of the Eastern Chin used to beat his gunwales, while
> vowing to regain territory from Chieh barbarians.

And the rebel-smiting tablet
That split the traitor-lackey's skull.

> The tablet used by the T'ang official, Tuan Hsiu-shih, to smash the fore-
> head of the would-be usurper, Chu Tz'u.

What is infused with this spirit,
With awesomeness lasts for eternity.
When it penetrates the sun or moon,

All question of life or death becomes immaterial.
Upon it depend the fundaments of earth;
Up from it soar the pillars of heaven.
It is the mainstay of human relations,
The very basis of morality!
Alas! Things have come to an awful pass;
I, a worthless one, have not done my best.
A Ch'u prisoner who tied his cap strings,[18]
I was transported by stages to the far north.
Being boiled alive would be sweet, like candy;
Indeed I requested it, to no avail.
Will-o'-the-wisps flicker in my dark cell;
The spring courtyard is shrouded in gloom.
I am a racehorse feeding from the same pail as oxen,
A phoenix eating together with chickens.
One morning, shrouded in poisonous miasma,
I will end up a skeleton in the gutter.
After two years of this heat and cold,
The noisome vapors have taken leave.
Alas! This dank quagmire
Has become my paradise!
I need no shoddy tricks
To hold the *yin* and *yang* harmless—for I have my Upright Spirit.
Reflecting on it glowing bright within me,
I gaze at the clouds above, floating, white.
Unending is my heart's affliction—
Oh, Heaven above! When will it end?
Greats of the past grow daily more distant,
But their example remains as long ago.
In the breeze from the eaves, I spread out a book to read;
Before me shines the bright virtue of the past!

This is not a poem fraught with despair. The line, "Oh, Heaven above! When will it end?" might be taken as momentary flinching, but Wen T'ien-hsiang recovers immediately and ends on a note of confidence about the future. The conquest of individual despair without resort to an epicurean kind of decadence had been a hall-

---

[18] [A reference to Chung I of the Warring States period, who, alone among Ch'u officials taken prisoner by the Chin, donned his official cap as a sign of loyalty to his state.]

mark of Su Shih's poetry.[19] But here the poet urges conquest of despair at a time when the future of the entire Chinese people was most in jeopardy!

Wen T'ien-hsiang's second and third poetic anthologies, the *Chih-nan hou-lu* and the *Yin-hsiao chi*, or *Collection of Wailings*, were written during his four years of incarceration. At the end of 1282, Qubilai personally summoned Wen for a final opportunity to render obeisance to the Yuan. Wen requested only that he be put to death. On the ninth day of the twelfth month,[20] at the age of forty-six, Wen T'ien-hsiang was taken to the vegetable market of Peking and publicly executed.[21]

During his imprisonment Wen T'ien-hsiang wrote two hundred poems composed entirely of lines rearranged from Tu Fu's poetry. The following example of one of these "Culled Line Poems," numbered 143, was written in the persona of his wife while thinking of her.

> I bound up my hair to become your wife;
> In a flurry we fled marauding forces.
> Parted in life, separation in death,
> I turn my head and tears stream down.

Each line is from a different Tu Fu poem. In his preface to the series Wen tells us:

[19] See *An Introduction to Sung Poetry*, pp. 104ff.

[20] [I.e., January 17, 1283; hence, Wen T'ien-hsiang's dates as given at the heading of this section.]

[21] The work most instrumental in introducing Wen T'ien-hsiang to Japan was the *Seiken igen* (Testaments concerning Those Who with Quiet Resolve Gave Their All to Past Sovereigns) by Asami Keisai (1652–1711), a pupil of Yamazaki Ansai (1618–1682). In the introduction to the volume, published in 1687, Keisai explains to the reader, "As for true men of devoted loyalty past and present, it is always the case that, once the alarm has sounded and destruction is near at hand, such men come to the fore." One chapter each in the work is devoted to Ch'ü Yuan, Chu-ko Liang, T'ao Ch'ien, and Yen Chen-ch'ing. The fifth deals with Wen T'ien-hsiang; others deal with poets treated below.

Also well known in Japan is the poem, "The Song of the Upright Spirit," written by Fujita Tōko (1806–1855) in imitation of the original; it begins:

> The grand, upright spirit,
> In its multifariousness culminates in this Land of the Gods;
> Towering upwards, it becomes Mt. Fuji's crest,
> And soars majestically for a thousand autumns.

Everything I want to say, Tu Fu earlier said for me. Daily entertaining myself with his poems, unable to put them down, I end up feeling they are my own and forget they are his. Thus I know it is not that Tu Fu, of his own accord, was able to write such poetry; his poetic lines, naturally, have the language of human nature and sentiment; they dogged Tu Fu, [it is not that he pursued them].

In other words, Tu Fu expressed the universal feelings of mankind everywhere as its representative. By simply assembling lines from his poems, one can write poetry of one's own.

## Other Poets of Resistance

In keeping with Qubilai's unification policy, the Mongol takeover of the Southern Sung was less harsh than that of the Chin dynasty in the north some forty years earlier. Still, the defeat amounted to an unprecedented humiliation for the Chinese. All of the empire, north and south, was under the control of an alien people. Moreover, this was the first time in history that all of South China had been forced to submit to non-Chinese rule.

Although the fierceness of the initial Mongol onslaught was largely blunted by the time it reached the south, its net effect was much the same: the life and livelihood of the people, especially those concerned with literature, became stifled. The ladder of success formerly open to men of letters, the examination system, was cut off. And those regional officials who replaced the Chinese, either Mongols or men from the Western Regions, were generally unreceptive to Chinese culture.

This engendered a fierce reaction among Chinese. Acts of resistance ensued which were accompanied by a poetry of resistance, or at least strong reaction. In some cases the poems they wrote are not in themselves particularly outstanding, but they have remained a historical fact of great significance in the consciousness of Chinese.

### *Wang Yuan-liang*
### *(fl. 1276)*

Wang Yuan-liang was a zither master at the Southern Sung imperial residence in Hangchow. In the second month of 1276 the city fell to the Mongols and the poet-minister Wen T'ien-hsiang was

sent captive to the north. A few days later Wang Yuan-liang ac-
companied a special group sent under escort to Peking. It in-
cluded the palace ladies in waiting, the six-year-old Sung emperor
Kung-tsung, and the two empress dowagers.

Wang Yuan-liang composed a series of ninety-eight seven-
character quatrains entitled "Songs of Hu-chou" that describe the
unhappy journey.

> Out the palace gates, they quickly board painted boats,
> Graceful nymphs, red against red, white on white.
> Mountains and streams stretch far away, a grief inconsolable—
> Again there appears a crescent of Southern moon rising.

A few weeks later when the entourage arrived in Peking, a
large welcoming reception lasting for days was hosted by the Yuan
empress, the wife of Qubilai. Although the guests had no need to
fear for their lives, it was only natural that they felt ill at ease. One
of the poems in Wang Yuan-liang's series describes the welcoming
banquet.

> Emperor Qubilai opens the first banquet;
> His Majesty solicitously thanks all for their trouble.
> The Great Yuan Empress shares with us Mongol fare;[22]
> The feast over, we return—the sky filled with moonlight.

During the first few of the many years he was to stay in Peking,
Wang Yuan-liang, zither in hand, often paid calls on the impris-
oned Wen T'ien-hsiang, and he later composed a poem mourning
his death. In addition, Wang authored several poems of farewell
to the young emperor and his mother when they withdrew from
secular life: the one to become a Buddhist monk in Tibet with the
name Moksa (i.e., Deliverance) Expounder (*Mu-po chiang-shih*),
the other to become a nun.[23]

In accordance with Qubilai's wish, the Sung palace ladies ac-
companying the two empress dowagers north were married off to
carpenters in Peking. When Wang Yuan-liang eventually returned
to the south, these former ladies in waiting composed poems for

---

[22] The "Mongol fare," as becomes clear from other poems in the series, included
butter, koumiss, raw onions, horsemeat, mutton, and grape wine.

[23] The legend that the last Sung emperor's son was later to become the Yuan
sovereign Shun-ti is purely apocryphal.

him as a parting gift, which later became available in booklet form as the *Sung chiu-kung-jen shih-tz'u*, or *Poems of Former Palace Ladies of the Sung*. The following is one by Wang Ch'ing-hui, ranked Lady of Bright Deportment.

> My fate fragile as a leaf,
> I am exiled on a road thousands of miles.
> In the yellow dust beyond Peking's walls,
> I sit and listen sadly to the sound of fulling cloth.[24]

After returning to the south, Wang Yuan-liang withdrew from the world to become a Taoist recluse. Looking like an unworldly holy man, with a flowing beard, broad nose, and imposing frame, he could be seen wandering Mt. Lu in Kiangsi. Local people were later to worship his portrait as that of a god.

A scholar-friend of Wang Yuan-liang, Ma T'ing-luan, praised his poetry for its similarity to Tu Fu's "history in poetry." Although it is only a suspicion of mine, it is indeed possible that the poetic-diary form, as found in Wang Yuan-liang's "Songs of Hu-chou" and in Wen T'ien-hsiang's *Chih-nan lu* and *Chih-nan hou-lu*, was influenced by the narrative recitations of traditional tales popular among the common people at the time.[25]

## Hsieh Ao
## (1249–1295)

The poet Hsieh Ao, originally from Ch'ang-hsi in Fukien, was a staff adviser to Wen T'ien-hsiang when the latter carried out anti-Mongol guerrilla activities in the south. After Wen's death, Hsieh paid respects to his leader's departed spirit on a fishing platform next to Fu-ch'un Mountain in Chekiang—the site where tradition had it that the commoner-friend of Emperor Kuang-wu of the Later Han, Yen Kuang, had enjoyed fishing. The matter is reported in a prose piece by Hsieh entitled "Teng Hsi-t'ai t'ung-k'u chi," or "An Account of Mounting the Western Platform to Carry Out Lamentations." Out of fear of discovery by the Mongols, Hsieh makes the nominal object of his sacrifice the T'ang official, Yen Chen-ch'ing. Sandwiched in the account is a song he sang

---

[24] [Cf. the translation by Watson, "Translator's Preface," *An Introduction to Sung Poetry*, p. vi.]

[25] Recitations in a form like that of *naniwa-bushi* in Japan.

while striking a rock with his monk's staff and calling out to Wen T'ien-hsiang's soul.

> At daybreak your spirit set out,
>     To what far region?
> Do not return!
>     The River Kuan has turned black.
> Become a red phoenix as you might,
>     There is nothing for your sacred beak to feed upon.

He recounts that, after repeating the incantation many times over, both staff and rock shattered.

### Lin Ching-hsi
### (1242–1310)

Lin Ching-hsi came from the P'ing-yang area of Chekiang. Some years after the fall of the Sung dynasty—the account varies as to when—a Tibetan lama by the name of Yang Lien-chen-chia (Byaṅ-spriṅ Caṅ-skya), who was associated with the Mongols, dug up the imperial tombs of the six Southern Sung emperors in Shao-hsing, so as to put a curse on the revival of the dynasty.[26] He removed the bones and, reburying them amid the ruins of the former imperial palace in Hangchow, erected a pagoda at the site.

Chinese were indignant at this outrageous act. Lin Ching-hsi and some of his companions disguised themselves as herb gatherers to search for the bones, and they had a fisherman recover Em-

---

[26] [The equivalent transcription given here of Yang Lien-chen-chia's name is the one used by Chan Hok-lam in his "Wei Su," in *Dictionary of Ming Biography, 1368–1644*, eds. L. Carrington Goodrich and Fang Chaoying (New York: Columbia University Press, 1976), p. 1466. Cf. Herbert Franke, "Tibetans in Yüan China," in *China under Mongol Rule*, ed. John J. Langlois, Jr. (Princeton: Princeton University Press, 1981), p. 321: "It is probable that Yang Lien-chen-chia . . . renders a Buddhist name. It might be reconstructed as Rin-čén skyabs, a name which is attested in Tibetan sources, but so far no person of this name can be identified with the Yang Lien-chen-chia of the Chinese sources." As Franke notes, Paul Ratchnevsky tentatively reconstructs the name as Rin-čén skya; "Die mongolischen Großkhane und die buddhistische Kirche," in *Asiatica: Festschrift Friedrich Weller zum 65. Geburtstag gewidmet*, eds. Johannes Schubert and Ulrich Unger (Leipzig: O. Harrassowitz, 1954) p. 494, n. 50. Note the study of the event by Paul Demiéville, "Les tombeaux des Song meridionaux," *Bulletin de l'Ecole Française d'Extrême-Orient* 25 (1925): 458–67; reprinted in Paul Demiéville, *Choix d'études sinologiques (1921–1970)* (Leiden: E. J. Brill, 1973), pp. 17–26.]

peror Li-tsung's skull, which had been thrown into a lake. Re-burying the remains near the site of the former tombs, they marked the location by planting holly, which was traditionally placed at emperors' tombs.[27] At the time, Lin Ching-hsi wrote the following old-style verse in irregular lines, entitled "Holly Blossoms." The dragons that are mentioned are symbols of the former emperors.

> When holly blossoms bloom,
> My heart grieves the day long.
> Across the Yangtze, a storm—to no avail, shadows under a clear sky;
> Deep in June mountains, we guard faint snow blossoms.
> Dragons lurk in the cloudy haze of stony roots
> Where no common ants dare bore.
> We have transplanted them here, to a world of immortals
> Who know eternity in a moon-reflecting cup.
> Here is the mournful nightjar, with all other birds in attendance;[28]
> At midnight with their single cry, mountain bamboo splits.

Lin Ching-hsi wrote a postscript, in the form of a seven-character old-style poem, to the collected poetry of Lu Yu. Lu Yu, of course, was the fiercely patriotic Southern Sung poet whose life-long wish had been to see the non-Chinese Chin dynasty driven out of the north and for all of China to be reunited under one sovereign. Eighty-five years old and on his deathbed, Lu Yu had written a poetic last will to his sons that ended with the words:

> The day the royal armies march north and seize the Central Plain,
> At the family sacrifice don't forget to report it to your father!

Seventy years later, during his great-great-grandsons' generation, the wish that China be reunited came true. But how ironic that the situation was completely the reverse of what Lu Yu had wished! Lin Ching-hsi concludes the poetic postscript with his own words of sorrow:

[27] Another tradition connects the heroic deed of reburial with T'ang Chueh rather than with Lin Ching-hsi. Hsieh Ao, for example, wrote a poem entitled "Song of the Holly, On Parting from T'ang Chueh." [See also pp. 134–35.]

[28] [The "mournful nightjar" is the bird, sometimes rendered in English as a "cuckoo," into which "the Shu soul," the soul of an ancient king of Shu, was said to have been transformed.]

Now that your grandsons have seen the Nine Provinces united,
What can they report when sacrificing to their father?

## Cheng Ssu-hsiao
## (1239?–1318)

Cheng Ssu-hsiao from Fukien presents an interesting example of
anti-Mongol sentiment. All of the names he bore, other than his
surname, were adopted after the fall of the Sung and, without ex-
ception, refer to the former dynasty. By adding one element to the
second character in his first name, Ssu-hsiao, the combination can
read "Ssu Chao," or Thinking of Chao, the family name of the
Sung ruling family. He was styled Suo-nan, meaning Residing in
the South, the territory of the former dynasty. And his literary
name, I-weng, signifying Recalling Father, can be understood to
mean that he is mindful of his Sung period ancestors. Similarly,
by slightly rearranging the elements in the first two characters of
the four-character inscription outside his residence in Soochow,
"Pen-hsueh shih-chieh" (meaning roughly Cave World), it could
read "Ta-Sung shih-chieh," or "The Great Sung Empire."

Whenever Cheng Ssu-hsiao heard Mongolian spoken in the
street, he is said to have covered his ears and fled. And although
he drew many paintings of orchids, he never painted in the
ground beneath them. Questioned about this, he retorted: "Don't
you know? The land's been stolen by barbarians!"

Among the few of his poems that have been preserved, the
series of twenty-four entitled "Brocade Cash, Last Chuckles" mer-
its attention. Containing interjections of vernacular language, the
poems reveal deep-seated resentment at the upsetting of the social
order by the Mongols. Cheng Ssu-hsiao's note accompanying the
series states in ironic self-deprecation, "Coins made from brocade
may look beautiful, but in fact are useless."

> For the past twenty years or so,
> It isn't that I don't enjoy a little wine.
> As of late, even Heaven has gone mad,
> And hounds this world of men.
> Reviled are bygone ice and snow,
> And praised, upstart flowers and willows.[29]

[29] ["Upstart flowers and willows" refer to the new Mongol nobility.]

No choice but to go it alone,
I stick the tip of my nose in my mouth.[30]

In the mid-seventeenth century history repeated itself. Instead of a Sung defeat at the hands of the Mongols, the Ming dynasty fell to non-Chinese Manchus. An iron box was discovered hidden in a temple well in Soochow, and the work it contained, purportedly a posthumous manuscript by Cheng Ssu-hsiao, became a

---

[30] To avoid the foul smell. [The painting reproduced on p. 2, from which the orchid on the cover to this volume is derived, is a famous one by Cheng Ssu-hsiao in which the ground has been left out. The poem to the right of the orchid is also by Cheng Ssu-hsiao (the one to the left by Ch'en Shen, another Sung loyalist). Inscribed as being by Suo-nan weng, or the Old Man Residing in the South, it reads as follows:

> With bowed head, I asked Fu-hsi,
> "Who are you that you came to this land?"
> Before setting brush to paper, I open my nostrils—
> Throughout the firmament, the fragrance of antiquity afloat.

Fu-hsi was the mythical sage-emperor associated with the introduction of culture to China (through the eight trigrams) and here, by implication, with the introduction of painting. The painter's strong identification with Fu-hsi in the poem carries an intense assertion of pride on the part of the poet in both himself and his culture. Cheng Ssu-hsiao is in effect saying: "You, Fu-hsi, brought China culture (including painting), transforming chaos to enlightenment; that is the sort of man you are. Well, so am I! The civilization of the past (through you) is alive (in me), and its fragrance will not only survive but flourish!" The "nostrils" in this poem stand in complementary opposition to the "nose" in the poem above, making the statement in each that much stronger. Cf. the translation (of the poem inscribed on the painting) by Ho Wai-kam, "Chinese under the Mongols," in *Chinese Art under the Mongols: The Yüan Dynasty (1279–1368)*, Sherman E. Lee and Ho Wai-kam (Cleveland: Cleveland Museum of Art, 1968), no. 236. The painting is discussed by James Cahill, who states that, of the extant works attributed to Cheng Ssu-hsiao, this is the only one that is genuine; *Hills beyond a River: Chinese Painting of the Yüan Dynasty, 1279–1368* (New York: Weatherhill, 1976), pp. 16–17. In addition to this painting, which is in the Abe Collection of the Osaka Municipal Museum of Art (and is here reproduced with its permission), "Another handscroll, with almost identical composition and similar inscriptions, is now in the Freer Gallery of Art, Washington, a possible copy of the Osaka scroll. A third handscroll, representing two small plants and epidendrum, is now in the Yale University Gallery. A fourth handscroll, representing bamboos, is in the Takashima Collection of Tokyo. Although there are many colophons by connoisseurs of [the] Yüan and Ming periods in these last two scrolls, their authenticity is still in doubt." Li Chu-tsing, "Cheng Ssu-hsiao," in *Sung Biographies: Painters*, ed. Herbert Franke (Wiesbaden: Franz Steiner, 1976), p. 22.]

popular subject of discussion. Entitled *Hsin shih*, or *A Heart's Story*, it is full of undisguised abuse and hatred for the Mongols.[31] Because the hostility directed at the Mongols in the work could just as easily be applied to the Manchus, some contend that the manuscript was a later forgery used for contemporary purposes; others find the work genuine. The following seven-character quatrain, one of a series of five entitled "Spring Day, Occasional Poems," appears in the work.

> Since this morning, I have dreaded climbing the highest tower;
> Spring spent, only an autumn cast remains.
> Plants and trees barren and cold, life's mood sour;
> Breezes fetid, rains greasy—an entire sky sad.

The abortive Mongol invasion of Japan, when *Genkō*, or "Yuan bandits," were driven back by *kamikaze*, or "divine winds," is scarcely mentioned in the works of other Chinese writers. Several poems in the *Hsin shih*, however, mention the invasion and revel in the Mongol defeat. If not a later forgery, the work might be used as a source for the period.

## Hsieh Fang-te
## (1226–1289)

Originally from Hsin-chou in Kiangsi, Hsieh Fang-te passed the Sung official examinations in 1256, the same year as Wen T'ien-hsiang. Although a straitlaced, unbending official, after the fall of the dynasty he raised an anti-Mongol resistance force in his home district. When it was defeated, he fled to Chien-yang in Fukien, where he became a fortune-teller.

Qubilai commanded his Chinese secretary, Ch'eng Chü-fu, to go to the south to encourage former Sung officials to serve the new regime. Hsieh Fang-te refused, referring to himself as a "wang-kuo chih ta-fu," or "Grand Master of the fallen dynasty." On the fifth summons, in 1288, he was finally compelled by Wei Yuan-yu to go to Peking.

When setting out on the journey, Hsieh Fang-te showed the following poem to his wife and children and to his friends. In this seven-character regulated verse he refers to Kung Sheng and Po-i,

---

[31] There exists a late Edo reprint of the work in Japan.

both of whom fasted themselves to death in the face of a change in government, the one refusing to serve the usurper-emperor Wang Mang (r. A.D. 9–23), the other withdrawing to a mountain in the west rather than eat grain provided by the new Chou dynasty. Nan Ch'i-yun, who is a figure found in Han Yü's writing, died maintaining his honor during the eighth-century An Lu-shan rebellion. References in the third couplet are to passages in the Confucian text, the *Meng-tzu*, or *Mencius*.

> Amid snows, pine and cedar turn ever greener;
> So too by a journey like this will my constancy grow firmer.
> Can the world be deprived of the purity of a Kung Sheng?
> Po-i's unsullied example is not alone among men.
> If one's principles are high-minded, life's loss can be endured;
> And if virtue is great, we learn how paltry a thing death is.
> That Nan Ch'i-yun was a man unbending to the end,
> The eyes of supreme Heaven see clearly.

The poet set about fasting en route to Peking and died upon arrival in the capital. His wife and children were executed as resisters.

Hsieh Fang-te is famous for editing the *Wen-chang kuei-fan*, or *Writing Models*, a collection of Chinese classical-prose pieces that has enjoyed wide popularity in Japan.[32] Also noteworthy is his correspondence with Liu Hsiu-yen that contains discussions of poetry.

There were other eminent men of letters among the ranks of Sung loyalists who, while not poets, devoted themselves to scholarship after the establishment of the Yuan dynasty. We owe them much for their great accomplishments: Wang Ying-lin (1223–1296) for the *K'un-hsueh chi-wen*, or *Information Recorded in Assiduous Study*; Hu San-hsing (1230–1302) for the *Tzu-chih t'ung-chien chu*, or *Commentary on the Comprehensive Mirror for Aid in Government*; and Ma T'ing-luan (1223–1289) and Ma Tuan-lin (1254–1325), father and son, for the *Wen-hsien t'ung-k'ao*, or *A Comprehensive Investigation of Official Documents*.

---

[32] Asami Keisai, the author of the *Seiken igen* collection of portraits of famous Chinese loyalists, devotes a chapter to Hsieh Fang-te.

## Poetry of Ordinary Townsmen

Acts of resistance from Wen T'ien-hsiang onward and the poetry of resistance that accompanied them are treated in Chinese history as events of great significance. They were to serve as important historical precedents. When the fortunes of the empire met with difficulty in later times—under Manchu pressure in the late Ming and from Western intrusions in the late Ch'ing—the example set by these Sung loyalists was never to be forgotten.[33]

Looking back at this period, it is easy to see the development of a spirit of resistance to non-Chinese rule. Yet there was another, less readily perceptible change taking place at the same time. In its quiet and far-reaching way it was to have great effect on the history of later Chinese culture and to reshape the history of Chinese poetry. Because of its impersonal nature this development has gone largely unmentioned in previous literary histories and has not been given the attention I feel it deserves.

Stated simply, under Mongol leadership the Yuan government restricted the participation of Chinese in governmental affairs. This forced Chinese to rechannel their energies, and many directed their efforts to literature. Thus the participation of ordinary townsmen in the writing of poetry broadened considerably.

A flourishing of poetry writing among townsmen was already much in evidence during the Southern Sung dynasty in the first half of the thirteenth century.[34] The Four Lings of Yung-chia and the poets of the Chiang-hu, or River and Lake School, were all ordinary townsmen. There was a shift; poetry was no longer the domain of government officials.

In the latter half of the century not only did Mongol subjugation not halt the tendency; in fact, it served to accelerate a development well under way. Suspension of the examination system signaled a curbing by Mongols of participation by Chinese in government. On the part of Chinese, there was on the one hand angry resentment and on the other energetic vitality. These could find an outlet in only one of two directions: either in participation in

---

[33] The writings of these men even served in late Edo Japan as a kind of bible among those nationalist advocates whose slogan was "*Sonnō jōi!*" or "Revere the emperor and expel the barbarians (i.e., foreigners)!"

[34] See the final chapter of *An Introduction to Sung Poetry*.

the commerce that had been developing in the region or in writing, especially the writing of poetry.

North China had experienced a similar situation during the first half of the century after the fall of the Chin dynasty. There, unemployed men of letters devoted themselves to producing works in the new literary genre of drama. Kuan Han-ch'ing, Ma Chih-yuan, and Po Jen-fu were in the forefront of those writing *tsa-chü* plays, the writing of which marked the first real flourishing of fiction in China.[35]

The situation was somewhat different in the south, where traditional literature was more firmly rooted. Fiction did not come into immediate prominence there; rather, poetry was the main outlet. Although no sources make this point explicitly, there are two kinds of material, treated respectively in the following sections, that indicate such was the case.

## Poetry Societies

The best evidence is offered by the short collection of a few dozen pages entitled *Yüeh-ch'üan yin-she*, or *Moon Springs Poetry Society*, edited by Wu Wei (dates uncertain) of P'u-chiang in Chekiang.[36] On the day of the harvest-moon festival, the fifteenth day of the tenth month, 1286,[37] Wu called for poetry contributions from literary groups throughout Chekiang, offering prizes for the best entries. The theme was to be "Fields and Gardens on a Spring Day, By Mood." The deadline for entries was set for the fifteenth day of the first month of the following year. No fewer than 2,735 people entered, 280 of whom qualified. According to an announcement on the third day of the third month, fifty participants were awarded prizes. The winner, a certain Lo Kung-fu (fl. 1287), belonged to the Hangchow Pure Recitation Society (*Ch'ing-yin*

---

[35] See my *Gen zatsugeki kenkyū*.

[36] [The "Moon Springs" of the collection's title was located near Wu Wei's home.]

[37] [Wu Wei uses the lunar-calendar term "Hsiao-ch'un yüeh," or "Minor-Spring Moon," to date the announcement. The fifteenth day of the tenth month, when the harvest festival traditionally took place, was associated with the balmy weather of spring—hence the appellation "minor spring." This and the two later dates noted in the text convert, respectively, into November 2, January 29, and April 16.]

*she*). By way of award, he received for public use seven pieces of silk, one piece of thin silk gauze, five writing brushes, and five ink slabs. His poem reads as follows:

> Growing old, no desire to appear at court or market,
> I wander free and easy in wooded valleys under an east wind.
> With a plow and good rain, I plant grain sprouts;
> Many a cold stream moistens the flowering plants.
> Calves let loose, in the morning I climb the plateau beyond the clouds,
> And listening to warblers, stand on the bridge beside the willow trees.
> Now that fresh grasses are growing by the poolside,
> Hsieh poetic ghosts can enter my dreams and beckon.[38]

The *Yueh-ch'üan yin-she* concludes with a poem by its sixtieth contributor, an anonymous entrant who styled himself Ch'ing-shan po-yun jen, or Man of Green Mountains and White Clouds. As appendices to the work, one finds the original announcement soliciting contributions, a description of responses, critiques of selections by Wu Wei, notes accompanying the prizes, and thank-you letters from the winners.

It is only by chance that such a work, which constitutes a sort of poetry-society magazine, has been preserved. Issued by one of many such societies throughout the region at the time, it hints broadly of a number of things. First, we know that there were at least 2,700 people of some poetic ability in the Chekiang region at the time. Second, with the exception of a few entrants like Ch'iu Yuan and Po T'ing whose poetic anthologies have been preserved, the great majority of entrants are otherwise unknown and can be assumed to have been ordinary townsmen. Third, it should be understood that such contests were initiated as a kind of privately sponsored imitation of the defunct examination system; in this respect, they sprang from a nostalgia for times past, a nostalgia that probably carried the implication of opposition to the Yuan government that had eliminated the examinations. And fourth, inasmuch as the sponsor of the event, Wu Wei, engaged Sung loyalist poets like Hsieh Ao, Fang Feng, and Wu Ssu-ch'i as advisers,

---

[38] [The final couplet refers to Hsieh Ling-yun (385–433) and his cousin, Hsieh Hui-lien. Hsieh Ling-yun related that it was while dreaming of his cousin that his most famous poetic line, one about spring grasses by the poolside, came to mind: "That expression came with divine help. It is not my own."]

we know that poets of resistance were the leaders of townsman poetry.

## Poetry-writing Manuals

The proliferation of simply and clearly written poetry-writing manuals aimed at the new class of townsman versifiers provides another indication of spreading interest in poetry; it also underscores the primacy of poetry writing at the time in the south. Two works of this kind had already appeared in the first half of the thirteenth century: the *San-t'i shih*, or *Poems in Three Forms*, by Chou Pi (fl. 1250), and the *Shih-jen yü-hsieh*, or *Jade Chips from the Poets*, by Wei Ch'ing-chih (fl. 1240).[39] In Yuan times, as illustrated by the following examples, these works were to multiply.

THE *YING-K'UEI LÜ-SUI*   In 1283 there appeared the forty-nine-chapter *Ying-k'uei lü-sui*, or *Aspiring to the Greats: The Pith of Regulated Verse*, compiled by Fang Hui. The work treats T'ang and Sung five-character and seven-character regulated verse by theme. Each chapter has a heading, beginning with "Panoramic Views after Climbing," "Palace Scenes," and "Remembrance of Things Past." Fang appends his own critiques to each poem. As his basis of judgment he uses the formula that for each couplet of "feeling" or "emotion" (*ch'ing*) there should be a couplet of "scene description" (*ching*). These concepts parallel those of "the intangible" or "felt" (*hsu*) and "the tangible" or "actual" (*shih*) in the *San-t'i shih*: "feeling" in Fang's work accords with "the intangible" or "felt" in the earlier volume, and "scene description" in the *Ying-k'uei lü-sui* is similar to "the tangible" or "actual" in the *San-t'i shih*. Fang also created a lineage for writers of regulated verse. He made Tu Fu the genre's Sole Founder (*I-tsu*) and the Sung poets, Huang T'ing-chien, Ch'en Shih-tao, and Ch'en Yü-i, the Three Patriarchs (*San-tsung*). Providing much detailed research on Sung poetry and on the lives of Sung poets, the *Ying-k'uei lü-sui* is a convenient work to use and for this reason has been widely popular both in China and Japan.

[39] See *An Introduction to Sung Poetry*, pp. 182–83. [Note also the study of the latter work by Volker Klöpsch, *Die Jadesplitter der Dichter: Die Welt der Dichtung in der Sicht eines Klassikers der chinesischen Literaturkritik* (Bochum: Brockmeyer, 1983).]

Fang Hui (1227–1306), the compiler of the work, was origi-
nally from Anhwei and had the literary name Hsu-ku chü-shih, or
Empty-Valleys Lay Believer. About Fang himself there has been a
great deal of criticism. There is the story concerning his governor-
ship of Yen-chou in Chekiang when the Mongol conquest of
South China was drawing to a close. While emerging from the city
gates to go to a parley with the Mongols, Fang urged the city's
defenders to fight to the death; a short while later he returned as
if in triumph, clad in the robes of a Mongol official. It is also re-
lated that during his later years when he was a leading literary fig-
ure in Hangchow, Fang Hui once engaged in excessive sport with
his young mistress; they knocked through a wall of the house,
crushing to death the Mongol who was sleeping next door—an
affair Fang managed to have settled out of court. Both anecdotes
are recorded by Fang Hui's fellow Sung loyalist, Chou Mi, in the
latter's *Kuei-hsin tsa-shih*, or *A Kuei-hsin Miscellany*.[40]

THE *LIEN-CHU SHIH-KO*    The year 1300 marks the date of pub-
lication of the twenty-chapter *Lien-chu shih-ko*, or *Linked-Pearl Po-
etry Types*. It classifies T'ang and Sung seven-character quatrains
according to three-hundred-odd *ko*, or "types," determined by
form of expression, the first being "the type in which all four lines
are parallel." The work's editor, Yü Chi (dates uncertain), was
from Po-yang in Kiangsi. Ts'ai Cheng-sun (fl. 1279) from Chien-
an in Fukien supplemented the work, occasionally inserting ex-
amples from his own writing. For example, under the heading
"the type in which repeated words are strung through the first
three lines," Ts'ai Cheng-sun offers his own poem, "Leaning on
the Balustrade," as the final illustration; the "repeated words
strung through the first three lines" are italicized.

How many times did I lean on the *balustrade* for a *midnight* tryst?
The feelings of *midnight* then cannot match my feelings *now*.
*Now* I must force myself to stand by the *balustrade*,
Empty steps bathed in moonlight, woods mantled in frost.

[40] Although Chou Mi, like Fang Hui, was a leading literary figure in Hangchow,
he was himself criticized by Yuan Chueh, the son of one of his friends, for making
huge profits dealing in rare art.

In his commentary to the poem Ts'ai Cheng-sun explains that it was written in 1276, the year the Sung dynasty fell, to express sorrow at its demise. Thus we gather that, like his teacher Hsieh Fang-te, Ts'ai was a Sung loyalist. In fact, when Hsieh was sent off to Peking, Ts'ai wrote a poem matching the rhyme words in the one his master wrote in farewell.[41]

The *Lien-chu shih-ko* soon disappeared in China, but it remained extant in Japan, having been transmitted there via Korea. After the publication of a critical edition in 1804 by Ōkubo Shibutsu (1767–1837)—one manifestation of the vogue for Sung poetry at the time in Japan—the work circulated widely.[42] In the preface to the edition, Yamamoto Hokuzan (1752–1812) states that there are reasons to believe the *Lien-chu shih-ko* was written to express resistance to the new Yuan regime: for one, the work contains numerous poems by Sung loyalist poets; for another, even though more than twenty years had passed since the fall of the Sung, the work initially bore a full title in which the name of the dynasty had prominence, *T'ang-Sung ch'ien-chia lien-chu shih-ko,* or *A Thousand T'ang and Sung Poets: Linked-Pearl Poetry Types.*

The material presented in this section, which will be elaborated upon in chapter 4, suggests that the fall of the Sung dynasty served to accelerate a remarkable increase in the number of townsman poets, especially in the lower reaches of the Yangtze, over the coming century and after.

# Liu Yin
## (1249–1293)

Attention thus far in this chapter has been focused mainly on developments in South China during the last quarter of the thirteenth century. We now shift to the north, to view happenings

---

[41] Cited above on p. 65. Ts'ai Cheng-sun also edited and published the *Shih-lin kuang-chi* (Extensive Record of the Forest of Poetry), a handy anthology that contains critical comments. The work is indicative of the increasing number of townsmen in need of such a compilation.

[42] The late Edo publishing world busily issued volumes like the edition of the *Lien-chu shih-ko* with a commentary by the Korean Sǒ Kǒjǒng, and the study by Abe Rekisai, the *Renju shikaku meibutsu zukō* (An Exploration of Famous Items in Linked-Pearl Poetry Types).

there over the same period. It has already been noted that Qubilai, having made Peking his Ta-tu, or Great Capital, energetically set about trying to attract Chinese scholar-officials to serve the new dynasty. In addition to Hsu Heng (1209–1281), the Confucian scholar close to Qubilai, the prime minister Liu Ping-chung (1216–1274) was also a Chinese official under the Mongols. From leading the life of a Buddhist monk, Liu returned to the secular world to serve the Yuan. His collection of poetry, the *Ts'ang-ch'un chü-shih chi*, or *Collection of the Lay Believer Storing Up Spring*, is still extant. The most prolific of Qubilai's scholar-officials, however, was Wang Yun (1227–1304), whose work is gathered in the *Ch'iu-chien hsien-sheng ta ch'üan-chi*, or *Great Collection of Writings by the Gentleman of the Autumn Streams*. All three Chinese were northerners, and none expresses particular animosity toward the Mongols. It was already half a century since the fall of the Chin, and that dynasty too, after all, had been one of non-Chinese rule. This was quite different from the situation in the south, where alien rule was unprecedented and the reaction was one of shock.

Liu Yin, a scholar from Pao-ting in Hopei who was styled Meng-chi and whose literary name was Ching-hsiu hsien-sheng, or Gentleman Quiescently Cultivating Himself, presents a case quite different from that of the three scholar-officials including Hsu Heng.[43] Liu Yin and Hsu Heng were similar in their pursuit of the philosophy of Chu Hsi, which had recently been transmitted to North China. When both were invited by Qubilai to serve the throne, however, Liu declined, claiming he must look after his aged mother; Hsu assented, a decision that met with Liu's disapproval. A famous exchange between the two took place when Hsu called upon Liu. Hsu Heng explained himself, "Unless I act this way, the Way cannot be carried out." To which Liu Yin replied, "Unless I act this way, the Way cannot be respected." As a result, all of Liu's years were spent in his native Pao-ting.

Liu Yin is second only to Yuan Hao-wen among poets of

---

[43] [For discussion of Liu Yin in particular, as well as several other figures examined in this chapter (Hsieh Fang-te, Cheng Ssu-hsiao, and Wen T'ien-hsiang), and of Chao Meng-fu, who is treated in chapter 4, see Frederick W. Mote, "Confucian Eremitism in the Yüan Period," in *The Confucian Persuasion*, ed. Arthur F. Wright (Stanford: Stanford University Press, 1960), pp. 202–40 and 348–53.]

North China during the century. His immersion in Neo-Confucian philosophical studies is reflected in his poetry, which is sometimes overly discursive but possesses great inner strength and energy. The following five-character regulated verse, entitled "Half My Life," is offered by way of example.

> Half my life I have eked out a living,
> Alone and beset by troubles.
> My few words come not from storing anything up;
> The eccentricity is a kind of pure laziness.
> I provision myself on the morning mist,
> My social life like night rain.
> No guests come to my thatched gate,
> Which is out-of-the-way and, besides, long shut.

The final couplet of the above stands in contrast with the one in the following seven-character regulated verse entitled "Autumn Suburbs." Leaving his precincts, the poet would sing of the austere natural beauty of the north.

> Walking through the green forest, about to turn back,
> I notice someone's thatched cottage in the woods.
> Clouds half laden with rain billow forth;
> Winds gradually blow them away, faintly revealing mountains.
> With experience of the world, one learns to value indifference;
> As the glitter of things wears off, one appreciates the calm of autumn.
> Heaven has made these fine landscapes to be a match for poetry,
> And not allow a hermit to stay behind firmly closed gates.

Liu Yin, like both Su Shih before him and his own senior contemporary Hao Ching, wrote a complete set of poems using the same rhyme words in the same order as that of T'ao Ch'ien's poetry. He was thus firmly in the Chin dynasty tradition of "Su studies." No example of this work will be offered here.

The next selection, a five-character regulated verse entitled "Staying Overnight at a Farmer's," is a poem that expresses Liu Yin's love of both unsullied nature and unsullied living.

> Happening to stay overnight with a farm family,
> I am given a welcome fitting an immortal:
> Food and drink spread out beside the door,
> Wife and children bow before the lamp.
> Where eyes flash love or hate, who can be at peace,

Or where emotions easily swing from fire to ice?
Who would have thought, here beyond the world of men,
There still are rustics of truehearted sympathy!

Liu Yin wrote a few five-character quatrains entitled "Miscellaneous Poems on Rural Life." Each has its special charm; witness the following.

Shouting, calling me out of bed from outside the window,
The old man next door ran over to say:
"The last few days you couldn't see the mountains;
This morning they're a freshly washed blue."

And:

Sunset was thick with the feel of rain
And a happy glow filled the southern acres.
Who expected an all-night wind
Would bring forth the willows beyond the gate?

Another poem, "The Wood Peony," from a series of eight entitled "Drinking at a Mountain Pavilion, Miscellaneous Plants," offers an observation more ironic in tone.

The world changes, daily becoming finer;
Flowers, too, must do the same.
I suspect that in remote antiquity
Their beauty could not equal that of today.

Liu Yin was not only opposed to the Mongols. He was also of the opinion, rare among northern Chinese of the time, that the three non-Chinese dynasties from the Liao and Chin onward were illegitimate, not just the Yuan. He expresses this view most clearly in a long old-style poem called "Song of Yen." The poem that follows hints at the same sentiment. Entitled "The I Terrace," it was written when Liu climbed the remains of the Gold Terrace (Huang-chin t'ai) in I-chou, Hopei, originally built by the Warring States monarch, King Shao of Yen. The poem is in seven-character regulated-verse form.

The lone bird in view sinks into sky-locked recesses,
While clouds carry parting's grief to weave evening shades.
The hills and streams of myriad states, once Yen and Chao,
For a hundred years were the sway of Liao and Chin.

The glitter of things wears off as autumn's glow fades;
No cup of wine can plumb the depths of the human heart.
When countless frosty pines sway in craggy ravines,
Heaven sets leaves aflutter to help purify our song.

In the poem "Ascending the Market Tower in Pao-ting," Liu Yin expresses naked resentment at the stationing of Mongol troops in the city: "Popular songs adulterated with the foreign, / The city's name is saddled with occupation." Among his poems, some seem to lament the fall of the only "orthodox" dynasty, the Southern Sung, not the Liao or Chin. The old-style poem entitled "Rising in the Morning to Record Events: *Ting-ch'ou* Year, Fifth Month, Twenty-Eighth Day" may be a case in point. (*Ting-ch'ou*, or 1277, came one year after the fall of the Southern Sung capital of Hangchow and two years before the end of the dynasty.) In it, Liu recounts his dream that two of the three moons in the southern sky disappeared, leaving only one central one, by implication the Southern Sung.[44]

From the fourteenth century onward, the preponderance of Chinese poetic activity was to be in the south. For a long period after Yuan Hao-wen and Liu Yin few poets were to emerge from their native Shansi and Hopei. Liu Yin was the last before the area's literature entered a period of extended decline.

---

[44] Treatment of Liu Yin in Asami Keisai's *Seiken igen* follows that of Wen T'ien-hsiang and Hsieh Fang-te. Hsu Heng's assent to Qubilai's request to serve the Yuan, in contrast with Liu Yin's refusal, prompted Keisai to consider Hsu a most disloyal subject who served barbarians.

At about the time Asami Keisai was recording this judgment, however, Hsu Heng was being praised by Itō Jinsai (1627–1705) as one of the Three Great Sages Past and Present (*Kokin san taiken*). It was Jinsai's view that Hsu's intentions were proper, so he ranked him together with Ch'eng Hao and Fan Chung-yen of the Sung.

# Chapter 4

# THE MATURATION OF YUAN POETRY, 1300–1350

## Two Developments Come to Fruition

The political history of the first half of the fourteenth century offers a period of respite. Although the effects of the Mongol depredations of the previous century continued in the form of rule carried out under the Mongols, there was peace throughout China.

After Qubilai died in 1294, his grandson, great-grandsons, and great-great-grandsons succeeded one another to the throne in periods of short reign. Only one later ruler, the last Yuan emperor, Shun-ti (Toghon-temür), was on the throne for an extended period, from 1332 to 1368. As before, leading government figures were either Mongols or peoples from the Western Regions; Han Chinese were unable to realize political aspirations. But as earlier Mongol intensity waned, the Chinese political system advanced. This is best symbolized by the reinstatement of the civil-service examinations in 1315, during the reign of Qubilai's great-grandson, Emperor Jen-tsung (Ayurbarwada, r. 1311–1320). Although Mongol emperors continued to be unskilled in Chinese and carried on their lives using Mongolian, their secretaries, who made up the Han-lin Academy, were Chinese civil officials. The Chinese classics were translated into Mongolian and lectures were given on them in the presence of the emperor. Qubilai's great-great-grandson, Emperor Wen-tsung (Tugh-temür, r. 1329–1332), was a lover of Chinese painting and calligraphy. And the final Yuan emperor, Shun-ti, as noted earlier, was non-Mongolian to the extent that he was rumored to be the illegitimate son of the last Sung emperor.[1]

Peace of the sort described above was maintained until the mid-fourteenth century, when disturbances broke out in various areas of the south to harass the final Yuan emperor. Largely cut off from government, Han Chinese devoted their full energy to literature. Several developments came to fruition at this time, including two that make the period a noteworthy starting point for later poetic history.

The most prominent of these developments is the maturation of poetry among ordinary townsmen, especially in the area along the lower Yangtze. A trend under way since the Southern Sung, it came to full maturation at this time and set the direction of later poetic development that was to be under townsman poets, particularly those from the south.

Also, the conscious use of T'ang poetry as a model for verse writing approached its final form. This was the solution to a problem outstanding since Southern Sung times and marked the beginning of a trend that became more pronounced in the poetry of the following Ming dynasty. It came to maturation largely under the direction of townsman poets of southern origins who had moved to the north to serve the Yuan court in Peking.

The Yuan dynasty was an abnormal age, one in which a non-Chinese people ruled China. In several respects Mongol force sought to cut off the earlier Chinese cultural tradition. An age with an unusual atmosphere, at the same time it was one with a new atmosphere in which several fresh developments took place. The birth of Yuan *tsa-chü* drama is the most prominent of these; developments in poetic history are others.

I will first discuss the process by which the poetry of ordinary

---

[1] For more detailed discussion, see my article, "Gen no shotei no bungaku" ("The Literature of the Various Yuan Emperors"), 1944–45; reprinted in *Yoshikawa Kōjirō zenshū*, 14: 232–313.

townsmen matured in the south. Townsman poetry of the
Yangtze Delta region originated with the Four Lings of Yung-chia
and the Chiang-hu, or River and Lake School, amid the regional
peace that prevailed under the Southern Sung during the first half
of the thirteenth century. As noted in the preceding chapter, the
destruction of the Southern Sung intensified its development in
the second half of the century. However, it is during the period
treated in this chapter, in the first half of the fourteenth century
toward the end of the Yuan dynasty, that townsman poetry be-
comes fully mature.

This process of maturation appears not only in a quantitative
increase in the number of those writing poetry but also, more re-
markably, in a qualitative improvement, at least in the desire for
such improvement. Previously, poetry by townsmen had been
limited to minor poems descriptive of minor themes. The works
of the Four Lings of Yung-chia and the River and Lake School are
representative of this. For poetic technique they used the minor
verse of late T'ang poets, the so-called late T'ang style. This pre-
dilection was one shared by writers included in the *Yueh-ch'üan
yin-she*, or *Moon Springs Poetry Society*, discussed in the previous
chapter.

But townsman poets gradually came to pursue a higher-level
poetry. No longer satisfied with writing verse that drew upon the
materials and sentiments of everyday life, they wanted to expand
their horizons and, as it were, take flight. What appeared in re-
sponse was the singular poet of the age, Yang Wei-chen. A towns-
man himself, he became the leader of the new townsman poetry.

## Yang Wei-chen (1296–1370): The Leader of Townsman Literature in the South

Yang Wei-chen came from what was probably a merchant family
in the small town of Chu-chi in the Shao-hsing area of Chekiang.
Although he passed the imperial examinations in Peking in 1327
at the age of thirty-one and served for a period as a tax official in
his native Chekiang, he soon resigned his post. Thereafter he lived
a free and unencumbered life as the leader of various poetry soci-
eties in the Chekiang area, dying at the age of seventy-four.

Yang Wei-chen undertook to write poetry beautiful in language, unfettered in spirit, and rich in imagination. For technique he modeled himself on the poetry of the past that tended in these directions, namely, the *yueh-fu* ballads of the Han and Six Dynasties and the poetry of Li Po and Li Ho during the T'ang—writings which since Northern Sung times had been long neglected.

In 1346 a ten-chapter collection of Yang Wei-chen's verse edited by his disciple, Wu Fu, was published, the *T'ieh-yai hsien-sheng ku-yueh-fu*, or *Old-Style Ballads by the Iron-Cliff Gentleman*, Iron Cliff being Yang's pen name. This first collection of Yang Wei-chen's poetry contains 409 poems, a few of which will be presented here.

One, entitled "Song of the Ching-wei," employs an old legend. In ancient times the daughter of Emperor Yen drowned in the Eastern Sea. To gain revenge on the sea for causing her death, she turned into a bird called the *ching-wei*, which daily picks up stones in its beak from mountains to the west, carries them over the ocean, and drops them in so as to fill the sea.[2]

> In the sea, water;
> On the mountain, stones.
> Seas don't contract, nor stones whittle down.
> In her beak she carries stones to level the sea;
> Blood dripping from her mouth will dry only when the seas do.

In the following comparatively long poem, Yang Wei-chen describes a nymph whom he imagines as coming to Lo-fu Mountain in Fukien, a place famous for its plums. It is entitled "Song of the Lo-fu Mountain Beauty."

> In the empty South Sea sky, the moon pure white,
> The Three Peaks resemble a fist, the sea a pond.
> In green robes singing and dancing, stirring no dust,
> The sea fairy is fish-borne on ripples slender.
> Airily she comes and alights on fragrant grasses,
> Lustrous as a moon ray passing through forest branches.
> Powder washed away, undarkened by tropical vapors,
> With white sleeves touching she is a heron about to fly.
> In her hand, the flute of the Old Man of Chün Mountain;

[2] In the title of the poem the character used for the word "song" indicates that the piece is a tune for the zither.

But few appreciate her new "Yellow Crane" tune.
In the Southland, her playing would break T'ao Yeh's heart;
Listening in the rain, I sit through the night until the Wu Mountain
dawn.

The poem is not intended to be followed logically. The "Three Peaks" in the second line refer to P'eng-lai and other mythical mountains in the sea. The "Old Man of Chün Mountain," "T'ao Yeh," and "Wu Mountain" are all names of legendary persons or places, the latter two associated with sexual adventure.

Yang Wei-chen's seven-character quatrains often imitated ballad-style "bamboo-branch" (*chu-chih*) love songs of the T'ang. The following two are from a series of nine composed at West Lake in Hangchow and are entitled "West Lake Bamboo-Branch Songs."

I warned you not to climb South High Peak;
You warned me not to climb North High Peak.
South Peak is cloudy, North Peak rainy;
Clouds and rains excite each other—to my grief![3]

South High and North High peaks are both names of mountains in the West Lake area. The second poem reads:

At lake's mouth—over the storied boat, lake skies cloudy;
At lake's center—under Broken Bridge, lake water deep.
Rudderless, the storied boat is your resolve;
Pillars still intact, Broken Bridge is my heart.

"Broken Bridge" is the name of a span near West Lake's Lone Mountain (Ku shan).

Feeling that the "Man-hsing," or "Casual Poems," of Tu Fu represented the earlier poet's freest expression, Yang Wei-chen used them as a model for writing his own verse. The following is one of a series of seven of his own "Casual Poems." It depicts a village wineshop scene, the "old lady" of the third line being the proprietor's wife.

Willow blossoms, white on white, tufts bursting;
Plums, green on green, kernels yet unformed.

---

[3] [Ever since the appearance of the "Kao-t'ang fu," or "Rhymeprose on Mt. Kao-t'ang" (attributed to the third-century B.C. author, Sung Yü), the term "clouds and rain" has normally had sexual connotations in Chinese literature.]

> My old lady tends the stove, her cap like a gourd;
> Kid sister is sipping wine, her mouth like a cherry.

Yang Wei-chen's boldest work is found in the collection of verse from his later years, the six-chapter *Fu-ku shih-chi*, or *Collection of Poems Restoring Ancient Style*, which was compiled when he was over seventy. Poems of his, like "The Toilette Box, Eight Themes" in seven-character regulated verse and "Twenty Supplementary Toilette Box Songs" in seven-character quatrains, imitate love poems by the T'ang poet Li Shang-yin called "Untitled Poems" and can be compared with "The Toilette Box Collection" by Han Wo of the late T'ang. Often they make use of the theme of a young girl's sensuality.

From "Twenty Supplementary Toilette Box Songs" two are presented here. The first is entitled "Manicuring." The newt (or water lizard) of the poem's first line is a small animal used as a love charm. Ground with buttercup stamens into a powder, it was used in painting nails.

> At night, newts ground with buttercup stamens,
> Ten fingernails change into red pelican beaks.
> Relaxedly they pick out a tune—
> Peach blossom specks floating on a stream.[4]

The second poem, entitled "Mating," is about pleasures of the night.

> Eyebrow mounds dark, facing the spluttering lamp,
> Her billowy half bun spills over pillow's edge.
> Arms and legs joined with another's, fetchingly about to sob,
> She grasps the fine silk, nearly kneading it to pieces.

Both of these poems have a freedom and unrestraint that broke ordinary bounds. Not only do they mark a break from the rationalistic, stiff poetry of the Northern Sung epitomized by Su Shih, they also mark a break from earlier townsman poetry that had been limited to what was ordinary and everyday.

Yang Wei-chen's life, like his writing, was stamped by a free

---

[4] [The special nail polish described here was said to change color if its wearer was unfaithful. Cf. the translation by Jonathan Chaves, trans. and ed., *The Columbia Book of Later Chinese Poetry: Yüan, Ming, and Ch'ing Dynasties (1279–1911)* (New York: Columbia University Press, 1986), p. 65.]

and generous spirit. In accord with his deathbed wish his funerary inscription was written by Sung Lien (1310–1381), a younger friend who became an important official at the beginning of the Ming dynasty. "At times, donning a Hua-yang turban and feathered jacket, floating his bright boat on Dragon Pool or Phoenix Shoal, he would play his iron flute. When the flute's sounds pierced the clouds, those who saw him wondered, might he be a banished immortal?" A "banished immortal" (i.e., one exiled from heaven to earth) refers to the T'ang poet Li Po. As Sung Lien's inscription adds, Yang Wei-chen lived the later years of his life at Sung-chiang in Kiangsu: "Not a day went by that he did not have guests, and not a day went by that they did not get drunk. . . . Calling the serving girls to sing the lyrics of "White Snow," he would accompany them on his phoenix lute. Some of the guests would stagger to their feet and dance." Everything here speaks of a style of life different from that of ordinary people, one insistent on there being special prerogatives for artists. Townsman literature had begun by describing what was common and ordinary in the life of average urban residents. With Yang Wei-chen, however, townsman literature went beyond such bounds in terms of both content and style of life.

Because both Yang Wei-chen's writing and way of life seemed so odd, Wang Wei (1323–1374), who became an important official under the following dynasty, criticized the poet for being a "literary devil" (*wen-yao*). But the majority of townsman poets looked up to Yang as a leader and in their writing emulated him or at least admired him. As the head of poetry societies throughout the area, dressed in unusual garb, he traveled back and forth throughout Chekiang and Kiangsu—to Hangchow, Sung-chiang, Wu-hsi, and other cities. He was always accompanied by a large contingent of young writers. As Sung Lien's funerary inscription relates: "The students of Wu and Yueh [the Chekiang-Kiangsu area] flocked to him in large numbers, much in the way mountains all pay homage to Mt. T'ai or rivers all flow to the sea. This continued for more than forty years." The superficial eccentricities of his life-style notwithstanding, Yang Wei-chen's popularity can be accounted for in part by his attractive personality. A more important reason, of course, is that his writings were widely supported and emulated by townsmen. His boldest love poems, including

"The Toilette Box, Eight Themes," were presented as poetic prac-
tice-models to the Yun-chien shih-she, or Yun-chien Poetry Soci-
ety, in Sung-chiang.[5] From references in various of Yang Wei-
chen's prose pieces, it is clear that the number of prose and poetry
societies throughout the area at the time was enormous.

Yang Wei-chen's character as a poet of the ordinary townsman
is reflected in the variety of people to whom he presented verses.
He gave poems to a fortune-teller, a physiognomist, the black-
smith who cast his beloved iron flute, a writing-brush craftsman,
a physician, and a cauterizer; and he presented prose pieces to a
female storyteller, a puppeteer, and a combmaker.

Toward the end of his long life, when Chu Yuan-chang, the
Founder Emperor of the Ming dynasty, ascended the throne,
Yang Wei-chen was summoned and strongly urged to serve as an
official of the new government. He refused on the grounds that
he had already served the Yuan dynasty. The following is from the
"Song of the Old Widow," which he presented in reply.

> Old Widow,
> Old Widow,
> Going on seventy plus nineteen;
> It's clear, when young you already had a husband.

Although the first Ming emperor, as will be described below,
treated men of letters with cruelty, he was unexpectedly magnan-
imous to this old man, allowing him to return home as a scholar
in retirement. In a poem presented to Yang at the time, Sung Lien
wrote, "Presented in white clothes, in white clothes you re-
turned," that is, you came to court and left it in the clothes of a
commoner, a nonofficial. In 1370, during the third year of Ming
rule, Yang Wei-chen's life as a townsman poet ended at the age of
seventy-four.

The advent of Yang Wei-chen, together with the flourishing in
the south of a townsman poetry centered around him, marks the
beginning of the Ming and Ch'ing poetic world, for poetry con-
tinues to evolve around townsman poets of this region. Although
there had been signs of such a development as early as the thir-
teenth century under the Southern Sung, it took definite form

---

[5] [Yun-chien is another name for Sung-chiang.]

during the latter part of the Yuan dynasty. Ironically, it was the abnormal situation of rule by non-Chinese Mongols which, by cutting Chinese off from political affairs, helped bring about the development.

## The Origins of *Wen-jen*

The writing and style of life of Yang Wei-chen mark the introduction of a new type of figure, one not found in earlier Chinese cultural history. Specifically, Yang Wei-chen's writings and those of the group associated with him, as well as their life-style, represent an attitude toward life in which literature and the arts were made supreme. Since they considered the arts supreme, these figures felt that, as artists, they had special prerogatives as to how they lived and so paid little heed to accepted norms. From this time on, those having such an attitude were called *wen-jen*, or "independent (free) artists."[6]

Earlier Chinese civilization had scarcely produced such figures. From early times literature had been considered an essential element in Chinese culture. But it was rare for other cultural elements to be swept aside and for literature alone to be accorded value. For most of the time throughout history, if measured against the other two realms with which it was united, philosophy and statecraft, literature would have been accorded a lower rank. Literary figures or poets were considered to be better as literary figures or poets by virtue of having talent and responsibility in political and philosophical affairs. The representative figures of Northern Sung poetry, Ou-yang Hsiu, Wang An-shih, and Su Shih—all of whom were philosophers and statesmen at the same time they were poets—embody this ideal especially well.

Yang Wei-chen and those centered around him, the *wen-jen* of South China at the end of the Yuan dynasty, were of a different view. They had no ties to philosophy and none with political affairs; or rather, the situation was such that they of necessity had no contact with the latter.

The term *wen-jen* had been used before. But its use to desig-

---

[6] [The author was explicit in wishing that the adjective "free" be part of the rendering of *wen-jen* into English.]

nate the type of person described here probably originates at this time. As such, it demanded a person who devoted himself solely to literature and the arts and who had no connection with politics. Consequently, a *wen-jen* had to be a pure townsman who was not a bureaucrat-official. Moreover, as a qualification for being an artist, one had to manifest a greater or lesser degree of eccentricity or deviation from accepted norms.

It was difficult to produce such a figure in the cultural milieu of earlier dynasties, when men of letters were expected to have some sort of connection with political affairs. There had been figures like the Chiang-hu, or River and Lake School poets, who had no political standing and were devoted to poetry writing. But in Southern Sung society the tripartite unity of literature, philosophy, and political affairs was universally accepted. Besides, poets of the Chiang-hu School were not the most important figures in their society. And among Chiang-hu poets there was no consciousness of dedicating oneself to a literature that held supreme position among the various activities in one's life.

In Yuan times, however, Chinese were cut off from politics. Because of this the period produced *wen-jen* whose attitude was one of devotion to literature and who, to give emphasis to this attitude, did not hesitate to make their life-style eccentric. The period also produced a society that accorded respect to such *wen-jen*, as illustrated by Yang Wei-chen and the relations he had with those around him. This was another new development brought about by alien rule.

The *wen-jen* ideal demanded proficiency not only in literature but in other arts as well, especially in painting and calligraphy. In cases where painting or calligraphy was an artist's special skill, the ideal demanded proficiency in poetry and prose writing as well. Ni Tsan, one of the Four Great Painters at the end of the Yuan dynasty, offers a good example of the *wen-jen* ideal.

## Ni Tsan
### (1301–1374)

Ni Tsan, being the wealthiest man in his native Wu-hsi in Kiangsu, was clearly of bourgeois origins. Having little interest in the family's business, he adopted the nicknames Lazy Tsan (*lan Tsan*) and Ni, the Perverse (*Ni yü*), and squandered his family's wealth principally through collecting paintings and calligraphy. He eventually converted all his possessions into cash, which he gave away to friends and acquaintances. When disorders later broke out in the lower Yangtze area, only Ni Tsan escaped the depredations that other men of wealth suffered.

As a manifestation of *wen-jen* eccentricity, Ni Tsan was fastidious to the point of being abnormal. Several anecdotes have been handed down about his compulsive cleanliness. For example, he is said to have spread out goose feathers under the open privy to soak up the feculence.

Ni Tsan, along with three other men of townsman origins—the Yellow-Heron Man of the Mountains, Wang Meng of Wu-hsing; the Crazy Older Brother, Huang Kung-wang of Ch'ang-shu; and the Plum-Blossom Man of the Way, Wu Chen of Chia-hsing—is commonly known as one of the Four Great Painters (*Ssu ta hua-chia*) of the Yuan dynasty.

Ni Tsan's poetry, like his painting, has great inner strength and energy. The following five-character quatrains are entitled "Inscribed on My Paintings, Two Poems."

> By the Eastern Sea is a man not well,
> Who styles himself "absurd," "perverse."
> He paints on walls, writes on silk and paper—
> Is this not an excess of madness?[7]

And:

> Green woods hide twisted thickets;
> Distant waters form an interval, then the indistinguishable.
> In this place of flying herons and bathing ducks—
> People's houses half-lit by the setting sun.

The following is a seven-character quatrain entitled "Sixth Month, Fifth Day—An Occasional Verse."

> I sit and watch the tint of moss about to climb my robes;
> On the pool's spring water, lingering light turns hazy.
> In the desolate village, all day long no carts or horses;
> Now and then a remnant cloud accompanies a wild crane home.

---

[7] [Cf. the translation by Chaves, *Later Chinese Poetry*, p. 69.]

Ni Tsan not only wrote ingenuous poetry of this sort to match his painting scenes, he also wrote romantic verse. In response to the prompting of his friend Yang Wei-chen, he tried his hand at "bamboo-branch" poems in the folk-song style. The following two verses are from a series of eight entitled "Bamboo-Branch Songs."

> Beside the lake is a young girl, fifteen or so,
> Hair tied with black damask, her makeup light.
> She has qualms about mom and dad using barbarian speech,
> So sings the latest Chinese tunes tending bar alone.

The girl takes a dim view of the way her parents, out of deference to their clientele, use Mongolian; when taking care of the shop alone, she sings "new tunes," which are in Chinese. In contrast, the girl in the next song is the daughter of one of the Mongol soldiers occupying the area.

> The girl in braids living beside the lake
> Sings barbarian songs at dance parties.[8]
> Her fine silk musk-scented, speech in Uighur—
> White cotton covers her head like a white mist.

In his preface to these "Bamboo-Branch Songs" Ni Tsan tells of gazing at the scenery of West Lake and being overcome with feeling. Presumably his sadness was prompted by seeing a locale of such beauty, the former capital of the Southern Sung, now under Mongol occupation. Even among romantically inclined *wen-jen* poets, there were conscious feelings of reaction to alien rule.

Ni Tsan's five-character old-style poem, "Expressing What Is in My Heart," serves as his autobiography. It relates how reality further conspired to bring him grief. The poem begins by telling the reader that Ni Tsan lost his father while still a boy and was brought up by an older brother. His ambition as a youth, he confesses, was to make his mark in history as a man of letters.

> Behind closed doors, I read classics and histories;
> Going out, I sought connections.
> With my brush, I dashed off compositions,
> And observing the times, had many a criticism.

---

[8] [Perhaps better rendered, "Sings barbarian songs, dancing on reed mats."]

I cast a cold eye on common men,
And with sophistries tripped up wise men of the age.
Riches and position seemed scarcely worth mention;
My true desire—to suspend a name through time.

But as Ni Tsan goes on to relate, his brother and mother died in
quick succession. And over the twenty years that have since en-
sued, as the head of a wealthy household, he has been beset by
heavy tax levies. Before dawn he must present himself at the gov-
ernment office and prostrate himself humbly before minor func-
tionaries.

Paying taxes uses up my blood and soul;
Doing government labor, I worry lest I fall ill.
Working hard, I am caught up in worldly affairs;
Pounding wildly, only my heart is dismayed.
Bent over humbly, I bow to petty officials;
Shouldering the stars, I call at the magistrate's.
Spring grasses were once resplendent;
They now resemble fragile sprouts laden with snow.

## Ku Ying
## (1310–1369)

Yang Wei-chen and Ni Tsan typify the way *wen-jen* figures formed
coteries in the lower Yangtze Delta region, in so-called Chiang-
nan, while it was under Mongol rule. In addition, there were fig-
ures who acted as patrons of these *wen-jen*. The most famous was
Ku Ying from K'un-shan in Kiangsu, a wealthy merchant whose
Jade-Mountain Thatched Pavilion (Yü-shan ts'ao-t'ang) was a
center of "elegant gatherings" of *wen-jen*—the foremost being
Yang Wei-chen and Ni Tsan. Those present at such assemblies
would compose poems; transcriptions of these compositions, in-
cluding some by Ku Ying himself, are still extant.

## Kao Ming
## (1305?–after 1368)

Kao Ming of Yung-chia in Kiangsu, the author of the famous play
*P'i-p'a chi*, or *Account of the Lute*,[9] was from this group of Chiang-

---

[9] [Translated into English by Jean Mulligan, *The Lute: Kao Ming's "P'i-p'a chi"*
(New York: Columbia University Press, 1980), and into German by Vincenz
Hundhausen, *Die Laute, von Gau Ming* (Peking: Pekinger Verlag, 1930).]

nan *wen-jen*. Kao Ming provides an excellent example of how the energies of writers of townsman literature were first poured into the writing of poetry before the excess was devoted to writing fiction. One of Kao Ming's poems appearing in the *Yuan-shih hsuan*, or *Anthology of Yuan Poetry*, is offered here by way of example. It was presented to a descendant of Empress Meng of the Sung dynasty; the descendant, Meng Tsung-chen, lived on Mt. Hui near Wu-hsi, a site famous for its springwater for tea.

> On the east bank of the River Pien, willow catkins
> Dispersed by spring breezes enter the five noble houses.[10]
> The brilliance is gone, Chiang-nan far away!
> Quietly you draw mountain springwater to boil tea.

## Peking Poets

The flourishing of poetry in the lower Yangtze area not only brought about the maturing of verse in that region, it also brought about a different kind of poetic maturation in the north as its effects spread there. The situation in the north was effected by writers of the same southern origins as those who carried out developments in the south, only the former were southerners who had moved to Peking to serve the Yuan court as important officials in the Han-lin Academy and History Bureau. Their poetry took a different direction from that of townsman poets who remained in the south, for they were more inclined to the use of T'ang poetry as the sole model for writing poetry.

That Chinese from the south went to Peking to serve the Mongols is attributable, above all, to the fact that conscious feelings of opposition to Mongol rule had gradually waned over the decades since the fall of the Southern Sung. Another factor was a nostalgia for the traditional Chinese cultural unity of literature and politics, whereby literary affairs were centered near the person of the emperor; there was a widespread desire that such a state of affairs somehow return, even under an alien ruler. On the part of the Mongol government as well, continuing sinification of the politi-

---

[10] The couplet refers to Kaifeng, the Northern Sung capital beside the River Pien. Like the thriving residences of the five marquises of the Wu clan in Han times, its days of glory are past.

cal system accommodated such nostalgia. In any event, the poetry of these Peking writers was qualitatively different from that of southern *wen-jen* of the period like Yang Wei-chen.

## Chao Meng-fu
## (1254–1322)

The first of the Peking poets to whom we turn our attention is Chao Meng-fu from Wu-hsing in Chekiang. Immediately after taking over South China, Qubilai ordered his confidant, Ch'eng Chü-fu, to make an inspection tour throughout the area to seek out men of talent and persuade them to serve the Mongol government. Although figures like Hsieh Fang-te, described in the previous chapter, repeatedly refused such offers, Chao Meng-fu accepted. Upon his arrival in Peking in 1286, Chao was accorded a cordial welcome by Qubilai.

Because Chao Meng-fu's government service took place at a time when the spirit of opposition to Mongol rule still waxed strong, he was widely criticized by people like his cousin Chao Meng-chien. The criticism was all the more intense because, as his surname indicates, he was a distant relative of the fallen Chao family of Sung rulers.

Chao Meng-fu is one of the great masters of Chinese calligraphy. In Sung times calligraphy, as typified by Su Shih and Huang T'ing-chien, was viewed more as an expression of inner spirit than of external formal beauty. Chao Meng-fu broke from this. He sought a return to the style of the great fourth-century father of the art, Wang Hsi-chih—one that strove for beauty through balance. Although Chao Meng-fu's calligraphy has been criticized for being tainted by his conduct, there is no denying its beauty. Similarly in his poetry, Chao broke from the "astringent" (*se*) and "stiff" (*ying*) qualities of Sung verse and sought a return to the pure lyricism of the T'ang. This marks the beginning of the approach taken by later Yuan court poets, who tried to approximate T'ang poetry. The following example of Chao's seven-character verse, entitled "Quatrain," was probably written while he was at the Peking court.

> Against spring's biting chill, I close the double doors,
> Scent lingering from the duck-shaped censer, the fire still warm.

Swallows do not come as petals again fall;
Rain and wind fill the garden, dusk descends.

After the death of Qubilai, Chao Meng-fu retired from government for a period, returning to the Han-lin Academy in the time of Emperor Jen-tsung. Chao himself seems to have had second thoughts about having served the Yuan at a time when the spirit of resistance to the dynasty was so high. In a five-character old-style poem entitled "It Was Wrong to Serve," he tells of his predicament: "Before, a seagull on the waters, / Now I am as a bird in a cage."[11]

As the spirit of opposition to the new regime abated and the Mongol government's adoption of Chinese ways became more routine, the number of southern Chinese who went to Peking to serve the government increased. They included those whose learning was commensurate with their key positions in the Han-lin Academy and who, at the same time, were proficient poets.

## *Yuan Chueh*
## *(1266–1327)*

First, there was Yuan Chueh from Ssu-ming in Chekiang (the present-day Ning-po); a disciple of the widely learned Wang Ying-lin, he adopted the literary name Ch'ing-jung chü-shih, or Pure Countenance Lay Believer. Yuan Chueh's poems, being scholarly in nature, are rich in descriptive power. Although he was like Sung dynasty poets in the way he actively adopted previously-unused subject matter from contemporary life, his style and diction, as illustrated by the poems cited below, are more akin to poetry of the T'ang than to that of the Sung.

Yuan Chueh responded to the call to serve the Peking court at the turn of the fourteenth century, in the Ta-te reign period (1297–1307) of Qubilai's grandson Temür, Emperor Ch'eng-tsung (r. 1294–1307). The series of five-character old-style poems, "Shipboard Songs," written as a journal of his trip to the capital, tells variously of scenes and products of the north that he was seeing for the first time. In the following poem, for example,

---

[11] It would be the talented woman of letters, Kuan Tao-sheng (1262–1319), to whom Chao is referring, when in the same poem he speaks of his spouse: "My sick wife carried our tiny child, / When I set out on the long trek."

the surface of the water on both sides of the boat as it approaches
"Yen-ching" (the Peking area), is covered with white reeds, the
capital's fuel source.

> White reeds grow on chilly sands;
> Their remnant flowers wave old brooms.
> A million houses of Yen-ching
> Depend on you for their kindling.
> Though unobtrusive and born of the lowest,
> Your usefulness is well worth praise.
> You outshine the peach and plum blossom,
> Each striving to appear prettiest of all.

In the reign of Emperor Jen-tsung, Yuan Chueh, like Chao
Meng-fu before him, became a high official in the Han-lin Acad-
emy. The emperor would spend summers at the Upper Capital
(Shang-tu) of K'ai-p'ing, or Doloonuur, and Yuan would some-
times accompany him and compose poems about desert scenes.
Yuan's poems were a response to conditions that made new sub-
ject matter available for poetry. For example, the next poem, the
third in a series of ten five-character regulated verses entitled
"Songs on the Upper Capital," is about the palaces and streets of
K'ai-p'ing.[12] Because the city walls mentioned in the poem's sec-
ond line are low, distant mountains come into view. "Dragon Bay"
in line four is a desert oasis, surrounded rather perfunctorily by
green vegetation. The poem was written in 1319, when Yuan
Chueh was fifty-three years old.

> Palace towers amid vast nothingness,
> City walls low, they draw in distant mountains.
> White elms blur Wild-Goose Fortress;
> Green plants fill out Dragon Bay.
> The market hemmed in, houses lie close together;
> My office work light, days are spent in leisure.
> If I come again, I'll inquire more about local customs;
> But to my regret, the splotches in my hair are growing whiter.

With the reinstatement of the examination system during Em-
peror Jen-tsung's reign in 1315, opportunities for Chinese to ad-

---

[12] Somewhat later another Han-lin official, Liu Kuan (1270–1342), also wrote
"A Poetic Diary of the Upper Capital."

vance in government increased. Of the more than 1,200 candidates who took the qualifying examination that year in the Chekiang-Kiangsu area, thirty-three passed, including twenty-eight Chinese and five Mongols or other non-Chinese from the Western Regions. They were among three hundred semifinalists who qualified to take the central metropolitan examination, one hundred of whom passed. The latter included Ma Tsu-ch'ang, Ou-yang Hsuan, Huang Chin, Hsu Yu-jen, and others, all of whom became Han-lin Academy officials at the end of the Yuan.

Although his was a short reign from 1329 to 1332 toward the end of the dynasty, Emperor Wen-tsung (Tugh-temür) had an extraordinary love of Chinese painting and calligraphy. His bureau for the collection and connoisseurship of art works, the K'uei-chang ko, or Hall of the Literary Constellation, was filled with Han-lin officials.

## Yü Chi
## (1272–1348)

Yü Chi, the most outstanding of the late Yuan officials in the Han-lin Academy, is also considered the greatest Yuan dynasty poet.[13] He compiled an anthology of prose and poetry entitled *Tao-yuan hsueh-ku lu*, or *A Record of Studies of the Past by Tao-yuan*, the latter being his pen name. Originally from Kiangsi, he was the most trusted government official for more than a quarter of a century—from the time he went to Peking during the Ta-te reign period (1297–1307) of Emperor Ch'eng-tsung until Emperor Wen-tsung ascended the throne in 1329.

Yü Chi's reputation as the outstanding poet of the Yuan dynasty derives from the great inner strength and energy that find an ideal balance in his verse—qualities for which he is in large part indebted to T'ang poetic models. The following five-character regulated verse was prompted by a painting entitled "Layered Peaks along the Yangtze" by Yü Chi's senior in the Han-lin Academy, Chao Meng-fu. It tells with feeling of how the Yangtze, the an-

[13] [Note the study by Magnus Michael Kriegeskorte, "Yu Ji (1272–1348): Ein Literatenbeamter unter der Mongolenherrschaft," Unpublished Ph.D. dissertation, Rheinische Friedrich-Wilhelms Universität zu Bonn, 1984.]

cient battleground between north and south, has become part of
a unified empire.

> In the past, Yangtze perils
> Brought a grief that turned hair white.
> A lifetime's official service over,
> I spend all day looking at the painting spread before me:
> Buddhist temples faintly visible,
> Fishing boats return over the broad expanse.
> Desolate appear a few trees—
> From time to time the tide comes in.

Yü Chi's poetry, like that of Yuan Chueh, contains previously-
untreated themes reflecting real-life situations of the time. I offer
the following five-character old-style poem, "Dedicated to the
Hatmaker," by way of example. Yü dedicated the poem to a Pe-
king hatter who was fond of learning.

> My horse and carriage enter a narrow lane,
> Here to visit the master hatter.
> You've locked yourself in and receive no visitors;
> Sitting erect, you recite books and poems.
> Not enough clothes to cover your legs,
> For lunch, poor fare is fine.[14]
> Making a hat sometimes takes a whole year;
> If it doesn't sell, you don't mind.
> Since I was a lad, I've enjoyed letters,
> And have tried everything with a brush.
> But I am put to shame before a solitude like yours;
> Hereafter I'll take your example to heart.

The "solitude" in the poem's penultimate line refers to the hatter's
modest persistence in his way of life. The poet, lazing amid
worldly concerns, feels put to shame before him.

The Four Masters of Yuan Poetry (*Yuan-shih ssu ta-chia*) are
generally taken to include two officials in the History Bureau dur-
ing Emperor Jen-tsung's time, Fan Heng (1272–1330) and Yang
Tsai (1271–1323), and two advisors who enjoyed Emperor Wen-

---

[14] [In the original the "poor fare" is betony and goosefoot plants, more accu-
rately rendered pogostemom and chenopodium.]

tsung's favor, Yü Chi and Chieh Hsi-ssu (1274–1344).[15] In the *Yuan shih*, or *History of the Yuan Dynasty*, Liu Kuan (1270–1342) and Huang Chin (1277–1357) are joined with Yü Chi and Chieh Hsi-ssu as the Four Masters of the Confucian Grove (*Ju-lin ssu-chieh*).

The overriding impression imparted by the poetry of these northern writers centered around Yü Chi is one of their consciously attempting to use the core of T'ang poetry as a model. The more this occurred, the greater was their departure from Sung poetry. The use of T'ang poetry as an exemplar solved a problem that had been outstanding for some time. To be more specific, Wang An-shih had early showed signs of feeling ill at ease with the excessively discursive and prosaic quality of Northern Sung poetry epitomized by his contemporary, Su Shih, and of wishing to redress the balance by returning to a more purely lyrical T'ang poetry. The great writers of the Southern Sung, Lu Yu and Yang Wan-li, displayed the same concern. Direct imitation of T'ang poetry had appeared with the townsman poets at the end of the Southern Sung, but it was late T'ang poetry that served as their model; the stiff, overly rationalistic poetry of the Northern Sung being neither to their liking nor within their capability, they took T'ang verse that dealt with minor descriptions of daily life as their model. Yet the poetry they used was but an offshoot of T'ang poetry; it did not form its core. Later, Yang Wei-chen used a better-quality T'ang poetry for his model, the verse of Li Po and Li Ho; but he drew only on its eccentric parts, leaving the heart of T'ang poetry untouched. The use of models from the central core of T'ang poetry was first attempted by Yü Chi and other late-Yuan Han-lin poets discussed here; their usage marks the beginning of the practice. Once started by them, poets of the subsequent Ming period intensified the use of poetic models from the heart of T'ang poetry.

It became common for Ming writers to criticize Yuan poets for having only imitated poetry from the T'ang that was "delicate and charming" (*hsien-yen*). Indeed, the poetry of Sa-tu-la, dis-

---

[15] Japanese editions of their collected works have appeared since Muromachi times, when they were reading material for Gozan poet-monks.

cussed in the next section, tends in this direction. But the move-
ment toward imitation of the mainstream of T'ang poetry ante-
dates the Ming dynasty, its direction being set by the group of late
Yuan poets treated here.

It should be noted additionally that Yü Chi and other late
Yuan poets of the north fell less victim to the vice common to later
advocates of T'ang poetry, especially Ming poets—that of merely
imitating T'ang poetic diction and thereby producing poetry
vapid in content. The poems by Yuan Chueh and Yü Chi cited
above illustrate how these poets, while dependent on T'ang poetry
for their diction and style, also sought to describe contemporary
realities. The Yuan dynasty itself, with its alien rule, was such a
reality, and the new life circumstances it brought about served to
sharpen the perspective of poets of the period.

The relationship between Yuan poetry and the rise and decline
of the period's new genre, *tsa-chü* drama, is of some significance
in this regard. During the early part of the dynasty (through the
reign of Qubilai) *tsa-chü*, as a newly flourishing fiction literature,
largely reflected current realities. But over the first half of the four-
teenth century, during the period treated in this chapter, *tsa-chü*
became mannered and lost their vitality. In contrast, poetry at the
end of the Yuan dynasty grew more realistic as *tsa-chü* became less
so. This was even truer of the prose of the period. The rise and
decline of fiction, on the one hand, and of poetry and nonfiction
prose, on the other, parallel each other in some cases and in others
do not. During the Yuan they do not.

There were literary figures serving the Mongol government
who, temporarily setting aside the fact that their rulers were not
Chinese, felt admiration for the unprecedented great empire that
had materialized. The seventy-chapter compendium of Yuan prose
and poetry, the *Kuo-ch'ao wen-lei*, or *The Dynasty's Literature by
Categories*, edited by the late-Yuan Han-lin official Su T'ien-chueh
(1294–1352), includes a preface by a scholar from the south,
Ch'en Lü (1288–1343); therein he states: "Our Empire encom-
passes the Six Directions. From of old 'an undifferentiated one,'
never has it had an all-encompassing unity equal to what it has
today. Never have the fortunes of Heaven and Earth flourished
more than they do now."

In the same vein Ou-yang Hsuan (1283–1357), a leading

Han-lin academician of the time, wrote that literature had recovered from its decline in the Southern Sung because of the atmosphere provided by Yuan unification. In one of his prose pieces he writes:

> Our Yuan dynasty arose like a dragon, transforming [the earlier decline] through its open generosity, so that a perfect literature has been born.
>
> In the Chung-t'ung and Chih-yuan reign periods [of Shih-tsu (i.e., the Generational Paterfamilias [Dynasty Founder], Qubilai), 1260–1264 and 1264–1294], literature was expansive and luxuriant.
>
> In the Yuan-chen and Ta-te periods [of Emperor Ch'eng-tsung (Temür), 1295–1297 and 1297–1307], literature was smooth flowing and fertile.
>
> In the Chih-ta and Yen-yu periods [of Emperors Wu-tsung and Jen-tsung (Qayshan and Ayurbarwada), 1308–1311 and 1314–1320], literature was pure and beautiful.
>
> And in the T'ai-ting and T'ien-li periods [of Yesön-temür and Emperor Wen-tsung (Tugh-temür), 1324–1328 and 1328–1330], literature was rich and heroic.[16]

A poem among Yuan Chueh's "Shipboard Songs," one written after his arrival in Peking, is best understood as being a product of the same mentality.

> In the clear night I gaze at the Dipper
> Flickering before me, its color so true.
> I now know the Central Land is truly exceptional,
> That I factiously misspoke matters astronomical.
> The Duke of Shao transformed the south;[17]
> Thus do fine teachings come from Yen.
> If the universe is a unity,
> How can there be bias toward any region?[18]

[16] [To maintain balanced prose style here, Ou-yang Hsuan omitted two reign periods: the Huang-ch'ing (1312–1313) era of Emperor Jen-tsung and the Chih-chih (1321–1323) period of Emperor Ying-tsung. The T'ien-li era started during the reign of Emperor Ming-tsung.]

[17] An allusion to the *Shih ching* (Classic of Songs).

[18] [The poem might be paraphrased along the following lines. The north's "fundamental colors," like those of the "northern ladle" (the Dipper), are true. I now know the empire's heartland, the "Central Land" (i.e., the north), is exceptional. Before when in the south, I spoke incorrectly of its correlation with the heav-

As described above, the latter part of the Yuan dynasty was a period of substantial cultural attainment. Men of the following Ming dynasty, considering the Yuan an age of barbarian rule, were contemptuous of the entire period. Yet the Ming was not without a writer like Yeh Sheng (1420–1474), who in his *Shui-tung jih-chi*, or *East of the Waters Diary*, looked back upon the late Yuan as a post-Northern Sung period of culture.

## Chinese Poetry by Non-Chinese

Yuan civilization also produced non-Chinese writers of Chinese poetry. The outstanding twentieth-century Chinese historian Ch'en Yuan, in his well-known work *Yuan Hsi-yü-jen Hua-hua k'ao*, or *A Study of the Sinification of Men of Western-Regions Origins during the Yuan Dynasty*,[19] gives several examples of such writers, including Ma Tsu-ch'ang, Kuan Yun-shih, Nai Hsien, and Ting Ho-nien.[20] Discussion of one of these, Sa-tu-la, brings this chapter to a close.

### Sa-tu-la
### (1272?–?)

There is some dispute about the origins of Sa-tu-la (Sadr). It is Ch'en Yuan's theory that because Sa-tu-la is recorded as being a Dānishmand (Ta-shih-man), he was of Muslim tribal origins. However, the rumor that Sa-tu-la, though born a Chinese, purposely adopted a foreign-sounding name so as to get on better in the world, appears in a work by K'ung Ch'i (fl. 1367) entitled the *Chih-cheng chih-chi*, or *True Record of the Chih-cheng Reign Period*—that is, 1341–1368. In any event, the place name of Yen-men in northern Shansi, a region bound up with the family history

---

ens. Fine teaching can come from the north (the ancient state of Yen) to transform the south, like the teaching the Duke of Shao instilled in ancient times. The universe being one, there cannot be bias in the geographically-bound cosmic energy accorded any particular region (specifically, the south).]

[19] [Translated into English by Ch'ien Hsing-hai and L. Carrington Goodrich as *Western and Central Asians in China under the Mongols* (Los Angeles: Monumenta Serica, 1966).]

[20] [Note the study by Richard John Lynn, *Kuan Yün-shih* (Boston: Twayne, 1980).]

of Sa-tu-la, provided the title for his collected verse, the *Yen-men chi*, or *Yen-men Collection*.[21]

Sa-tu-la's life includes a period spent as a townsman in the south and one spent as a Han-lin official in Peking. Similarly, his writing appears to be a mixture of the two strains. According to his chronological biography Sa-tu-la was born in 1272,[22] the same year as Yü Chi, and spent his early years as an itinerant merchant traveling throughout the south. The following is one of two seven-character quatrains entitled "On the Double-Ninth Festival, Away from Home." According to the same biography the work was written in 1302, when Sa-tu-la was aged thirty.

> This festive day, on business far away,
> Chrysanthemums scarcely differ from those at home.
> No money to buy wine next door,
> With each lonely recitation my heart breaks.

[21] Sa-tu-la's *Yen-men chi* was read by China's most famous twentieth-century writer, Lu Hsun, as is clear from the latter's *Yeh-ts'ao* (Wild Grasses). See my *Zoku ningen shiwa* (Poetry Talks on Personalities, Continued), 1961; reprinted in *Yoshikawa Kōjirō zenshū*, 1: 537–39.

In Japan, the *Yen-men chi* was reprinted early, during the period of division between the Northern and Southern Courts (1336–1392). The following poem appears in a work published in early Edo times entitled *Sa Tenshaku chōsen kō* (Draft of a Selection from Sa-tu-la).

> To speak of impermanence reveals spiritual insight—
> Plum blossoms aloft for hundreds of miles, a pine through the night.
> Waking from my worldly dream, clouds spit forth the moon;
> In the Kuan-yin Shrine, the lone sound of a bell.

A Gozan priest in Muromachi times, taking advantage of the circumstance that a story about the soul of Sugawara no Michizane (845–903) having crossed to China was currently popular, made up the lines and attributed them to Sa-tu-la. I am indebted to Prof. Kanda Kiichirō for this information. [The title of the poem is "Tenmangū," or "Shrine to the Heaven-Filling One," a name given to Shinto shrines dedicated to the deified Michizane, one of whose appellations is "Heaven-Filling One."]

[22] [Most scholars prefer 1308 as the date of Sa-tu-la's birth: see Chiang Liang-fu, *Li-tai jen-wu nien-li t'ung-p'u* (A Comprehensive Table of Dates of Figures through the Ages) (1937; rpt. Taipei: Shih-chieh shu-chü, 1974), p. 392; Tanaka Kenji, "Satsutora" ("Sa-tu-la"), in *Ajia rekishi jiten* (An Encyclopedia of Asian History) (Tokyo: Heibonsha, 1959–62), 4: 45; and Yoshikawa Kōjirō himself, in the study cited in the preceding note.]

The following two poems are from a series of seven entitled "Verses Written While Sick."

> A traveler a thousand miles from home,
> I long to return, my room filled with moonlight.
> The cassias' bloom about to fade,
> In sickness I pass the midautumn festival.

And:

> In the wind, leaves fall high and low;
> Autumn sounds of fulling cloth heard near and far.
> At this end of the earth, afflicted by much sickness,
> I lean on my cane and gaze at a lone cloud.

Although Sa-tu-la was a low-level clerk for a period in the Yuan Branch-Censorate in the south, he passed the imperial examinations in 1327 at the age of fifty-five and became a civil official under Emperor Wen-tsung. He probably wrote the following seven-character quatrain, entitled alternatively "A Palace Lyric" or "An Autumn Lyric," while at court.

> In the clear night, the imperial carriage goes out the Chien-chang
>    Gate—
> In two or three files, a retinue of purple-clad palace ladies.
> As silver lanterns pass along the stone balustrade,
> Their light reveals the frost on lotus leaves.

It is unclear what Sa-tu-la did after leaving Emperor Wen-tsung's court. The poems handed down to us as being from his later work include pieces with most alluring titles like "The Handkerchief," "The Beauty's Silken Sash," and "Embroidered Shoes," which suggest the same proclivities seen in Yang Wei-chen's romantic poems.

Another non-Chinese writer active during this period was Hsin Wen-fang (fl. 1300), whose family was of Western-Regions origins. He authored the superb collection of biographies of T'ang dynasty poets, *T'ang ts'ai-tzu chuan*, or *Biographies of Talented Masters of the T'ang*. After being transmitted to Japan, the work was lost for a period in China. Under the direction of Hayashi Jussai (1768–1841), principal of the Bakufu academy, it was reprinted in Japan during the Kansei reign era (1789–1801) of the

Edo period as a volume in the *Itsuzon sōsho*,[23] or *Collectanea of Works Lost in China But Extant in Japan*, and thus became known again in its homeland.

The most copious collection of poetry from the Mongol period is the *Yuan-shih hsuan*, or *Anthology of Yuan Poetry*, edited in Ch'ing times by Ku Ssu-li (1665–1722). Being divided into four separate collections, it took several decades to complete. One night Ku Ssu-li dreamed that dozens of men dressed in ancient court garb surrounded him and bowed, thanking him for his efforts in making their writings again available to the world.

[23] [Also called *Isson sōsho.*]

# Chapter 5

# The Early Ming,
# 1350–1400

## The Ming at Its Inception

The prediction that the Mongol barbarians would not last a century proved true.[1] Fewer than one hundred years after Qubilai successfully united all of China, the Yuan dynasty collapsed. For the greater part of his thirty-six-year reign the last Yuan emperor, Shun-ti (Toghon-temür), was harassed by rebellions in the south. Rebel leaders initially suffered from rivalry among themselves, but the leader from Feng-yang in Anhwei, Chu Yuan-chang, was successful in overcoming all rivals. Having consolidated control in the south, he turned his forces northward and sent Shun-ti fleeing from Peking to the desert wastes further north. The year was 1368.

The date marked the founding of a new, unified empire under Chinese rule that was to last three hundred years, the Ming (or "bright") dynasty. Its inaugural Hung-wu reign period (1368–1398) signified that it was to be Overflowing in Martial Spirit.

[1] [The prediction, as noted by Sung Lien (1310–1381), appears in the *Huang-ming wen-heng* (A Literary Scale for the Imperial Ming), edited by Ch'eng Ming-cheng (fl. 1466), Ssu-pu ts'ung-k'an ed., p. 1.1b.]

The new dynasty's capital, initially the Kiangsu city of Nanking, was eventually moved to Peking.

The Founder Emperor of the Ming dynasty,[2] Chu Yuan-chang, can only be characterized as having been inflexibly single-minded. He valued simple unadornment, frankness, direct action, and authoritativeness. He hated delicate refinement, effeminacy, pretentiousness, and anything smacking of these. His frame of mind was related to his personal background. Chu Yuan-chang was the first Chinese emperor to emerge from the common people in over 1,500 years, the last having been Liu Pang, who became Emperor Kao-tsu of the Han (r. 206–194 B.C.). As a young man Chu Yuan-chang had even for a period been a member of the occupational group despised by most Chinese, Buddhist monks. This forms a sharp contrast with earlier dynasties. The founding emperors of the T'ang and Sung periods had been high officials in the dynasties preceding them. Even the first emperors of the Chin and Yuan eras had been nobles among their respective Jurchen and Mongol peoples. The Founder Emperor of the Ming, however, had little use for the nobility and all that was associated with it; nor were the trappings of urban life to his taste.

Yet Chu Yuan-chang was not as lacking in learning as was Han Emperor Kao-tsu, who in a famous incident urinated into a Confucian scholar's cap. Chu wanted the new Ming empire to be an enlightened one. He simply did not want its culture to fall victim to the overrefinement, effeminacy, and pretentiousness that so often marred earlier ages. For this reason he took a dim view of the fact that the traditional guardians of cultural life, the intelligentsia, had been the mainstay of literature. He wanted more practical men of action, individually or as a class, to emerge as cultural leaders.

Chu Yuan-chang gave the matter some thought before deciding to institute a new examination system, one in which literary ability would no longer be emphasized. A short passage was to be selected from the Confucian canon as a topic for discussion, usually from the *Four Books* (the *Analects, Great Learning, Doctrine of*

---

[2] [Chu Yuan-chang was posthumously designated T'ai-tsu, or Ultimate Paterfamilias, of the Ming dynasty. Also widely known as the Hung-wu emperor, he is here consistently referred to by his given name or as the Founder Emperor.]

*the Mean*, and *Mencius*). Examinees were then to write an essay in a set literary form, the so-called *pa-ku wen*, or "eight-legged essay" style.[3] This exercise formed the central part of the new examination system. Poetry writing, traditionally given much weight, was excluded from the subjects examined. This resulted in an official examination much easier to pass than earlier ones had been, one in which even people of low-class origins, through self-study, had a chance to succeed and thereby become officials.

It can be argued that the simplification of the examination system was essentially a response to the growing influence of townsmen in the empire, that it was a means of affording this increasingly powerful stratum of society greater participation in government. Inasmuch as many townsmen had well-developed literary taste and writing ability and were thus already equipped to pass the old-style examination, it would be more correct to say that the new system provided opportunity for advancement to those among them who had no bent for literature. Rather, if anything, Chu Yuan-chang sought to give impetus to the advancement, individually or as a class, of an altogether nonurban sector of the population—namely, unsophisticated people who, like himself, came from rural villages. In this way, a check could be put on townsmen whose literary talents were in the ascendant; future culture was to be put in the hands of a new stratum of society whose members would act as officials and form a new intelligentsia. It is in this light that the thinking behind the Founder Emperor's simplification of the examination system should be viewed.

Given his tough, strong personality, Chu Yuan-chang was not averse to using any methods, including indiscriminate murder, to further his aims.[4] He was especially cruel in his treatment of those

---

[3] [For a useful introduction to the genre, including a translation of a sample eight-legged essay (with accompanying Chinese text), see Tu Ching-I, "The Chinese Examination Essay: Some Literary Considerations," *Monumenta Serica* 31 (1974–75), 393–406.]

[4] ["He became extremely suspicious of his associates who had helped him to power and got rid of most of them in a number of bloody purges. The first great purge took place in 1380 when the chancellor Hu Wei-yung was accused of plotting rebellion and executed. Thousands of allegedly involved persons were sentenced to death. The next great purge took place in 1385, and another great purge occurred in 1393, when the veteran general Lan Yü was accused of rebellion and when reportedly fifteen thousand people were executed." W. L. Idema, *The Dra-*

who, to his mind, represented the old-fashioned intelligentsia. Kao Ch'i and many other early Ming poets, as we shall see, were to become his victims.

I will here relate two incidents that illustrate Chu Yuan-chang's cold-bloodedness. In the days before he became emperor, while fighting against Ch'en Yu-liang on the upper Yangtze, Chu learned that one of his civil officials, Hsia Yü, had engaged in the illicit trade of salt with the enemy. Chu had him tied naked in a small boat and set afloat on the Yangtze in front of the Yellow-Crane Tower (Huang-ho lou) of Wu-ch'ang for three days and nights, before finally having him executed. There is also the story of the wife of one of Chu Yuan-chang's powerful generals, said to be a jealous woman. Even after her husband had achieved great success she refused to let him take any concubines. One day Chu held a great banquet and had a large, red lacquer tray brought before his guest, the general. Urged to remove the lid, he discovered he had been served a woman's pair of hands, his wife's bracelet still intact on one of the wrists.

The first of these tales is found in the *Lieh-ch'ao shih-chi hsiao-chuan*, or *Short Biographies from the Poetry Collection of Successive Reigns*, by Ch'ien Ch'ien-i (1582–1664). The second is in one of the unofficial histories (the exact title of which I do not recall). But regardless of whether the facts related are strictly true or not, Chu Yuan-chang had a character that gave rise to such stories.

Chu Yuan-chang's successors carried on his same basic policies, bringing them to their full, logical conclusion. Thus the three hundred years during which he and his descendants ruled have a single, basic underlying tone or theme, one that is characteristically simple, direct, and uninhibited, and which sometimes turns brash and violent. It is the diametrical opposite of the culture of the following Ch'ing dynasty, when delicacy and refinement were most prized.

In the realm of philosophy Wang Yang-ming's (1472–1529) "learning of the mind" (*hsin hsueh*) typified the age. With the phrase from Mencius, "All things are already complete in us,"[5] as

---

matic *Oeuvre of Chu Yu-tun (1379–1439)* (Leiden: E. J. Brill, 1985), p. 6 (citing passages in the *Dictionary of Ming Biography*).]

[5] [Mencius VIIA.4. Translation by James Legge, *The Chinese Classics*, 5 vols. (rev.

its byword, more precise erudition was cast aside. Wang Yang-ming is the most simple and straightforward of all Chinese Confucian thinkers. In literature as well, because drama and vernacular fiction were simple, straightforward, and uninhibited in both diction and content, these genres flourished during the Ming as never before.

Such developments in philosophy and literature can be attributed to the fact that, in accord with Chu Yuan-chang's wishes, men of a social stratum broader than that which had previously been in charge of Chinese civilization became the dynasty's cultural leaders. They were from a class for which straightforward simplicity was second nature. Even if one feels that Chu Yuan-chang's policies alone could hardly have dominated the spirit of the dynasty so effectively, the time was ripe for the change of direction that he initiated. Chu Yuan-chang perceptively sized up the situation and was the first to act on it.

With the banishment of the alien Mongols, Chinese prided themselves on the recovery of their sovereignty and civilization. The dynasty's emphasis on unadorned simplicity, however, was really a continuation of a Yuan phenomenon, one that had been forced upon China through violence. It was a Yuan legacy, simply carried on and skillfully used by the later dynasty for its own ends. This was recognized even during Ming times. Chang Chü-cheng (1525–1582), who was prime minister under the Wan-li emperor late in the dynasty (and who has gained a high reputation among historians in modern times), argues that the Ming was really successor to the Yuan dynasty and not to the Sung.[6]

The poetry of the age followed the general Ming pattern of simplicity and directness. And an extraordinary number of ordinary townsmen participated in writing verse. Each of these tendencies—the simplification of poetic style and the increase in townsman poets—reinforced the other. The general anthology of Ming poetry edited during the Ch'ing by Chu I-tsun (1629–1709), the *Ming-shih tsung*, or *A Ming Poetry Compendium*, con-

---

ed. Oxford, 1893–95; rpt. Taipei: Wen-hsing, 1966), vol. 2, *The Works of Mencius*, p. 450.]

   [6] See the *Chang T'ai-yüeh chi* (Collected Writings of Chang Chü-cheng), chap. 18, "Tsa-chu" ("Essays"). [Note also chap. 7, n. 49.]

tains works by more than 3,400 writers. The majority are ordinary townsmen, only a minority being government officials.

In keeping with the overall simplicity and directness of Ming verse, which strove toward a pure lyricism, T'ang poetry, especially that period's more open and forthright lyrical verse, became the standard Ming poetic model. Calmness and intellect, which had been the hallmarks of a richly discursive and narrative Sung poetry, were scarcely paid heed. This direction in the development of poetry is already in evidence at the beginning of the Ming dynasty. Influential poets of the time were townsmen in the south, especially the area around Soochow. But because these figures treated literature as the proper focus of men's talents, or at least were perceived by Chu Yuan-chang as doing so, this worked to their misfortune. Viewed by the Founder Emperor as incorrigibly old-fashioned intellectuals, many fell victim to his purges. Among their number was the foremost poet of the early Ming, Kao Ch'i.

# Kao Ch'i
## (1336–1374)

The poet Kao Ch'i, who graces the early period of Ming poetry, is considered by some the finest poet of the three-hundred-year dynasty. Yet he was a Ming subject for a brief six years before being executed by the Founder Emperor in 1374, at the age of thirty-eight.[7] His earlier years had been spent as a townsman in the city of Soochow, which was under Chang Shih-ch'eng's control during the disturbances at the end of the Yuan dynasty.

At an early age Kao Ch'i showed signs of precocity. In 1351, at the age of fifteen, he formed a poetic group with some neighbor youths, called alternatively the Ten Friends on the Northern Outskirts (*Pei-kuo shih-yu*) or the Ten Talented Ones (*Shih ts'ai-tzu*).[8] The *Ming shih*, or official *History of the Ming Dynasty*, mentions that one of the neighbor youths among the Ten Friends group, Wang Hsing, was the son of an apothecary; this gives us some idea of Kao Ch'i's social origins. The history further relates that Kao

---

[7] [Note the study by Frederick W. Mote, *The Poet Kao Ch'i, 1336–1374* (Princeton: Princeton University Press, 1962).]

[8] The "northern outskirts" is the area where Kao Ch'i lived, near the city wall in the northern sector of Soochow.

won second-place and prize money in a Soochow city-wide po-
etry-writing competition.

Kao Ch'i was thus very much a part of the tradition of towns-
man poetry that had been developing in the Soochow area since
Southern Sung times. Yet his poetry soars in mental flights never
seen before in townsman poetry, which were owing to his unusual
temperament. Kao spoke of sometimes being overcome by an in-
explicable sadness; we find this expressed in the opening lines of a
five-character poem entitled "Whence This Melancholy?"

> Whence this melancholy
> That with the autumn so suddenly appears?

As he states later in the same poem:

> Neither is it the sigh of a poor scholar,
> Nor the sadness of one sent afar.

The following "Song of Sadness" reveals the same temperament.

> Floating clouds in the breeze's wake
> Are scattered to the four wilds.
> As I turn to heaven in sad song,
> Tears come down in streaks.

In having such a temperament Kao Ch'i was different from earlier
townsman poets, who had consistently been down-to-earth in
their poetic themes. He sought to transcend the bounds of the
mundane and everyday in his verse and, as it were, to take flight.
His representative work, "Song of the Green-Hill Master," is an
expression of this. Ch'ing-ch'iu, or Green Hill, was Kao Ch'i's lit-
erary name, the name of the manor near Soochow where he lived;
it was also a name associated with the South-Sea locale of fairy
goddesses. For Kao the poet's task is to shape poetry out of his
mental peregrinations.

> The Green-Hill Master,
> Thin but clean,[9]

---

[9] [Consonant with the witty, self-deprecatory tone of the poem, this line might
be rendered alternatively, "Skinny but squeaky clean," or "Threadbare but well
laundered."]

Was first a fairy courtier in the Five-Cloud Pavilion;
When was he banished to the world of men?[10]

.   .   .   .   .   .   .   .   .   .   .   .   .   .

Among the Eight Extremes indistinct, his mental wits do roam,
And cause the formless to fashion sound.[11]

Some groundwork for such mental flights had been laid by earlier townman poets. Yang Wei-chen (discussed in the preceding chapter) is a prime example. But Yang had merely dressed up his verse in the superficial language of earlier poetic greats who had taken such flights, Li Po and Li Ho. It was only with Kao Ch'i and his peculiar genius that true poetic flights of fancy, or at least comparatively more of them, were achieved. In this Kao marks the culmination of a century and a half of the tradition of townsman poetry.

Kao Ch'i differed from earlier townsman poets in still another way that reflected his desire to transcend everyday bounds. He was deeply concerned about political affairs. The disintegration of the Yuan dynasty made this possible, enabling Chinese political consciousness, long repressed under the Mongols, to come fully to life again. The following five-character old-style poem entitled "Autumn Wind" illustrates such awareness.

> Autumn winds enter my chamber
> To scatter fallen leaves by my side.
> I have not been out for several days—
> The trees already this yellow!
> I feel myself growing more listless,
> Indifferent to the haste of destructive time.
> For the morning meal, a single bowl;
> For night's rest, a lone bed.
> When Confucius set out to implement the Way,
> His wagon tracks led off in all directions.
> But as for me, what am I doing,
> That I am unable to forget the world?

[10] [Like Li Po, the "banished immortal"; p. 82 above.]
[11] [For complete translations of the poem, see Mote, *The Poet Kao Ch'i*, pp. 69–72, and Chaves, *Later Chinese Poetry*, pp. 123–25.]

Compare the following five-character quatrain entitled "Year's End."

> Past regretting—too late to seek the Way,
> Upon reflection—how hard to save the age!
> A mediocrity, what can he accomplish?[12]
> At this edge of the world, another year passes.

From the last line of the poem we know that Kao was en route somewhere; as in many other such poems, the goal of his journey remains indefinite and unstated.

The man of power in Soochow at the time was Chang Shih-ch'eng, one in whom Kao Ch'i had little confidence. In response to Chang's invitations to serve, Kao remained noncommittal. It is related in the biographies of the poet written by his friend Li Chih-kuang and by his pupil Lü Mien that he would frequently discuss current affairs with Jao Chieh, one of Chang Shih-ch'eng's staff officers.

Kao Ch'i was quite self-assured about his unique talents and consequently felt isolated. Both attitudes are in evidence in the following five-character regulated verse that can be read as his poetic self-portrait, "A Lone Wild Goose." Therein the poet remains aloof, it being beneath his dignity to pass the night with "common fowl," literally "mallards and common gulls," that is, ordinary poets.

> Over Heng-yang I lost my companions,[13]
> And set back alone on the long flight homeward.
> Passing the Lung Range, diffident to take a letter,[14]
> Cleaving the sky, I have difficulty joining formations.
> I call to the flock beyond the clouds in urgency,
> And mourn my shadow disappearing in the moonlight.
> Since I will not join common fowl to spend the night,
> In reed straw, night after night it is cold.

[12] ["A mediocrity" is a self-deprecating reference by the poet to himself.]

[13] Heng-yang in Hunan was said to be the southern terminus of migrating wild geese. [The Ssu-pu pei-yao edition of Kao's poems followed here has *pan* as the last character in the line.]

[14] In Chinese poetry one often finds letters being entrusted to winged messengers like the wild goose in this poem. Here Kao, in the person of the bird, hesitates to transmit such a message because of the political uncertainties of the time.

Many of Kao Ch'i's Ten Friends on the Northern Outskirts received the patronage of Yang Wei-chen. But we have no evidence that Kao himself did. Perhaps Kao, Yang's junior by some forty years, considered his elder one of the common flock with whom he refused to consort. Yet he did form a friendship with Ni Tsan, thirty-five years his senior; we have several poems dedicated by Kao Ch'i to Ni Tsan during Ni's later years.

Before the establishment of the Ming regime Kao Ch'i enjoyed a reputation as a young poetic genius. His first two poetic anthologies, *Lou-chiang yin-kao*, or *Lou-River Poetry Manuscript*, and *Fu-ming chi*, or *Clay-Pot Soundings Collection*, both date from this period. A friend of Kao's, Wang Wei (1323–1374), wrote the following in his preface to the latter collection. "Kao Ch'i's poetry, in its superb abandon and pure beauty, is like a hawk soaring through autumn skies. Performing a hundred twisting maneuvers, even if summoned, it will not descend. Like a lotus in blue-green waters, of unadorned beauty and undefiled by things worldly, it has the true air of a gentleman."

In the second year of the new dynasty, in 1369, the thirty-three-year-old Kao Ch'i was summoned to the capital of Nanking to serve on the board compiling the official history of the preceding Yuan dynasty. The call to serve was far from welcome; the Founder Emperor was already notorious for his harshness toward men of letters. And to compound matters Kao came from Soochow, the stronghold which had held out the longest against the victorious emperor.[15]

During the boat trip of about ten days from Soochow to Nanking, Kao Ch'i felt deeply uneasy, as revealed in the following five-character quatrain entitled "En Route to the Capital, Meeting a Friend on His Way Back to Our Hometown."

> I am off and you are on your way back;
> Here we meet and stand by the road.
> I want to send word home by you,
> But first tell me about affairs in the capital.[16]

[15] The situation is similar to relations in Meiji period Japan between the government in Tokyo and various *han* in the Tōhoku region.

[16] [Cf. the translation by Mote, *The Poet Kao Ch'i*, p. 153.]

The disquiet, unhappiness, and fear that attended his year and more in the capital come through in Kao Ch'i's poetry from the time. The worst of his fears eventually proved true. After resigning from office and returning to Soochow he was arrested on trumped-up charges nearly four years later and, at the age of thirty-eight, executed. Ironically, the portrait of Kao that has been passed on to us has him dressed in the robes of a Ming official.[17]

Notwithstanding Kao Ch'i's few unfortunate years as a Ming subject, his poetry was the first to display the characteristics that were to remain consistent over the following three centuries of the Ming dynasty. For one, Kao's verse is that of a pure poet—an always plainly lyrical poetry that expresses deeply felt emotions. Learning and philosophical thinking are not directly reflected in his verse. We have spoken before of Kao's concern about political affairs; and as a scholar, although not widely learned, he was of a caliber good enough to be selected as a compiler of the official Yuan history; thus, unlike so many later Ming poets, he was not devoid of learning. But to the extent that ideas are expressed in Kao's poetry, as in the "Song of the Green-Hill Master," they derive from deeply felt emotion rather than from the intellect.

Kao Ch'i was a forerunner of later Ming poetic style in an additional way. He drew on the poetry of the past richest in emotional feeling as his literary model. Discussing Kao's poetic models, his friend Li Chih-kuang stated, "Going back in time, he descried the Chien-an period (196–220); coming toward the present, he reached as far as the K'ai-yuan era (713–741) of the High T'ang; the Ta-li (766–780) and later periods he ignored." Kao Ch'i viewed such later periods of T'ang poetry as having lost the passion of the earlier ones. Another friend of the poet, Chang Yü (1333–1385), in a seven-character regulated verse entitled "A Lament for Kao Ch'i," makes the same point when mourning Kao's untimely death.

> His was the will of a lifetime, and to what end?
> Deprived of salary, deprived of land—most tragic!
> Yet he may well rest on fame inextinguishable—
> Ballads in the style of Han and poems à la High T'ang.[18]

[17] [It is reproduced in ibid., p. 183.]
[18] [Cf. the translation by Chaves, *Later Chinese Poetry*, p. 93.]

Han and Wei dynasty *yueh-fu* ballads and High T'ang poetry were not only Kao Ch'i's poetic models; for Old Phraseology poets in the sixteenth century as well, they served as exclusive models for poetry. Here again Kao took the ground first.

As to what extent Kao Ch'i's poems in fact approximate his models, that is another question. Employing terms analogous to ones he used to describe the Green-Hill Master (saying he was "thin but clean"), we can say of Kao's poetry that it is refreshing and pure, but lacking in complexity and richness. Rather, the poetry of Kao Ch'i is plain and unadorned. It stands at the head of later Ming poetic style in its simplicity and straightforwardness.[19]

Kao Ch'i's poetic theory appears in the preface he wrote to the *Tu-an chi*, or *Lone-Monastery Collection*, which contains poems by his monk-friend Yao Kuang-hsiao (1335–1418), better known by his monastic name Tao-yen. Poetry is said to have three essentials: *ko*, *i*, and *ch'ü*. *Ko* is the "poetic framework," the rhythmic feeling that derives from a poem's sound and meaning. *I*, or "meaning," refers to the content of a poem. And the "atmosphere" of a verse is expressed by *ch'ü*.

> There are three requisites for poetry. The "poetic framework" differentiates the style of a poem; "meaning" communicates its sentiment; and through "atmosphere" it achieves the marvelous. Unless a poem's framework is differentiated properly, it will degenerate into baseness and go contrary to the way of taking the past as a guide. Unless sentiment is communicated, a poem will fall into vague emptiness and its capacity to move people will be slight. And unless marvelousness is achieved, verse will slip into banality and its tone will scarcely transcend the vulgar.

*Ko*, *i*, and *ch'ü* find their analogues in the critical terms later made famous by the literary theorists Shen Te-ch'ien (1673–1769), Yuan Mei (1716–1797), and Wang Shyh-chen (1634–1711): "formal style" (*ko-tiao*), "native sensibility" (*hsing-ling*), and "ineffable personal tone or flavor" (*shen-yun*), respectively.[20] It is

---

[19] [The author mentions the "thin" side of Kao Ch'i partly to counter the tradition of overestimating him that was especially strong among early Meiji *kanshi* poets in Japan. Kao had been similarly criticized by the author's teachers as part of their reaction to traditional Chinese studies (*kangaku*) of the Meiji period.]

[20] The classic study by Suzuki Torao, *Shina shiron shi* (A History of Chinese

noteworthy that the "way" Kao Ch'i advocates as the basic prin-
ciple for achieving a poetic framework, that of "taking the past as
a guide," is one dependent on poetic models.

## The Four Outstanding Talents of Wu-chung and Yüan K'ai

Townsman literature of the area around Soochow produced many
poets of talent in late Yuan and early Ming times in addition to
Kao Ch'i. Yang Chi (ca. 1334–ca. 1383), Chang Yü (1333–
1385), and Hsu Pen (1335–1380), together with Kao Ch'i, be-
came known as the Four Outstanding Talents of Wu-chung (*Wu-
chung ssu-chieh*), Wu-chung being a designation for the Soochow
area. (Both Chang and Hsu had been among Kao's boyhood Ten
Friends on the Northern Outskirts.) Their poetic style, although
similar to that of Kao Ch'i, did not measure up to his. Like Kao,
they all fell victim to Chu Yuan-chang's purge: Yang Chi and Hsu
Pen died in prison,[21] and Chang Yü drowned himself after being
recalled from exile in Kwangtung. The term the Four Outstanding
Talents of Wu-chung is intended to call to mind the Four Out-
standing Talents of the Early T'ang (*Ch'u-T'ang ssu-chieh*)—Wang
Po, Yang Chiung, Lu Chao-lin, and Lo Pin-wang—who similarly
met untimely deaths.

By way of example I would like to cite a five-character regu-
lated verse by Chang Yü entitled "Presented to a Monk Returning
to Japan," which was probably written for a Zen monk of the early
Muromachi period (1338–1573).

With tin-knobbed staff, you depart to follow your fate,
To your native mountains lying near the sun.
You revere the Dharma of the lands of the East,
And have the enlightenment of Greater-Vehicle Zen.
Cast spells on the water, and dragons will come to your begging bowl;
Recite the scriptures, and waves will spare your boat.
In truth, there is no departing or staying;
But as I part from you, tears cascade.

---

Poetic Theory) (Tokyo: Kōbundō, 1927; rpt. 1967), is indispensable for discus-
sion of these poetic theories.

[21] [It is doubtful that Hsu Pen died in prison; see T. W. Weng, "Hsü Pen," in
*Dictionary of Ming Biography*, p. 596.]

The Yangtze-Delta city of Sung-chiang near modern Shang-hai, along with Soochow, was a center for townsman poetry from Yang Wei-chen's time onward. One of Sung-chiang's young native sons, Yuan K'ai (fl. 1367), came under the aegis of Yang Wei-chen. Because he wrote the following seven-character regulated verse entitled "White Swallow," he earned the nickname White-Swallow Yuan (*Yuan po-yen*).

> The ancient land is ruined, its affairs turned to naught;
> One rarely sees the showy mansions of old first families.
> With the moon bright on Han waters, not a trace of your shadow;
> Snow filling the Liang garden, you still have not returned.
> Willow tufts on the pond, their scent enters dreams;
> Pear blossoms in the courtyard, a chill that invades the clothing.
> The Chao sisters were indeed jealous of one other;
> Do not fly into Bright-Sun Lodge![22]

Called upon to serve the Ming government, Yuan K'ai managed to avoid the summons by feigning insanity.

# Liu Chi
# (1311–1375)

Although the majority of literary figures at the beginning of the Ming dynasty suffered persecution at the hands of Chu Yuan-chang, there were two notable exceptions, Sung Lien and Liu Chi, who were treated most favorably. Neither was simply a litterateur; both were men of considerable acumen in practical affairs. Sung Lien (1310–1381) is well known as an outstanding prose writer,

---

[22] [In this poem Yuan K'ai hangs together several allusions that have reference to swallows, the most notable being the one in the final couplet. After Lady Chao Fei-yen (Flying Swallow), consort of Emperor Ch'eng of the Han dynasty, "had become empress, she declined somewhat in favor; all the emperor's attentions now became fixed upon her younger sister, who was promoted to the rank of Bright Companion and assigned to quarters in the Bright Sun Lodge." Burton Watson, trans., *Courtier and Commoner: Selections from the "History of the Former Han" by Pan Ku* (New York: Columbia University Press, 1974), p. 266. Cf. the translation of the poem by Daniel Bryant, "Selected Ming Poems," *Renditions* 8 (Autumn 1977): 87.]

but his reputation as a poet is not high.[23] Liu Chi, however, was outstanding as both.

Coming from Ch'ing-t'ien in eastern Chekiang, Liu Chi became a Presented Scholar in 1333 and served as an official under the Yuan dynasty. During the disorders that marked the south at the end of the Yuan when the rebel leader Fang Kuo-chen was harassing Liu's region, the latter worked as adviser to Shih-mo I-sun, the Yuan general whose family was of Western-Regions origins. Liu was to write several poems lamenting the defeat and death of this leader.

Liu Chi's poetic style differed greatly from the gifted, impassioned verse of Kao Ch'i and other urban poets. His origins in the out-of-the-way countryside and his meditative temperament probably account for this. The following poem from Liu's early years illustrates the point; it is the fourth in a series of five-character old-style poems entitled "Thoughts, Thirty-One Poems."

> The ancients robbed Heaven and Earth,
> But nature's resources were beyond exhaustion.
> Nowadays people rob farm folk,
> So by year's end marsh and hill are bare.
> All is noisy along the nine thoroughfares,
> Sleeves of gowns linked in a long rainbow.
> People laugh at country hicks like Chü and Ni,[24]
> And get on proudly with their pleasurable pursuits.
> This is where it starts, the commotion;
> When will it end, the seething?

The poet speaks of a contradiction between the countryside, where farmers are bled dry (and by year's end, when all debts fall due, even mountains and marshes are denuded), and cities, where people in colorful clothes throng the thoroughfares. Liu Chi wonders when the "seething," that is, the desperate confusion or chaos that follows upon "commotion," that is, disorder or anarchy, will end. The thought expressed here is consonant with that behind the policy Chu Yuan-chang adopted in his later years, of emphasizing rural areas while curbing urban districts.

The contemplative side of Liu Chi takes a more complex form

---

[23] Sung Lien's poetry has drawn the attention of Japanese because he wrote various pieces referring to Japanese monks.

[24] *Analects* XVIII.6.

in the following poem, nineteenth in a series of forty-one five-character old-style verses entitled "Miscellaneous Poems."

> The yellow hawk preys on birds and sparrows;
> Mountain roosters eat insects and reptiles;
> Bees consume the honey of flowers;
> Shrimp ingest moss-bound sediment;
> Rabbits eat grass- and reed roots;
> Phoenixes feed on dryandra seeds.
> The taste of each is formed by its nature;
> Change it, and all die.
> These pensive thoughts I dismiss with a laugh;
> With whom can I pursue the mystery?

Liu Chi's laugh, of course, is an ironic one. He dearly wishes he had a kindred spirit with whom he could investigate the mystery and how to deal with it.

Both of the poems offered above were written before Liu Chi entered Chu Yuan-chang's service. He did so as a strategist in 1359—the same year as Sung Lien—at the age of forty-eight, nine years before the establishment of the Ming dynasty. In his later years Liu's relations with the Founder Emperor were a delicate affair.[25] The late Ming and early Ch'ing critic, Ch'ien Ch'ien-i, who edited the *Lieh-ch'ao shih-chi*, or *Poetry Anthology of Successive Reigns*, not only divided Liu Chi's selections into two separate Yuan and Ming sections, he also commented that the poet in the later poems had lost his openhearted frankness and seemed "rueful and spent." This is no exaggeration, as we see in the following "River Song," one of a series of four seven-character quatrains from the later period.

> Red smartweed and crimson maple, a single autumn hue;
> Ch'u clouds and Wu waters merge in the distance.
> Life's countless affairs, with the west wind, pass;
> Only the blue Yangtze, day and night, flows on.

Liu seems to be reflecting on changes that he himself helped bring about. His point here may be that, with the successful establishment of the new order, much in the old has been lost.

---

[25] His later position in government was analogous to the positions in Japan of Hayashi Razan (1583–1657) and the abbot Tenkai (d. 1643) under Tokugawa Ieyasu (1542–1616).

Although Liu Chi's verse is the most contemplative of the period, his style is closer to that of T'ang poetry than to that of the Sung. The two old-style poems quoted above seem to be based on such T'ang models as Ch'en Tzu-ang's "Reflections on Life's Vicissitudes" and Li Po's "Poems in an Old Mode." Thus we see that the conscious use of T'ang poetic models appears not only in poems from the time that express feeling, like those of Kao Ch'i, but also in poems like Liu Ch'i's that express thought.[26]

## The *T'ang-shih p'in-hui*

The conscious use of T'ang poetic models progressively increased from the time of Yü Chi and other late Yuan court poets in the north, to that of Kao Ch'i and Liu Chi in the early Ming, and beyond. Eventually, by mid-Ming times, T'ang poetry became the clearly established orthodox model for writing poetry.

The writing of T'ang-style poems was complemented in the realm of literary criticism by developments in poetic theory. The early Ming marks the appearance of the *T'ang-shih p'in-hui*, or *A Graded Anthology of T'ang Poetry*, a work that strongly asserts the supremacy of T'ang poetry and urges the imitation of its central core. This ninety-chapter work, compiled by Kao Ping (1350–1423) from Ch'ang-lo in Fukien, dominates later poetic theory of the Ming.[27]

The *T'ang-shih p'in-hui* does not take the form of abstract poetic theory. Rather, it is a large-scale anthology of T'ang verse. Some 5,769 poems by several hundred writers are arranged chronologically under seven formal categories:[28] five- and seven-

---

[26] Two items concerning Liu Chi might be added. First, because of his reputation as an ingenious and resourceful minister, books of prognostications circulated among the common people under his name. [For discussion of these works, see Chan Hok-lam, "Liu Chi," in *Dictionary of Ming Biography*, pp. 937–38.] Second, as we can tell from the series of poems he wrote referring to Kao Ming, Liu Chi was a friend of the author of the famous play, the *P'i-p'a chi* (Account of the Lute).

[27] The *T'ang-shih p'in-hui* was completed in 1393. An abridged version by the author in twenty-two chapters also appeared under the title *T'ang-shih cheng-sheng* (The Correct Strains of T'ang Poetry).

[28] [According to Cheng Ch'ing-mao, the 5,769 poems are by 610 writers, and the ten-chapter *Shih-i* (Supplement) to the work adds 954 poems by 61 writers. *Yuan Ming shih kai-shuo* (Chinese-language translation of this volume) (Taipei: Yu-shih wen-hua shih-yeh kung-ssu, 1986), p. 159.]

character old-style verse; five- and seven-character quatrains; five-
and seven-character regulated verse; and five-character long verses
in regulated meter.

For Kao Ping there are four periods of T'ang poetry com-
prised of nine groupings of authors, all of which, periods and
groupings, are given names that by their usage have evaluative sig-
nificance. He outlines the scheme in the introduction to the work.
Seventh-century verse is called Early T'ang (*Ch'u-T'ang*) poetry;
its writers are the Orthodox Founders (*Cheng-shih*) of the dynas-
ty's poetry. The High T'ang (*Sheng-T'ang*) period, covering the
K'ai-yuan and T'ien-pao reign periods (713–741 and 742–756),
is divided into four categories: Orthodox Patriarchs (*Cheng-
tsung*), Great Masters (*Ta-chia*), Famous Masters (*Ming-chia*), and
Right-Hand Assistants (*Yü-i*). The High T'ang—the age of Li Po,
Tu Fu, Meng Hao-jan, Wang Wei, Ch'u Kuang-hsi, Wang
Ch'ang-ling, Kao Shih, Ts'en Shen, Li Ch'i, and Ch'ang Chien—
is the zenith of T'ang poetry. The Middle T'ang (*Chung-T'ang*)—
the age of Han Yü, Po Chü-i, and others—extends from the mid-
eighth until the beginning of the ninth century. Poets of this pe-
riod were Immediate Successors (*Chieh-wu*, i.e., ones who half fol-
lowed others' footsteps), and mark the beginning of a decline.
Late T'ang (*Wan-T'ang*) poetry comprises the remainder of the
ninth century. Its practitioners—Tu Mu, Li Shang-yin, and
others—are Properly Transformed Ones (*Cheng-pien*) and Linger-
ing Echoes (*Yü-hsiang*), who represent a marked decline.[29] Put
simply, poets of the High T'ang like Li Po and Tu Fu are consid-
ered the zenith of poetry and the best subject for emulation.

This view of High T'ang poetry dates back one hundred and
fifty years to Yen Yü's (1180–1235) *Ts'ang-lang shih-hua*, or *Po-
etry Talks by Ts'ang-lang*. Drawing on Ch'an (i.e., Zen) Buddhist
terminology, Yen Yü had viewed the poetry of the High T'ang,
together with that of the Han, Wei, and Chin dynasties, as being
"Primary Truth" (*ti-i i*); poetry by Po Chü-i and other Middle
T'ang poets embodied "Ancillary Truth" (*ti-erh i*); and poetry of
the Late T'ang was said to result from Pratyeka Yana and Sravaka
Yana (*sheng-wen pi-chih kuo*).[30]

---

[29] [The ninth category is the Overflowing Ones (*P'ang-liu*), comprised mostly
of Buddhist and Taoist priests.]

[30] [Pratyeka Yana and Sravaka Yana are, respectively, "the erroneous method of

But Yen Yü's views, appearing as they did at the end of the Southern Sung dynasty when late T'ang poetry was the rage, had been comparatively fragmentary and isolated. By contrast, Kao Ping set out to prove systematically with his more than five thousand verse selections that T'ang poetry could be clearly divided into four periods with qualitative rankings: Early, High, Middle, and Late T'ang. Also, Kao Ping took another step that went beyond Yen Yü: he removed Han, Wei, and Chin verse from "Primary Truth," leaving only High T'ang poetry preeminent. After consultation with Lin Hung from his hometown area in Fukien, Kao determined that pre-T'ang poetry formed a transitionary stage, the "incomplete" elements of which led to fulfillment in the "completed" verse of the T'ang. This was not only a departure from Yen Yü; it was unprecedented in Chinese poetic theory.

Kao Ping's praise of T'ang poetry is stated with greater decisiveness than it had been by earlier critics. It is noteworthy, moreover, that the ideas he expressed emerged from Fukien and not from the Chekiang-Kiangsu center of literary activity. Perhaps it was easier to reach such clear-cut views in a locale somewhat removed from the center of poetic activity. This is not to say that poetic activity in Fukien was dormant. Poetry societies not only flourished there, with Lin Hung as the leading figure, but also in Kwangtung as well. Thus we know that early Ming townsman poetry flourished as far as the southern extreme of the empire; but the quality of such poetry was not necessarily high.[31]

---

attempting to attain individual enlightenment in isolation without any teacher and apart from the true *P'u-sa Sheng* (*Bodhisattva Yana*), . . . [and] the equally erroneous method of attempting to attain enlightenment through the (mere) chanting of the scriptures and listening to doctrine." Richard John Lynn, "Alternate Routes to Self-Realization in Ming Theories of Poetry," in *Theories of the Arts in China*, eds. Susan Bush and Christian Murck (Princeton: Princeton University Press, 1983), p. 318.]

[31] In Japan the *T'ang-shih p'in-hui* was widely read in the mid-Edo period as part of the emphasis on T'ang verse advocated by Ogyū Sorai (1666–1728). Its five-character quatrain and seven-character regulated-verse sections were published in separate editions, in 1733 and 1738, respectively. The former was collated by Hattori Nankaku (1683–1759), and the latter contains an introduction by him. A volume comprising the section of five-character long verses in regulated meter appeared in 1816. An edition of the *T'ang-shih cheng-sheng*, with annotation by Higashi Mutei (1796–1849) of Ise, was published in 1843.

# Chapter 6

# THE MIDDLE MING (I):
## STAGNATION AND REVIVAL,
## 1400–1500

## A Half-Century Hiatus

The two preceding chapters dealt with the late Yuan and early Ming period, when Yang Wei-chen, Yü Chi, Kao Ch'i, and Liu Chi were luminaries. Not only did poetry flourish, the new vernacular genres of drama and vernacular fiction also came to maturity. The great works of "southern-style drama" (*nan-hsi*), including Kao Ming's *P'i-p'a chi*, or *Account of the Lute*, as well as the compilation of China's first full-length novels, the *Shui-hu chuan* and *San-kuo-chih yen-i*, date from this fourteenth-century period.[1] Ch'ü Yu's series of stories of the supernatural, the *Chien-teng hsin-hua*, or *New Stories for When the Lampwicks Are Trimmed*, also dates from the time.

When we enter upon the fifteenth century, however, all turns to silence. The first fifty years of the century are a virtual blank with regard to literature. Political life, by contrast, was of some event; the consolidation of the regime, except for a few incidents, continued apace. After the thirty-year reign of the Founder Em-

---

[1] I here follow Lo Kuan-chung. [For translated titles of the novels, see Introduction, n. 2.]

peror came to an end in 1398, his grandson, the Chien-wen emperor, took over the throne for four years before it was usurped by the latter's uncle, the Yung-lo emperor (r. 1402–1424).[2] Interestingly, one of the army commanders under the usurper was Tao-yen, the onetime monk and literary companion of Kao Ch'i.[3] The transference of the Ming capital to Peking further consolidated the Yung-lo emperor's hold on the empire. In his cruel treatment of men of letters he resembled his father, the founder of the dynasty. He once forced one of his personal secretaries, Hsieh Chin, to get drunk and then had him buried alive in the snow. The son and grandsons of the Yung-lo emperor—the Hung-hsi (r. 1424–1425), Hsuan-te (r. 1425–1435), and Cheng-t'ung (r. 1435–1449)[4] emperors—were heirs to an era of peace. Although the last of the three was taken captive while carrying out a campaign against the Oirat Mongol chieftain, Esen, the empire's midcentury internal peace was scarcely disturbed; his younger brother, the Ching-t'ai emperor, took over the throne from 1449 to 1457 during his temporary absence. Incidentally, the fact that Ming emperors took only one reign-period title per sovereign is a manifestation of the dynasty's emphasis on plainness.[5]

While government grew more tightly consolidated, literature continued in a moribund state. Three civil officials at court, the Three Yangs (*San Yang*)—Yang Shih-ch'i (1365–1444) from Kiangsi, Yang Jung (1371–1440) from Fukien, and Yang Fu (1372–1446) from Hupei—wrote extremely tedious verse in a so-

[2] The brave loyalty rendered the Chien-wen emperor at the time by Fang Hsiao-ju (1357–1402) provides the subject for the last chapter in Asami Keisai's series of portraits of loyalists, the *Seiken igen*.

[3] Details of the event, along with a description of its aftermath, are related in the Japanese historical novel by Kōda Rohan (1869–1947), *Unmei* (Fate).

[4] Restored under the T'ien-shun reign period from 1457 to 1464.

[5] [Because only one reign period is used per emperor in Ming and Ch'ing times—with the sole exception of the Cheng-t'ung emperor (n. 4 above)—rulers of the two dynasties are commonly referred to by their reign-period names, e.g., the Yung-lo emperor. Thus Chu Yuan-chang, posthumously designated the dynasty's T'ai-tsu, or Ultimate Paterfamilias (adapted here to Founder Emperor [see chap. 5, n. 2]), is also known, in accord with his reign-period title, as the Hung-wu emperor. For a chart giving all three names for each Ming ruler—original name, reign-period title, and posthumous name—see *Dictionary of Ming Biography*, p. xxi.]

called secretariat style (*t'ai-ko t'i*). Their work, along with that of the unfortunate Hsieh Chin (1369–1415), has been relegated to oblivion. The earlier flourishing of townsman poetry came to a halt. Verse writing continued to be part of the educational training of townsmen, but virtually no one from this fifty-year period is worthy of attention.

One might ask what brought about such a cultural hiatus. Apparently it was caused by the very success of the Founder Emperor's political policies, as implemented both by him and his successors. We must await further historical study for more detailed understanding of the process at work. It is my surmise, however, that the simplification of the examination system, with the result that all one had to do to become an official was to learn how to write an eight-legged essay, effected precisely the social change desired by its institutor: namely, a class of people too unsophisticated to have entered such positions before was now qualified to become officials and men of cultural affairs. Educated up to a point, they simply lacked the necessary ability to write poetry.

Also, because the traditional center of townsman poetry around Soochow had been an enclave of Chu Yuan-chang's bitter enemy Chang Shih-ch'eng, the area suffered the displeasure of the Founder Emperor in the form of the highest tax rate in the empire. This sapped the people's spirit and robbed them of the surplus energy needed for letters.

The cultural hiatus in the period's poetry had its effect on other genres as well. The flourishing of vernacular fiction, of the sort noted during the preceding century, is nowhere to be seen. All that we have from the period are Li Chen's (1376–1452) collection of short stories, the *Chien-teng yü-hua*, or *Further Stories for When the Lampwicks Are Trimmed*, and a few *tsa-chü* plays written by the Founder Emperor's grandson, Chu Yu-tun (d. 1439).[6]

It was not until the second half of the fifteenth century that the cultural stagnation of the earlier period was overcome. The Cheng-t'ung emperor, who had been taken captive by Esen, was returned to the throne in 1457, under the reign-period title T'ien-shun, or Heavenly Course. His son and grandson, the Ch'eng-hua and Hung-chih emperors (r. 1464–1487 and 1487–1505), were

---

[6] [See Idema, *The Dramatic Oeuvre of Chu Yu-tun.*]

heirs to an era of peace that extended over the second half of the sixteenth century. Also, the newly ascendant class of simple, unsophisticated leaders that had emerged through the Founder Emperor's political policies remedied their lack of sophistication by mastering literary skills. Cultural revival began among the townsmen of South China, particularly Soochow, earlier the center of townsman culture. The leader of the revival there was a wealthy landholder named Shen Chou.

## Shen Chou
## (1427–1509)

Shen Chou is known as the greatest painter of the Ming Dynasty.[7] Yet his fame as a poet was second only to that he enjoyed as a painter. Shen's background is noteworthy. He was born the son of a landowner in 1427, in the riverside village of Hsiang-ch'eng just to the north of Soochow. He died in 1509 at the age of eighty-two, having lived his entire life as a true townsman. Although Shen had the requisite talent to pass the imperial examinations and become a high official, he chose not to do so. His only connection with government was his role as chief of provisions for his hamlet, a position that involved collecting local taxes. It was as a painter and poet that his name dominated the age.

Shen Chou's poems are rich in a visual description consonant with his talent as a painter. His depictions often deal with life in surrounding farm villages. The seven-character old-style poem, "Women of the Low-lying Fields," is offered here by way of example. It depicts the strenuous efforts of farm women using waterwheels to bail out water that has flowed from a lake into nearby low-lying fields. The "crows' tails" referred to in the poem's fifth line are unclear; perhaps they were pieces of cloth attached to waterwheels scooping out water.

> Lakeside fields, in ten years only one crop;
> This year again, lake waves at the brink.
> Men build up dikes, women tread waterwheels;

---

[7] [Note the study by Richard Edwards, *The Field of Stones: A Study of the Art of Shen Chou (1427–1509)* (Washington, D.C.: Freer Gallery of Art, Smithsonian Institution, 1962).]

Days long and treading endless—no energy left to draw on.
Revolving crows' tails flutter on a hundred spokes;
Muddy feet, unkempt hair, awash in wind and rain.
Don't you see, farmers don't mind a life of toil;
The daughters they bear also marry farmers.

As village head Shen Chou did not have to perform physical labor himself. Yet this poem has much less the air of an indifferent on-looker than do earlier poems in the style. Perhaps this was be-cause, as noted earlier, the farm villages in the Soochow area were assessed at the highest tax rate in the empire and Shen had respon-sibility for collecting local taxes.

As an artist Shen Chou often drew highly colorful landscapes. The following seven-character quatrain entitled "A Painting of Peach-Blossom Spring" may reveal the secret to his artistry. The title, of course, like the poem's final line, refers to T'ao Ch'ien's tale of an idyllic rustic scene.[8] Repelled by the reality of his own wretched village, Shen would paint an imagined one.

Cries of hungry boys and girls throughout the village,
To say nothing of tax collectors' pounding at the gates.
All night long unable to sleep, this old man
Gets up to find some paper to paint a Peach-Blossom Spring.[9]

Shen Chou's artistic mastery, especially his achievement in painting, not only brought about a revival of Soochow's long-dor-mant culture, it was also universally applauded as that of the finest artist of the age. Yet in terms of social position Shen was ever proud of being a townsman. The following is a five-character reg-ulated verse written at year's end, when Shen was returning by boat from the scenic spot of Kuang-fu Village on the outskirts of Soochow. The "poles" in the opening line are a gauge of height. The poem concludes with an expression of the dignity the author feels in being "one in cotton dress," that is, a commoner who is not an official.

Two poles high, the sun lowering in the west;
Paddles carry us home to the east.
As an old fisherman crosses the bridge,

---

[8] [See chap. 3, n. 10.]
[9] [Cf. the translation by Chaves, *Later Chinese Poetry*, p. 172.]

Wild birds shuttle through trees in flight.
Together with the water, my eyes turn clear;
With the leaves, my hair grows thin.
Between all-inclusive Heaven and Earth—
An autumn breeze and one in cotton dress!

As a townsman who devoted his life to the arts, Shen Chou
comes within the definition of *wen-jen* discussed in chapter 4. Yet
he was not eccentric in his behavior, which probably enhanced his
reputation.[10]

As Shen Chou's life illustrates, townsman culture had devel-
oped to the point where it could produce the following: a talented
townsman deserving of respect from society, a society that hon-
ored such a talent as the outstanding man of the age, and positive
pride on the part of that figure in being a townsman.

## Shen Chou's Disciples

Shen Chou attracted many talented townsmen from the Soochow
area as his disciples. Some were occasionally eccentric. What
prompted their eccentricity, however, differed from what had oc-
casioned such behavior in late Yuan *wen-jen* like Yang Wei-chen
and Ni Tsan. Shen Chou's disciples were like their predecessors in
advocating special privileges for themselves as artists; yet there
was no feeling of friction between them and the government, as
there had been between late Yuan *wen-jen* and their Mongol rul-
ers. As an expression of their burgeoning power as townsmen, the
eccentric behavior of Shen Chou's disciples seems rather to have
been in assertion of their freedom as townsmen.

### Chu Yun-ming
### (1461–1527)

Chu Yun-ming is most remembered for his skill at "mad-grass"
(*k'uang-ts'ao*) style calligraphy. His actions were as free and unin-
hibited as his calligraphic style. In return for his services as a callig-
rapher he most welcomed being recompensed with female com-

---

[10] For a more detailed biography of the painter-poet, see my "Shin Sekiden"
("Shen Shih-t'ien [i.e., Shen Chou]"), 1960; reprinted in *Yoshikawa Kōjirō zenshū*,
15: 562–612.

panionship. If the payment happened to be in cash, he would squander it drinking with his cohorts, which may account for why he was pursued by creditors whenever he stepped out the door.

Chu Yun-ming had six fingers on one hand, hence his literary name of Chih-shan, or Extra Knob. His family seems to have been of merchant origins in Soochow. His father became a Presented Scholar, and Chu himself passed the regional examinations and was an official for a time.

Of the poems by Chu Yun-ming to be cited here, the first sings the praises of his native Soochow. It is a five-character regulated verse entitled "Late Spring, A Mountain Outing."

> A small skiff sets out from the bank that cuts across the scene;
> In mountains to the west, blue is the touch of dawn.
> At waterwheels, toiling women;
> On the sedan chair, a young gadabout.[11]
> The sound of grain—in every house a mortar.
> Tea being picked—baskets all about.
> Of the beautiful sights of Soochow,
> Farming and sericulture are the finest.[12]

As dissolute as Chu Yun-ming was, even he shows awareness of the difference between those who do the work in society and those who live off it.

Chu Yun-ming's seven-character regulated verse, "Early Third Month, On the Hsia Mountain Road," contains the following lines:

> Spring clouds, spring rains, spring winds—
> Mountain on top of mountain, misty in an atmosphere suffused with blue.
> A fine landscape in our beautiful South—
> How hard to bear, being a sojourner!

The most uninhibited of Chu Yun-ming's poetic couplets appears in the five-character old-style verse, "In Imitation of Li Po's 'Lying Drunk on a Spring Day' "; it reads, "If man were without dreams, / Till the end of his days there would be no primordial

---

[11] [Presumably a reference by the poet to himself.]
[12] [Cf. the translation by Chaves, *Later Chinese Poetry*, p. 191.]

darkness." Chu Yun-ming's own unconventional behavior was in conscious pursuit of such a primordial state.

## T'ang Yin
## (1470–1523)

T'ang Yin styled himself Liu-ju chü-shih, or Six Similes Lay Believer.[13] His unbridled license was such as to startle even his senior fellow disciple, Chu Yun-ming. The vernacular short-story collection, the *Ku-chin ch'i-kuan*, or *Unusual Events Past and Present*, records an episode that may not be wholly fictional. Once, upon seeing a beautiful girl on the street, T'ang Yin was able to learn she worked as a maid for the owner of a large pawnshop. Concealing his identity, he gained a position in the household and eventually won the girl.

The following excerpt is from a comparatively long poem by T'ang Yin entitled "An Air":

> Future days so few!
> Past days so many!
> Man's life is for enjoyment,
> Why bother with the rest?

In 1498 at the age of twenty-eight, T'ang Yin came in first in the regional examinations in Nanking, only to become implicated the following year in a scandal over the leaking of metropolitan-examination questions. He was barred for life from officialdom. This only served to make his conduct more dissipated. One of his seven-character quatrains refers to these events in the opening couplet.

> The winner, Number One in the regional exams;
> Later, after cutting loose, I returned to my thatched roof.
> Don't laugh, the place can barely fit an awl stood upright;
> But under my brush, thousands of miles of rivers and mountains
>     come to life.[14]

The author of the final line was, of course, a famous painter, in addition to being a poet.

---

[13] [Note the study by T. C. Lai, *T'ang Yin: Poet/Painter, 1470–1524* (Hong Kong: Kelly and Walsh, n.d. [1971]).]

[14] [Cf. the translation by Chaves, *Later Chinese Poetry*, p. 210.]

T'ang Yin had a character all his own. After agreeing to join the service of the Prince of Ning, Chu Ch'en-hao, he learned that the latter was plotting revolt. So T'ang drank excessively and feigned stupidity, even sitting cross-legged and naked, so as to force Chu to withdraw the invitation for him to serve.

As recorded in the official history of the Ming dynasty, T'ang Yin's deathbed words in 1523 at the age of fifty-three were that later generations, too, would misunderstand him.

## Wen Cheng-ming
## (1470–1559)

Born in 1470, the same year as T'ang Yin, Wen Cheng-ming is best known for his calligraphy.[15] His personality—warm, refined, mild—was like his calligraphic style. After the death of Shen Chou in 1509, he became the leader of the arts in Soochow, living to the age of eighty-nine. Because of his skill as a painter Wen Cheng-ming became an official in the Han-lin Academy in Peking. Sensing the hostility of those around him, he returned to Soochow after three years.[16]

Wen Cheng-ming's prose and poetry are collected in a volume entitled the *Fu-t'ien chi*, or *Large-Field Collection*.[17] The following is a five-character regulated verse entitled "Sitting Alone."

[15] [Note the studies by Anne DeCoursey Clapp, *Wen Cheng-ming: The Ming Artist and Antiquity* (Ascona: Switz.: Artibus Asiae, 1975); Richard Edwards, *The Art of Wen Cheng-ming (1470–1559)* (Ann Arbor: University of Michigan Museum of Art, 1976); and Marc F. Wilson and Kwan S. Wong, *Friends of Wen Cheng-ming: A View from the Crawford Collection* (New York: China House Gallery, 1975).]

[16] ["Wen was resented by others who felt that a painter had no place in the Han-lin Academy. . . . Another reason why, within the Academy, respect for Wen's literary and artistic abilities was mixed with resentment was that scholars of longer standing at court and with far more practical experience were placed under him." James Cahill, *Parting at the Shore: Chinese Painting of the Early and Middle Ming Dynasty, 1368–1580* (New York: Weatherhill, 1978), p. 215.]

[17] [The title comes from a poem (#102) in the *Shih ching* (Classic of Songs), the opening line of which reads, "Do not till too large a field." Bernhard Karlgren explicates the poem as follows: "A girl is admonished not to long for a 'faraway person,' who cannot be reached or obtained; to 'think of' that unattainable person is too ambitious, just as to cultivate a field too large for your working resources." *The Book of Odes* (Stockholm: Museum of Far Eastern Antiquities, 1950), pp. 66–67.]

> I sit alone in the quiet under thatched eaves;
> Once the mind settles, the Way can be savored long.
> My life's days given over to books,
> In retirement I add incense to the burner.
> When the sun rises, birds and ravens turn cheerful;
> As rains cease, refreshed are flowers and bamboo.
> In this leisurely way I have cultivated a certain laziness;
> Not that I have few visitors to greet.

Many visitors would come to Wen Cheng-ming's Soochow residence to request paintings and calligraphy. Like his mentor Shen Chou, Wen always managed to maintain a leisured composure, enjoying the special advantages of being a townsman. For example, the following seven-character regulated verse, "Up Early," describes the pure morning dawn in this metropolis of several hundred thousand residents.

> Lingering reverberations of last-watch drums—dark blue the sky;
> Night about to fade, I open the front gate to draw water.
> Roosters' crowing, people's voices, far off in the distance;
> Setting moon and aureole dawn turn light together.
> My short hair, turned to the wind, stays free of dust;
> Green leaves, touched by dew, turn slightly cooler.
> Once the sun rises above the rooftops, countless affairs will coalesce;
> How I cherish this quiet moment, and stroll for a while.

### Yang Hsun-chi
### (1456–1544)

In Soochow and its environs there were probably several thousand people writing poetry at the time whose activities were centered around Shen Chou and his disciples. Two of the more interesting deserve mention. One, Sang Yueh (1447–1503) from Ch'ang-shou (a prefecture adjacent to Soochow), earned quite a reputation for pretentiousness. Once, when calling on a district inspector of schools, he presented a namecard inscribed "Genius of the South." He also had the interesting habit of burning books after reading them.

Yang Hsun-chi is another personality. Born into a trading family without a single volume in the house, he turned into a true bibliophile. A few years after becoming a Presented Scholar in 1484, he feigned illness and returned to Soochow to devote himself to his books rather than continue to serve as an official. In a five-character old-style poem, "Inscribed on the Doors of My Bookshelves," he relates his progress from bookless son to literary scholar.

> Mine was a trading family
> Living in Nan-hao district for a hundred years.
> I was the first to become a scholar,
> Our house being without a single book.
> Applying myself for a full decade,
> I set my heart on building a collection.
> Though not fully stocked with minor writings,
> Of major works, I have nearly everything:
> Classics, history, philosophy, belles lettres—
> Nothing lacking from the heritage of the past.
> Binding up the volumes one by one in red covers,
> I painstakingly sew them by hand.
> When angry, I read and become happy.
> When sick, I read and am cured.
> Piled helter-skelter in front of me,
> Books have become my life.
> The people of the past who wrote these tomes,
> If not sages, were certainly men of great wisdom.
> Even without opening their pages,
> Joy comes to me just fondling them.
> As for my foolish family, they can't be helped;
> Their hearts are set on money alone.
> If a book falls on the floor, they don't pick it up;
> What do they care if they get dirty or tattered?
> I'll do my best by these books all my days,
> And die not leaving a single one behind.
> There are some readers among my friends—
> To them I'll give them all away.
> Better that than have my unworthy sons
> Haul them off to turn into cash.

In his devotion to scholarship Yang Hsun-chi was rather the exception among Ming poets. The simplicity and directness that characterized Ming poetic style were based on an approach to writing that did not encourage such wide reading.

According to an anecdote current in Ming times, whenever Yang Hsun-chi came across a particularly interesting passage in his reading, his arms and legs would wave in the air. His biography in the official Ming history records another anecdote. Once, when the high official Ku Lin paid him a visit, their discussion was interrupted by a messenger sent from the local governor urging Ku to come at once. Ku seemed undecided whether to break off their interview, so Yang Hsun-chi angrily told him to leave. The following day Ku Lin came to apologize, but was refused admittance at the door.

# Li Tung-yang
## (1447–1516)

The regeneration of poetry in the latter half of the fifteenth century was not confined to the townsman poets of the south. With the appearance of Li Tung-yang poetry came to life again at the Peking court, bringing an end to the tedium of the Three Yangs.

Li Tung-yang chose the literary name Hsi-yai, or Western Shore, because his residence was located on the west bank of the scenic Lake of the Ten Monasteries (Shih-ch'a hai) in Peking. For more than forty years Li served as an important official under the Ch'eng-hua, Hung-chih, and Cheng-te emperors—ninth, tenth, and eleventh in the Ming line. Because of his high position and because he frequently served as chief examiner for the metropolitan examinations, many junior officials became his disciples. Thus he was a man of considerable influence, exercising great power in both the literary and political world.

Li Tung-yang was himself of humble origins. Although his ancestral home was Ch'a-ling in Hunan, his more immediate ancestors resided in Peking. His grandfather, who attained the low rank of corporal, was assigned to the imperial household and acted as a foreman in charge of laborers. Recognized as a child prodigy, Li Tung-yang was presented to the emperor at the age of three, and when only seven was placed in the service of the palace. After becoming a Presented Scholar at the unusually young age of sixteen, he served as a leading official in the emperor's entourage and eventually became a man of great influence.[18] He illustrates well how,

---

[18] [The preceding three sentences, partially revised from the original, draw on

even in literary affairs, the social stratum that the dynasty's Founder Emperor wished to have come to the fore eventually matured to the point of producing such a prominent poet.

A characteristic of Li Tung-yang's poetry is its large scale, which was commensurate with his high position. For example, the following seven-character old-style poem, "On a Painting of Fish Being Caught, A Song," opens with scenes viewed in a scroll painting.

> Poor people fish mostly with snare nets;
> Rich people fish mostly with seine nets.
> The poor don't manage as well as the rich;
> One seine net can bring in tens of feet of fish.
> When river flowers line the banks and the river is low,
> That is when a foot-long fish is worth an inch of gold.
> With banks high and snare nets small, not enough gets heaved in,
> And the stifled sobs of fishermen's songs sadden the heart.
> Along the riverbank, family after family sells its catch;
> Large boats, small boats, too numerous to count.
> Large boats bearing good fish bring in lots of cash;
> Small boats linger on, through day and night.
> A Ch'ang-sha wanderer, I think of my native land—
> How I'd like to be there, sitting and watching along the stream:
> I'd buy some fish, purchase wine, and, facing the bright moon,
> Bring myself to raise a cup, though hardly a drinker myself.
> Living here west of Lake Bridge,
> Court messengers bring fish long as large chopsticks.
> But can I, by myself, eat food most residents have never tasted?
> From my railing, I have them tossed back in.
> There are things in life that interest me, but not fish;
> Enough now of unrolling this scroll to look at the scene.
> With neither home nor land to call my own, one need hardly ask—
> My only wish: with the common people of the Four Seas to share fat,
> fresh fish.[19]

In his regulated verses Li Tung-yang is often good at giving the telling details of a scene or event. The following poem was written in 1479 while returning from Ch'ang-p'ing, north of Pe-

---

material (in part quoted) from Fang Chaoying, "Li Tung-yang," in *Dictionary of Ming Biography*, p. 877.]

[19] [Cf. the translation by Chaves, *Later Chinese Poetry*, pp. 179–80.]

king, where the poet had been in the Ch'eng-hua emperor's entourage on a visit to the tombs of earlier Ming emperors. The poem follows the rhyme scheme of one written by Yang T'ing-ho, who accompanied the party.

> Past all the post stations, the way at last enters the capital;
> Waterside villages, hillside towns, how many passed along the way?
> We'd lodge with those we happened to meet—I don't recall their names;
> Trusting the way to my horse, I wrote poems, unheedful of the leagues.
> The wind suddenly still, geese return to the sandy shore;
> As waters clear, fish plunge near stone weirs.
> Gemlike towers should be beyond those layers of sky—
> Let not the faintest clouds obscure the moon's brightness.[20]

As the title suggests, Li Tung-yang's hundred-verse collection, *Ni ku-yueh-fu*, or *In Imitation of Old-Style Ballads*, was written in the style of early folk songs; it relates historical events through the ages.[21] The story of the Tibetan lama who desecrated the Sung imperial tombs has been related earlier.[22] Two different loyalists, T'ang Chueh and Lin Ching-hsi, were later credited with reburying the remains and marking the spot with holly. One of Li Tung-yang's ballads, "Song of the Holly," tells of the event.

> Kao-tsung's tomb,
> Hsiao-tsung's tomb,
> Scales and bones all cast off, those dragons now spiritless.
> Was it Loyal T'ang,
> Or Loyal Lin?
> Reports in unofficial histories, uncertain as to which.
> Jade fish and golden grain, all turned to dust;[23]
> One need hardly ask about holly buds, as well.
> Hui-tsung and Ch'in-tsung never returned, just their coffins;
> For two hundred years only the wood has been rotting.

---

[20] The compound "gemlike towers" is one that had been used by Su Shih. The implication of the final couplet is, "May there be no wrong around the emperor." [Cf. the translation by Chaves, *Later Chinese Poetry*, p. 181.]

[21] Li Tung-yang's work was to influence Japanese literature, serving as the model for Rai San'yō's (1780–1832) *Nihon gafu* (Japanese Ballads), which includes the famous couplet, "The Honnō Temple, / How wide the moat?" A Japanese edition of the *Ni ku-yueh-fu* was published in the Ansei period (1854–60) of the late Edo.

[22] See pp. 60–61.

[23] The fish and grain were burial articles.

As for Li-tsung's skull, no need to grieve;
It got reburied in the south, a scoop of earth sufficed.

The final four lines need clarification. The last two Northern Sung emperors, Hui-tsung and Ch'in-tsung, were captured by Chin dynasty troops and held captive in Manchuria until they died; only their coffins were later returned. The skull of Emperor Li-tsung of the Southern Sung, said to have been used as a drinking vessel by the Mongols and later thrown into a lake, had been recovered and buried nearby. Upon the suggestion of Wei Su, an official under Chu Yuan-chang, the Founder Emperor had the skull excavated and restored to its original tomb in Shao-hsing. In this poem Li Tung-yang is in effect telling the loyal servants T'ang Chueh and Lin Ching-hsi to rest in peace, their task is over.

Ch'ien Ch'ien-i, the compiler of the *Lieh-ch'ao shih-chi*, or *Poetry Collection of Successive Reigns*, considered Li Tung-yang the finest poet of the mid-Ming period. He notes that while Li's collected verse, the *Huai-lu-t'ang chi*, or *Collection of the Hall Embracing the Foothills*, draws on a wide range of poetic sources— Tu Fu, Liu Ch'ang-ch'ing, and Po Chü-i of the T'ang, Su Shih of the Sung, and Yü Chi of the Yuan—the poet displays an individual quality all his own. Ch'ien's disciple, Wang Shyh-chen, took exception with his mentor, saying Ch'ien had overly praised Li. It is fair to say, however, that Li Tung-yang is rare among Ming poets for the suppleness of his poetic vision.

Because Li Tung-yang dominated the literary affairs of government officials for so many years, it was natural that a reaction set in. What added fuel to the resentment felt toward him by younger officials of the bureaucracy was his accommodating manner as a politician (which was matched by a pliancy in his verse). In his later years Li Tung-yang served the Cheng-te emperor, a rough, coarse youth who to some extent embodied the spirit of the Ming. The favor the young emperor accorded the eunuch Liu Chin served only to stimulate the latter's unruliness; whereas other leading officials quit the government in protest, Li vacillated and stayed on. It was with the specific intention of giving vent to such grievances against Li Tung-yang that the Old Phraseology movement, which was to dominate the following century, was born.

In summary, the entire fifteenth century was a period of transition. It began with a half century of stagnation, but a gradual revival in the writing of poetry, which developed over the latter half of the period, led into the sixteenth century when the Old Phraseology movement held sway.

Drama and vernacular fiction, unlike poetry, did not enjoy a revival during the latter half of the fifteenth century; few works were produced in these genres. It was poetry that continued to be the first interest of men of talent throughout the empire; drama and vernacular fiction flourished again only when an excess of talent overflowed from poetry into these genres, a process that required time. The revival of drama and fiction had to await the flourishing of Old Phraseology in the sixteenth century.

# Chapter 7

## THE MIDDLE MING (II): THE AGE OF OLD PHRASEOLOGY, 1500–1600

### Old Phraseology

Sixteenth-century China was dominated by an archaist literary movement called Old Phraseology (*Ku-wen-tz'u*). The movement advocated the use of models to recapture the intensity and strength of past literature. Only a very limited range of works from the core of the classical tradition was considered acceptable for imitation. Specifically, writings of the Ch'in and Han dynasties were deemed the proper model for prose writing, especially the *Shih chi*, or *Records of the Historian*, completed in the first century B.C. For poetry eighth-century High T'ang verse was the ideal, particularly the poetry of Tu Fu; also acceptable as a model, but only secondarily so, was second- and third-century Han and Wei dynasties verse. The movement's advocates regarded all other past literature as being totally improper, special disdain being reserved for the writings of the Sung dynasty. The dictum of the age was "prose must follow the Ch'in and Han, and poetry the High T'ang; all else is not the Way." To this was added the strong injunction, "Do not read anything after the T'ang."[1] The role of

---

[1] Li Meng-yang, as cited by Ch'ien Ch'ien-i in the latter's *Lieh-ch'ao shih-chi*, Li Meng-yang biography.

these classical models was crucial. A writer's aim was to strive for congruence between his own work and the model; not only was he to employ the same diction and phraseology of the original, it was also incumbent upon him to reproduce the pattern of feeling embodied in the model.

Old Phraseology swept the empire, completely dominating sixteenth-century China. People from a broad range of social strata welcomed, supported, and participated in the movement. Its precepts became dogma not only for the literary world of the time but also for virtually every facet of sixteenth-century Chinese cultural life. It is in this period that Ming poetry expanded to its full, at least in terms of quantity.

Leading Old Phraseology figures for the first half of the century were the Earlier Seven Masters (*Ch'ien ch'i-tzu*), including Li Meng-yang and Ho Ching-ming. The second half of the century was the age of the Later Seven Masters (*Hou ch'i-tzu*), the most prominent among them being Li P'an-lung and Wang Shih-chen. The term "seven masters" evoked the energy and spirit of the original "seven masters" of the Chien-an period (196–220). Ming poets adopted it in conscious self-assurance that they measured up to their namesakes, the terms "earlier" and "later" being added afterwards.

Inasmuch as it was so concerned with the imitation of classical literary models, Old Phraseology offered a certain aristocratic surface appeal. Moreoever, emphasis on the strict congruence between one's own writing and classical models gave the illusion that detailed intricacy was the movement's underlying principle. In fact, just the opposite was the case. The spirit of the age being one of simplicity, directness, and intensity, the same characteristics were operative in its literary works.

The following factors contributed to this. First, the exclusive models chosen for imitation—the *Shih chi* for prose and High T'ang verse for poetry—were the most intense in all past literature. Second, although congruence with past models was advocated as the sole approach to writing, in practice it was reducible to the following: all one had to do to write poetry or prose was to have read the proper models. In other words, once you read the *Shih chi*, you could write prose; and if you simply read some High T'ang verse, you could write poetry. This was hardly a subtle, learned approach to writing. Since the works of Sung authors, many of whom were men of immense learning, were rejected in toto as debased writing, it was considered unnecessary to read them. And third, the actual method of poetic imitation employed, that of simply tracing verbally over the linguistic patterns of earlier models, was a very simple and direct approach.

The two leading figures of the Old Phraseology movement, Li Meng-yang and Li P'an-lung, were men of strong passion who came from the newly ascendant social stratum of the Ming. It is a striking coincidence that both came from families of rural origin that had included *hsia-k'o* (Robin Hood-like figures) in their background.[2] The personalities of the two help account for the spirit of the Old Phraseology movement. That factor and their background help explain why the movement attracted so many townsmen and dominated the century. By the same token they and their writing are the logical outcome of the social policies instituted by the dynasty's Founder Emperor.

Domestic tranquility continued to prevail throughout the sixteenth century; it is only against this background that the literary development of the period was possible. After the shorter reigns of the Hung-chih (r. 1488–1506) and Cheng-te (r. 1506–1522) emperors, the Chia-ching emperor's forty-four-year span (r. 1522–1566) highlighted the early-middle part of the century. Following the short rule of the the Lung-ch'ing emperor (r. 1567–1573), the forty-eight-year reign of the Wan-li emperor (r. 1572–1620) formed another long period, one that led into the following century.

Though an era of tranquility, the age was not completely free of disruption. Around midcentury, during the Chia-ching emperor's rule, Japanese pirates frequently plundered the coastal region of South China. And during the rule of the Wan-li emperor at the

---

[2] [*Hsia-k'o* were men with a reputation for quarreling and gambling who would take justice into their hands as champions of the poor and distressed. Although outside the Confucian pale, they had a humanitarian streak and preferred fighting to submitting to injustice. In his study of these figures as they appear in Chinese literature, James J.Y. Liu lists the ideals of the *hsia-k'o* as follows: altruism, justice, individual freedom, personal loyalty, courage, truthfulness and mutual faith, honor and fame, and generosity and contempt for wealth. *The Chinese Knight-Errant* (London: Routledge and Kegan Paul, 1967), pp. 4–6.]

end of the century, Toyotomi Hideyoshi invaded China's neighbor, Korea, in 1592 and again in 1597. Although these were the most prominent events of the period, they were not enough to disrupt the atmosphere of domestic tranquility that prevailed.[3]

## The Earlier Seven Masters

### Li Meng-yang (1475–1531)

Li Meng-yang was the first theorist, polemicist, and practitioner of the Old Phraseology movement. The origins of the poet are noteworthy. His ancestral home was Ch'ing-yang in Shensi, a backward region in North China far from well-established literary centers in the south like Soochow. Li Meng-yang's grandfather was a local grocer, moneylender, and *hsia-k'o*. One of his uncles was a clerk handling household registers for the military district, and another was a fortune-teller. Li entered these items in a "family genealogy" (*tsu-p'u*) he composed in the writing style of the *Shih chi*. Only with his father does there appear a Li of more intellectual bent; although the latter became instructor in the household of the Prince of Kaifeng, his main function was to serve as the prince's drinking partner. Thus Kaifeng, itself scarcely a literary center at the time, became the second ancestral home of the Li family.

We are told the future poet was given the first name Mengyang, or Dreaming of the Sun, because his mother conceived him while dreaming of its orb. As a youth of seventeen Li Meng-yang placed first in the Shensi regional examinations and entered the world of officialdom the following year, in 1493, upon passing the metropolitan examinations. The man in charge of the metropolitan examinations was Li Tung-yang, the figure of enormous influence discussed in the previous chapter.

Li Tung-yang's literary style was not to Li Meng-yang's liking. He found it to be the way he found the man's politics—too flexible, overly compromising, and unduly accommodating. Nor were

---

[3] The situation is quite different from that in Japan of the time, which was in the throes of civil war at the end of the Muromachi period.

the writings of the southerners, Shen Chou and his disciples, to young Li Meng-yang's taste; for someone like Li, who had grown up in a rural family of *hsia-k'o* background, their work was too delicate, too urban, too tepid. He wanted a more intense and vital kind of writing—hence the literary models he advocated.

Li Meng-yang's approach to literature was revolutionary. First, he completely rejected as prose models the writings of more recent dynasties; thus he discarded the corpus of Han Yü of the T'ang and Ou-yang Hsiu of the Sung, even though theirs was certainly "old-style prose" (*ku-wen*). Li stated categorically, "Prose must follow the Ch'in and Han." The *Shih chi* provided the best such model, and the *Chan-kuo ts'e*, or *Intrigues of the Warring States*, was considered secondarily acceptable. As for later writing, as noted before, his dictum was "Do not read anything after the T'ang." Sung and later writing was rejected as being anemic, sluggish, and having lost proper "rhythm": "The writing that is popular nowadays is devoid of any order whatsoever; it resembles nothing so much as packed sand or a manipulated snake."

Equally revolutionary was Li Meng-yang's doctrine concerning verse, "Poetry must follow the High T'ang." Recognition of the outstanding quality of that period's verse was nothing new; more than one hundred years earlier Kao Ping in his *T'ang-shih p'in-hui*, or *A Graded Anthology of T'ang Poetry*, had pointed to the High T'ang as being the zenith of poetry. Li Meng-yang differed from Kao Ping, however, in his evaluation of Middle T'ang poets like Po Chü-i. Even though for Kao their work represented a decline from earlier writing, he had still included Middle and Late T'ang poets in his scheme; Li, however, completely rejected all T'ang poetry after the High T'ang.

Li Meng-yang's attitude toward Sung poetry also marks a sharp break from earlier views. Even though Ming poets rarely drew on Sung writings as poetic models, preferring to select from the entire range of T'ang verse, they had always held Sung poetry in respect. Also Su Shih's disciple, Huang T'ing-chien, was recognized by earlier Ming writers as having been the finest of the poets modeling themselves on the style of Tu Fu. With Li Meng-yang, however, there was a marked change in attitude; he completely rejected Sung poetry in any form. In his view, "Sung writers put great stock on 'argument' (*li*), while slighting 'rhythm' (*tiao*)." By "rhythm" Li meant both an external musical rhythm produced by the sound of the words and an internal one issuing from the breaks and flows in meaning. Li was not denying the importance of argumentation; rather, he felt that its conscious employ was more proper to prose than to poetry. "Has poetry ever been without its own argument? No! Yet if one concentrates on argument, why write poetry instead of prose?" In Li Meng-yang's view, since Sung verse was argumentation run rampant, it had lost "rhythm" and therefore was not poetry.

Li Meng-yang emphasized that verse must have feeling and that it must appeal to the senses. Paucity of feeling, he argued, goes hand in hand with an excess of logic or with too much analytical discussion, precisely the defects of Sung poetry. He makes this point in a piece entitled "Ch'ien-ch'iu shan-jen chi," or "An Account of the Hidden-Dragon Recluse," which he presented to an Anhwei merchant by the name of She Yü. Therein he lists what he refers to as the "seven difficulties of poetic composition." Specifically he says, it is difficult to write poetry that is "ancient in form, untrammeled in rhythm, relaxed in spirit, full in line, rounded in sound, and transcendent in thought"; finally, "all of these must be given expression through feeling." To this he adds the proviso, "Even given these, without 'color' (*se*), it will not be 'godlike' (*shen*)." That is to say, unless verse has elements that appeal to the senses, it will never be marvelous or divine. "Sung writers lost these qualities and thus wrote no poetry worthy of the name."

Li Meng-yang advocated as close an adherence to original poetic models as possible. In reply to a request for guidance from a certain Chou Tso in Chekiang, he wrote, "The way people today imitate men of the past is not [real] imitation of them. . . . Patterns in fact exist of their own accord [in past literature]." Li is here arguing that it is not the antiquity of a model that makes it important; rather, it is the completeness and naturalness with which it is an actual embodiment of literary principle that gives it its value.

Li Meng-yang wrote verse based on his theories. One example is the following old-style poem written in 1505, from a series of seventeen entitled "Expressing My Indignation." Li had criticized a maternal relative of the Hung-chih emperor, Chang Huo-ling, the Duke of Shou-ning. As blunt in politics as he was in the advocacy of his literary theory, Li Meng-yang was thrown into the palace-guard jail no fewer than three times for his temerarious outspokenness. The fifth line of this poem dating from his second incarceration can be interpreted as a complaint that others equally blameworthy have escaped punishment.

> Under cramped eaves, evening turning dark,
> The cold lamp's flame does not lengthen.
> Its faint brilliance, flickering as the breeze settles,
> With a gust of wind is like bright frost.
> Others are free of the wide net;
> How did I end up here?
> Rats from the wall chatter beside my bed;
> Bats fly through empty rafters.
> An unexpected gust stirs at the south window,
> And suddenly the passing night is over.
> Alas! Still unable to sleep,
> I toss and turn, my heart grieved.

Li Meng-yang's five-character and seven-character regulated verse is mostly imitative of Tu Fu, the High T'ang poet he most admired. Although Li felt that regulated verse should fully re-create the original Tu Fu, what he in fact re-created was the vitality and intensity of Tu Fu's verse and not its fine detail. The following, which was likely composed in the second Li-family native home, Kaifeng, is the second of two five-character poems entitled "Climbing for a View."

> Though to retreat is indeed my nature,
> On the right occasion I am in high spirits.
> Flowers fraught with mist of days past,
> Willow shadows differ from years gone by.
> I stroll and sit among the lush green—
> My old haunt, these familiar woods.
> From the tall pavilion, a view extending far,
> Not a day goes by but I climb to gaze.

Much the same thematic material employing the same diction is repeated over and over in Li Meng-yang's poems. Phrases like "Heaven and Earth" and the "Central Plain" are among the poet's favorite expressions, as illustrated in the following poem written in Li's later years, "Summer, Climbing the Pavilion East of the Kaifeng City Walls."

> On this frame, old age setting in;
> Here on the Central Plain, a tower to climb.
> Cycles of *yin* and *yang*—a horse come and gone;
> Heaven and Earth—in essence an empty boat.[4]
> The thousand peaks of Wang-wu lying low,
> The Yellow River's single stream in flow.
> Clear sands stretch on and on at dusk;
> I envy you freewheeling gulls!

Fixed poetic models and fixed phraseology make for repetition of theme in poem after poem, resulting in a style that can be termed "a thousand compositions all in a single pattern." This drawback, scarcely limited to Li Meng-yang, is one common to all Old Phraseology writers.

The best of Li Meng-yang's work is illustrated by the following, one of a series of three five-character regulated verses written in his later years. It was composed on a trip through the central Yangtze area where Chin Island dominates the scene.

> Mad waves daily eastward tumbling,
> This islet suddenly athwart their flow—
> Where clams learn to craft mirages,
> And dragons freely roam heron caves.
> Bathed in light, the sky rises, only to fall;
> As shadows shift, the land sinks, only to bob back up.
> Knowledge untangled surpasses the Three Appearances;
> What need to search for the Ten Continents?[5]

The following poem, probably written while in Kaifeng, illustrates Li Meng-yang's seven-character regulated-verse style. It is

[4] The "empty boat" is a famous image found in *Chuang-tzu*. ["When lashed boats are crossing the river, and some empty boat comes and bumps against them, even a hot-tempered man will not get angry. . . . If a man can roam in the world with emptied self, who can interfere with him?" Chap. 20, "Shan mu" ("The Mountain Tree"). A. C. Graham, trans., *Chuang-tzu: The Seven Inner Chapters and Other Writings from the Book "Chuang-tzu"* (London: George Allen & Unwin, 1981), p. 142.]

[5] "Knowledge untangled" and the "Three Appearances" are probably Buddhist terms. The "Ten Continents" are mythical fairy lands beyond the sea.

one of a series of five celebrating "Year's End." The precise meaning of the individual lines remains unclear; but rather than seek an overall integrity of meaning to this (as well as to the last-quoted) poem, the reader would do best to keep in mind that it was the writer's intention to re-create the "rhythm" of Tu Fu's verse.

> While countless other plants stand bare at year's end,
> Spare plum and long bamboo are delightful in the breeze.
> Shadows of flying geese on fresh snow over Three Rivers—
> The loneliest city of the Four Seas in the setting sun's rays.
> All is stillness in the garden of this white-haired one;
> Let carriages and horses rush elsewhere through purple dust.
> Who can bear, with the change of season, the astonishment of recent events?
> All the worse when, leaning from on high, one counts the ruined palaces of yesteryear!

In his quatrains, especially his seven-character quatrains, Li Meng-yang sought to recapture the strength and vigor of the High T'ang poets Li Po and Wang Ch'ang-ling. For example, the following is one of two seven-character poems entitled "Going over the Frontier Pass," composed while visiting Chü-yung Pass along China's Mongolian frontier:

> Heaven created Chü-yung, a two-against-one-hundred pass;
> And Ch'i-nien is still further off, thousands of mountains away.
> I do not know who let Hu-yen make his way in,
> But it seems only yesterday we fought at Yang-ho and returned.

The strategic pass of Chü-yung was said to be able to hold invaders off at a ratio of fifty to one. Ch'i-nien had been a stronghold of barbarian Hsiung-nu tribesmen led by Hu-yen during Han times. And Yang-ho denotes a desert locale. Although couched in terms of the Han, the poem is in fact describing the Mongolia of the poet's time.

To commemorate the Chia-ching emperor's ascent to the throne in 1522, Li Meng-yang composed two seven-character poems entitled "Songs for the First Year of the Chia-ching Reign Period." The first reads:

First month of a new reign, again a royal spring;
People of the Four Seas bow in praise of our sagacious one.
Already reported from Mt. Ch'i, a colorful phoenix singing;
Word from this side of the passes, a unicorn has appeared.[6]

Another weak point of Li Meng-yang's verse, other than the repetitiveness mentioned earlier, is its hyperbole. The following poem on lowly "Grapes" illustrates the tendency.

Under the west wind for thousands of miles, the season when geese
    pass—
Green clouds and dark jade, a jumble of shadows.[7]
Waking from my stupor, I pick an icy globe to chew;
Tell me not of lichees under southern skies!

The rare lichees of faraway Kwangtung may be famous, the poet says, but they are nothing compared with cool-tasting grapes. The phrase "thousands of miles," like the "Four Seas" in the preceding poem, is one of Li's beloved expressions.

Li Meng-yang's penchant for exaggeration sometimes resulted in humorous overstatement. Witness the following seven-character quatrain, "Prison Rain," wherein Li exaggeratedly compares himself with two of China's greatest poets. It is from a series of two written during one of his incarcerations.

In the eighth month, cold rains hold sway across the sky;
Black clouds come and go, as red clouds unfold.[8]
For Li Po in Hsun-yang, it was never so trying;
Nor was Sung Yü's autumn lament ever so sad.

The lines also illustrate Li's fundamental desire that poetry have both amplitude of feeling and intensity.

Although Li Meng-yang's poetry carried tremendous authority in his own time, in the following century and especially in Ch'ing times critics were to look down upon it for sometimes falling into exaggerated braggadocio devoid of any real content. Even in his own time Li Meng-yang's poetry was tagged "rough and hard" (*tsu-kang*) by Hsueh Hui (1489–1541). Such a "rough and

---

[6] [The appearance of a phoenix or unicorn was an auspicious sign of the inauguration of a reign of peace.]

[7] ["Green clouds and dark jade" are presumably light- and dark-colored grapes.]

[8] ["Red clouds," in this context, are lightning.]

hard" quality doubtless stemmed from the poet's passionate temperament, one that gave rise not only to his frequent arrests, his simple and direct literary theory, and his rough and hard verse, but also to his own kind of philosophy.

According to Li Meng-yang's philosophy, it is elements of sensation or feeling and their movement that make up the fundamental features of the universe, and it is through them that the world is being formed. He expounds these views in a work entitled *K'ung-t'ung tzu*, or *Master K'ung-t'ung*, the title being the author's pen name. The chapter "Hua-li," or "Principles of Transformation," contains the following passage, one in which "colors" and "sounds" refer to sense perceptions: "In Heaven and Earth there are only colors and sounds. How can one not drown in them? . . . To transcend colors and sounds without becoming estranged from them, that is how one can avoid drowning in them."

The same work also contains a theory of growth based on two homophonous characters, here labeled A and B, one of which is used in more than one sense. "It is because the kernel (*jen* A) of the peach and apricot has the potential of giving life to life that it is called *jen* (*jen* A). Mencius says, 'Righteousness (*jen* A) is the heart of man (*jen* B).' He also says, 'Righteousness (*jen* A) means man (*jen* B),' because it refers to giving birth to life." According to Li Meng-yang, it is this growth, this movement, that forms the basis of man and the world.

If one carries Li Meng-yang's philosophical ideas to their logical conclusion, literature becomes supreme. Literature as he defined it—the sensate expression of feelings and emotions forming a mental state that is itself in motion—is the truest undertaking of man; it must be man's indispensable concern. Li does not state this view explicitly. But the Old Phraseology movement that he headed should be seen as involving more than a statement of principles of literary composition; it contains the idea of the supremacy of literature as well.

Li Meng-yang's ideas carried earlier discussions on the place of literature a step further. We have discussed before the views of Yang Wei-chen, Ni Tsan, and other late Yuan *wen-jen* artists and poets who, demanding complete dedication to literature and the arts, made these supreme. Their attitude, however, was more a negative one of escape from political reality or an expression of political reaction or opposition to the Mongols than it was a forth-right statement of principle. Even Li Meng-yang's contemporaries in Soochow, Chu Yun-ming and T'ang Yin, were passive in their resistance to authority. In contrast, Li was very outspoken and direct in the way he expressed his views. Because of this, and given his position as a high government official, he was able to turn the entire sixteenth century in his direction.

In further developing his theory emphasizing natural human emotion and sensate feeling as being proper to literature, Li Meng-yang sometimes appears to argue that the songs of ordinary working men make for truer literature than the writings of *wen-jen* scholars.[9] In the preface to his collected poems he recounts that his friend Wang Shu-wu (dates uncertain) once stated the following, to which Li later in the same passage adds his assent: "Poetry consists of the natural sounds of Heaven and Earth. The moaning of people by the wayside, their singing in the lanes, the groans of work, the strains of play—whatever, once expressed in song, finds wide response—these constitute what is True." It is ironic to find such an emphasis on natural feeling and sentiment at the heart of a movement that, in fact, advocated the strict imitation of only a narrow selection of classical literary models. The theoretical reso-lution of this contradiction lay in the movement's conception of what these classical models constituted. They were considered the very embodiment of universal human principles, truth in and of themselves.

Final mention should be made of Li Meng-yang's connection with the philosophy of Wang Yang-ming. Once a friend of Li, Wang was counted among Old Phraseology advocates until he left the movement, arguing that its approach could not lead to truth. There is little doubt, however, that Li Meng-yang's literary theory and writings were of some bearing on the philosophical idealism of Wang Yang-ming.[10]

[9] The twentieth-century writer Mao Tun (1896–1981) points this out in his work, *Yeh-tu ou-chi* (Nighttime Reading, Occasional Notes).

[10] Specialists may wish to consult my article, "Li Bōyō no ichi sokumen: 'Ko-bunji' no shominsei" ("A Profile of Li Meng-yang: The Populist Nature of 'Old Phraseology' "), 1960; reprinted in *Yoshikawa Kōjirō zenshū*, 15: 614–33. [Chinese translation by Cheng Ch'ing-mao, appended to *Yuan Ming shih kai-shuo*, pp. 259–81.]

Li Meng-yang's bold, straightforward theory, as well as his actual writing, won wide acclaim in the sixteenth century. He prided himself on being one the finest poets since Li Po and Tu Fu, and such an estimation was widely accepted at the time. Li Meng-yang and his most influential followers and supporters were later called the Earlier Seven Masters. Besides Li they included two other poets from Shensi, K'ang Hai and Wang Chiu-ssu; two from Honan, Ho Ching-ming and Wang T'ing-hsiang; and one each from Shantung and Kiangsu, Pien Kung and Hsu Chen-ch'ing. Thus, with the exception of Hsu Chen-ch'ing, all were from the north, an area that long had not been a center of literature.[11]

## Ho Ching-ming
### (1483–1521)

Ho Ching-ming and Li Meng-yang are linked together as "Li and Ho" (in contrast with "Li and Wang" of the Later Seven Masters, discussed below). From Hsin-yang in Honan, Ho Ching-ming was much like Li Meng-yang, being a brilliant young man of low-class origins from a poor family. At the age of fifteen he placed first in the regional examinations, and four years later, in 1502, passed the metropolitan examinations and became a Presented Scholar and official in Peking.

Ho Ching-ming's views are very much in accord with those of Li Meng-yang, as is clear from the numerous letters they exchanged. Unlike Li, however, Ho did not wish to limit poetic models to the High T'ang alone; he also held poetry of the Early T'ang in high esteem, especially its old-style seven-character verse. Ho Ching-ming imitated Early T'ang seven-character poems, as illustrated by his "Song of the Bright Moon." In the preface to that long work Ho Ching-ming states that poetry must be based on "personal nature and emotion" (*hsing-ch'ing*). The keenest expression of "personal nature and emotion," he argues, is the love between man and wife. Tu Fu's seven-character old-style poems, he says, are comparatively weak in this area; they do not measure up to those of the Four Outstanding Talents of the Early T'ang;[12]

---

[11] Li Meng-yang, Ho Ching-ming, Hsu Chen-ch'ing, and Pien Kung were also known as the Four Outstanding Talents of the Hung and Cheng Periods—that is, of the Hung-chih and Cheng-te reign periods, 1488–1506 and 1506–1522.

[12] [See p. 114.]

and the Early T'ang masters, in turn, are not on a par with the *Shih ching*, or *Classic of Songs*, the classic par excellence in this respect.[13]

The following passages from Ho Ching-ming's "Song of the Bright Moon" may serve to clarify the difference between him and Li Meng-yang. Hsueh Hui, a contemporary of the two, characterized them by contrasting the "wonderfully untrammeled" (*hsun-i*) quality of Ho's verse with Li's "rustically heroic" (*tsu-hao*) poetry.

> The Ch'ang-an moon
> Emerges hazily from the sea peak.
> Far-off layered walls conceal its half orb;
> Gradually visible, the palaces that bear its first rays.
> Slender, the waves of gold;
> Round, a basin of jade.[14]
>
> .　.　.　.　.　.　.　.　.
>
> Gleaming is the lotus growing in jade marshes,
> Graceful the willows covering golden dikes.
> In phoenix tower, a girl plays the pipes;
> In cricket hall, a wife weaves brocade.
> And shut away deep in the deep palace's courtyard
> Is one who, year after year, pines for her lord.
>
> .　.　.　.　.　.　.　.　.
>
> At such a time, leaning on the railing, tears fall long as jade chopsticks;
> At such a time, candles go out and dark eyebrows frown.
> Long jadelike tears and dark eyebrows conceal a deep chagrin;
> Chagrin concealed, her real feelings cannot be expressed.
>
> .　.　.　.　.　.　.　.　.　.　.　.　.

## Hsu Chen-ch'ing
## (1479–1511)

Coming as he did from Soochow, Hsu Chen-ch'ing was the exception among Old Phraseology masters. Initially one of the Four Outstanding Talents of Wu-chung,[15] Hsu showed a preference for the softer, more pliant poems of Po Chü-i, Liu Yü-hsi, and other Middle T'ang poets. Among the Earlier Seven Masters, his writing is the most florid. The following seven-character regulated verse,

---

[13] Motoori Norinaga (1730–1801), in chap. 10 of his *Tama katsuma* (Basket of Jade), offers a critique of Ho Ching-ming's preface.

[14] [The sun's rays are "waves of gold," the still-visible moon "a basin of jade."]

[15] The others were Chu Yun-ming, T'ang Yin, and Wen Cheng-ming.

"Writing and the Hazy Moon," is a well-known poem from his early period.

> In wind and frost, I take it easy sick in bed;
> The season presses on, like a snake going to its hole.
> Fallen petals beneath the hedge, I gather half a handful in autumn;
> Fresh from a dream beside the lamp, I see temples turned grey.
> The literature of the Southland—in every house a gem;
> The hazy moon of Yangchow—every tree bears a flower.
> I expect all such attachments will disappear,
> When I carry a monk's bowl and obey vinaya commandments.[16]

In 1505 Hsu Chen-ch'ing became a Presented Scholar in Peking where, upon hearing the disquisitions of Li Meng-yang and Ho Ching-ming, he became a great advocate of their archaism. Full of promise, Hsu Chen-ch'ing died at the age of thirty-two. His tomb inscription was written by his friend Wang Yang-ming.

## K'ang Hai
## (1475–1540)

K'ang Hai was from Wu-kung prefecture in Shensi, an area long barren of literary talent. The son of a farm family, he was born in 1475, the same year as Li Meng-yang; and he was First-Place Graduate in the metropolitan examinations the same year that Ho Ching-ming passed. Six years later, in 1508, when Li Meng-yang was imprisoned upon incurring the hatred of Liu Chin, a eunuch in the Cheng-te emperor's service, Li had a brief four-character note smuggled out to K'ang Hai that said, "Save me, Tui-shan!"— Tui-shan being the latter's pen name. K'ang Hai sought an interview with Liu Chin and managed to effect Li Meng-yang's release by saying that there were three great men from Shensi at the time—Liu Chin himself, Li Meng-yang, and another official—and that it was Liu's duty to spare such a person from his native region. Although Li Meng-yang thus managed to avoid death, K'ang Hai himself did not escape unscathed. When Liu Chin's fortunes went into eclipse, K'ang Hai was damned by association

---

[16] [This poem is in fact about literature and women, the hazy moon of the poem's title referring to the latter. Note the parallel treatment of the two topics in the third couplet. In the fourth couplet the poet makes an unconvincing vow to renounce both "attachments."]

and exiled to a faraway region, where he remained in obscurity the remainder of his life.

K'ang Hai often invited another of the Earlier Seven Masters, Wang Chiu-ssu, a farmer living in the village of Mi-p'i in nearby Hu prefecture, to visit him. By the thrashing ground in front of K'ang's house the two would discuss literature over wine. In a five-character regulated verse entitled "Brewing Wine," K'ang Hai relates:

> My Way still needs wine;
> The autumn solstice makes for even better brewing.
> But heating up a hundred piculs of grain
> Still will not produce a thousand goblets.
> In pleasant pursuits, the years draw to a close with little to show;
> I hear a tune, the time is late.
> As for style, dear Tu Fu
> Is the one I am devoted to as my master.

Although K'ang Hai was devoted to his "master," his poetry is certainly a far cry from that of Tu Fu. Given the simple, manly, intense kind of verse that was the aim of the Earlier Seven Masters—indeed of Ming poets in general—this poem is more an example of the vice such poetry was prone to, rusticity.

K'ang Hai and Wang Chiu-ssu were composers of *san-ch'ü* vernacular songs. Moreover, as dramatists, their *tsa-chü* plays—K'ang Hai's *Chung-shan lang*, or *The Wolf of Chung Mountain*, and Wang Chiu-ssu's *Tu Tzu-mei ku-chiu yu-ch'un*, or *Tu Fu Purchases Wine for a Spring Outing*—broke the silence that had marked the genre over the preceding century. Recent literary historians have pointed to these two figures as being forerunners of the sixteenth-century flourishing of Chinese drama. Thus one notes that a flourishing in vernacular literature was brought parallel with that of poetry.

Notwithstanding the high reputation the Earlier Seven Masters had in their own time,[17] their writing became distinctly unpopular in the next and following centuries. As a result collected

---

[17] I will forego discussion of the other Earlier Seven Masters. [The dates for those not treated are as follows: Wang Chiu-ssu (1468–1551), Wang T'ing-hsiang (1474–1544), and Pien Kung (1476–1532).]

editions of their work have become rare books, some especially difficult to find.

# Wang Yang-ming
# (1472–1529)

The famous philosopher Wang Yang-ming, who for a period was a member of the Old Phraseology movement, has standing as a poet as well as a thinker.[18] His writings are distinguished by their abundance of mental energy. His famous seven-character quatrain, "Floating on the Sea," displays a philosophically analytical strain.

> Be there danger or safety, my breast remains untroubled,
> For how does either differ from clouds adrift in the sky?
> The night still, ocean billows for thirty thousand *li*,
> Under the bright moon a traveling monk descends on a heavenly
>     wind.[19]

The following poem, one of two five-character regulated verses entitled "Li Po's Shrine," is richer in suggestiveness. It was written when Wang Yang-ming, no less capable as a military figure than as a philosopher, visited a shrine to the T'ang poet on his

---

[18] [Note the following studies: Julia Ching, *To Acquire Wisdom: The Way of Wang Yang-ming* (New York: Columbia University Press, 1976); Tu Wei-ming, *Neo-Confucian Thought in Action: Wang Yang-ming's Youth (1472–1509)* (Berkeley: University of California Press, 1976); Chan Wing-tsit, *Instructions for Living and Other Neo-Confucian Writings by Wang Yang-ming* (New York: Columbia University Press, 1963); Carsun Chang, *Wang Yang-ming* (New York, 1962); and Frederick Goodrich Henke, *The Philosophy of Wang Yang-ming* (1916; 2d ed., New York: Paragon Book Reprint Corp., 1964). The Julia Ching volume includes a selection of Wang Yang-ming's poems in translation.]

[19] [A *li* is approximately one-third of a mile. The expression "traveling monk" in line four renders the set phrase *fei hsi*, or "[a monk] riding his walking stick [through the firmament]." Morohashi Tetsuji, *Dai Kan-Wa jiten* (Comprehensive Chinese-Japanese Dictionary) 13 vols. (Tokyo: Taishūkan, 1955–60), entry no. 44000.180. Cf. the translations of the poem by Ching (p. 225), Tu Wei-ming (p. 110), and Chang (p. 4) in the works cited in the preceding note. Tu Wei-ming comments as follows (p. 191, n. 60, and p. 110): "The poem is widely acclaimed as a vivid demonstration of [Wang] Yang-ming's courage." "It may also symbolize Yang-ming's own decision to stop roaming about and come down to face the reality of life."]

triumphal return from quelling a rebellion by the Prince of Ning, Chu Ch'en-hao. An old monk at the site had been badgering him to write a poem—hence the light touch of humor at the end of the poem.

> That great of all time is no more,
> But on this deserted mountain his shrine still stands.
> Bamboo thick, it overruns the pathway;
> Moss creeps together, covering what remains of the stele.
> Clouds and rain—arrayed in literary beauty;
> Brooks and streams—bound up with dreamy thought.
> An old monk, quite missing the point,
> Is still after me to inscribe a poem.[20]

In 1531 Li Meng-yang, the first Old Phraseology advocate and leading figure of the Former Seven Masters, died at the age of fifty-six. Hsu Chen-ch'ing and Ho Ching-ming had already passed from the scene. The figure of the group to live the longest was Wang Chiu-ssu, who died near midcentury (in 1551), at the age of eighty-three.

## The Later Seven Masters

Over the first half of the sixteenth century the Old Phraseology movement was already a force in society, welcomed and supported by participants from a wide variety of social backgrounds. But over the latter half of the century—from the middle of the Chia-ching emperor's reign (r. 1521–1566), passing through the years of the Lung-ch'ing emperor (r. 1566–1572), until the middle of the Wan-li emperor's rule (r. 1572–1620)—its influence grew enormous, such that it completely dominated China.

The two leading Old Phraseology figures of the latter half of the sixteenth century were Li P'an-lung and Wang Shih-chen. Not only were they leaders in literary affairs, they also virtually dictated the cultural life of the empire. Their approval or disapproval was such as to make or undo the reputation of any talent of the age.

---

[20] [The old monk does not understand that, as suggested in lines five and six, all is already complete in Nature; at its best poetry can display natural beauty like that of clouds and rain, just as dreamy thoughts are bound up with brooks and streams.]

Although both were examination graduates and officials, they were not always central political figures in the world of the time. Yet simply by being the top literary figures of the age they were able to command enormous influence, their every word and gesture given attention. The concept that literature is supreme, which was implicit in the earlier Old Phraseology movement, became the accepted fashion throughout the period, a development that served to enhance the respect shown these two.

The Old Phraseology movement was without leadership following the death of Li Meng-yang in 1531. Although Li P'an-lung had not come into direct contact with the earlier figure, he took it upon himself to act as his successor, gathering a circle of young fellow officials. In the triennial examinations for entrance into the civil service Wang Shih-chen, who was to be Li P'an-lung's lifelong friend, was a successful candidate in 1547 (three years after Li passed) and became an official in the same government ministry. Three years later, in 1550, Hsu Chung-hsing (1517–1578) from Kiangsu, Tsung Ch'en (1525–1560) from Kiangsu, Liang Yu-yü (ca. 1520–1556) from Kwangtung, and Wu Kuo-lun (1529–1593) from Hupei passed the examination and became members of the same literary group as Li P'an-lung and Wang Shih-chen. Five of the six (that is, all except Li P'an-lung) were from the south, which indicates how effectively the Old Phraseology movement, originally a northern movement, had penetrated the empire.

These successors to the Earlier Seven Masters were called the Later Seven Masters. In addition to the ones named above, an older poet was part of the group, Hsieh Chen (1495–1575) from Lin-ch'ing in Shantung. The only nonofficial in their number, distinctive with his one eye, Hsieh lived the life of a wanderer; he was also a famous *hsia-k'o* and was well known for his popular-song tunes—qualities all of which attracted his junior fellow poets.[21]

---

[21] One incident surrounding Hsieh Chen is especially well known. Once when the literary talent Lu Nan was thrown into prison after earning the hatred of the local governor, the man who came to his rescue was the elderly Hsieh, who addressed his fellow writers, "Are you going to let Lu Nan be done away with before your very eyes and simply write poems lamenting the death of Ch'ü Yuan a thousand years ago?!" [As Fang Lienche Tu explains, "In pleading for Lu, Hsieh de-

*Li P'an-lung*
*(1514–1570)*

By his own words Li P'an-lung came from a "peasant family" (*nung-chia*).[22] His father was a wine-loving gambler who purchased a post under the imperial prince who was resident in Te-chou, Shantung. The father died when the son was eight years old, mention often being made in the latter's prose writing of the hardship his mother later suffered. From his early years Li P'an-lung enjoyed writing literary pieces in a peculiar, archaic style, on account of which people told him he was crazy; he would retort, "If I'm not crazy, who is?"

Four years after placing second in the regional examinations Li P'an-lung became a Presented Scholar in 1544, at the age of thirty, and served as an official in the Ministry of Justice. He was already an adherent of the Old Phraseology dictum, "Prose must follow the Ch'in and Han, and poetry the High T'ang."

The following poem by Li P'an-lung was written while serving at the Ministry of Justice. It is the first in a series entitled "With Wang Shih-chen and Other Justice Officials, on 'South of the City-Wall Lake' in Early Summer." The poem describes an excursion to a small lake south of Peking, a pleasant pause in the hectic life of these officials.

> Who would have thought men caught up in worldly affairs
> Could still enjoy such a carefree excursion?
> At this edge of the world, only my scanty hair left;
> Within the seas, a small boat for release.
> Our official record is poor in this time of peace,
> While gentlemen in painted chambers excel.
> Life's hundred years—all green brew;
> This one day—floating free for a while.

clared that if the literati could not even save a Lu Nan of their own time, they had better not lament any more over the ill fate of Ch'ü Yüan, . . .''; "Lu Nan," *Dictionary of Ming Biography*, p. 996.] Hsieh was successful in saving Lu.

[22] Like Li Meng-yang, Li P'an-lung was apocryphally said to have been conceived when his mother dreamt of the sun. We are told in the biography of Li P'an-lung written by his friend Wang Shih-chen that, boastful though two of his names might be—P'an-lung, or Holding onto a Dragon, and Yü-lin, or By Its Scales—they were intended to reflect the auspicious circumstances of this birth; and that he chose the pen name Ts'ang-ming, or Vast Sea, because his home was near the sea.

For a decade Li P'an-lung and his group of Peking cohorts flourished. By the time he was transferred to the governorship of Shun-te in Hopei, Li was recognized, by others as well as himself, as the leader of their circle. Li P'an-lung had a falling out with Hsieh Chen, but he and Wang Shih-chen were mutually deferential in their recognition of each other's talent. The following is a poem composed by Li when Wang paid him a visit at his post in Shun-te. It is one of two entitled "Climbing the Chün Tower with Wang Shih-chen."

> We open the window to face for hundreds of miles an autumn past its
> peak,
> And wine in hand watch the River Chang flow northward.
> My beloved green hills I offer you;
> But how can one bear it, turning grey, to remain here?[23]
> Shadows of floating clouds do not blot out the dying hues;
> The setting sun overlooks our disdainful frowns.
> The empire in its trouble calls on the sword;
> You and I in the Central Plain again climb this tower.

The "trouble" in the final couplet probably refers to one of the many times martial law was imposed in Peking as a precaution against Mongol incursions. This would account for the poets' "disdainful frowns."

Wang Shih-chen praised Li P'an-lung's seven-character regulated verse (of the sort just cited) as being the finest since Tu Fu. But the repeated use of clichés like "edge of the world," "hundreds of miles," "within the seas," and "hundred years"—used in the above two poems—make all of his poetry sound the same. They account for Hu Ying-lin's comment, "Except for about ten of them, I can't bear reading many of his poems."

Li P'an-lung was promoted to the rank of Vice-Superintendent of Instruction in Shensi. But when his superior, a fellow official from Shantung, told him to write an essay, Li is reported to have angrily replied, "How can the writing of an essay be done by official order?"[24] and resigned that very day. The many earth-

---

[23] In the original, Shun-te [the "here" of the translation] is referred to by its alternate name of Hsing-chou.

[24] [As translated by Lo Chin-tang, "Li P'an-lung," in *Dictionary of Ming Biography*, p. 846.]

quakes that were then plaguing Shensi doubtless also helped prompt his resignation.

Li P'an-lung later built a residence in Shantung not far from the family's native area of Chi-nan and called it White-Snow Tower (Pai-hsueh lou). In his own words: "The tower is about ten miles east of Chi-nan, in Pao-ch'eng. Before me I look out on the foothills of Mt. T'ai. To the northwest the Hua-pu-chu Hills are in view, along whose base the Yellow and Ch'ing rivers converge. And to the left I command a view of the plains of Ch'ang-po and P'ing-ling; the sea air extends this far. Each time I climb to gaze, I become sad at the magnificent sight." Once, after being sick, Li P'an-lung wrote a seven-character regulated verse about the pavilion.

As I lean on my pillow, in the lonely wood the extended rain lets up;
Feeling suddenly revived, I decide to climb the tower.
Big Ch'ing River, hugging a solitary city-wall, makes its bend;
Long White Mountain, bathed in the late sun's rays, seems to revolve.
There is no cure for a Hsi K'ang laziness,
And I well understand T'ao Ch'ien's writing "The Return."[25]
After all, who can explain the meaning of floating clouds,
Whose swatches of shadow, swinging, drop into my wine cup?

In the *Hsi-shan jih-chi*, or *West-Mountain Diary*, Li P'an-lung describes White-Snow Tower as being a three-story building surrounded by a moat. On the top floor the poet would compose poems, the second story housed the poet's concubines, and the ground floor served as a reception area. Would-be visitors first had to present a poem. Only those whose poems were considered good enough were transported to the reception area by boat; others were told they ought to read more and turned away. Such is what the diary recounts.

Li P'an-lung was even more forceful than Li Meng-yang in arguing that making one's compositions congruent with a limited number of models is the only way to write. He based his argument on the latter part of the following passage from the *I ching*, or *Classic of Change*:

[25] Li P'an-lung is likening himself to these earlier poets of retiring disposition. [For the latter's "The Return," see Hightower, *The Poetry of T'ao Ch'ien*, pp. 268–70.]

The Images and Judgments sections [of the *I ching*] speak of the most confused diversities without arousing aversion. They speak of what is most mobile without causing confusion.

This comes from the fact that the holy sages who discerned the Images and Judgments in phenomena emulated them before they spoke and discussed them before they moved. Through emulation and discussion they perfected the changes and transformations.[26]

These words are interpreted by Li P'an-lung to mean that dependence on or imitation of models gives rise to transformations that are free; and even to mean the greater the imitation, the freer one's writing.

The most striking example of this principle's being put into practice is offered by poems Li P'an-lung wrote in his later years in imitation of the old-style poems and folk songs of the Han and Wei dynasties. Note first the following, an anonymous Han period verse from among the "Nineteen Old Poems" in the *Wen hsuan*, or *Literary Selections*.

> Green, green, the grass by the river-bank;
> Thick, thick, the willow trees in the garden.
> Sad, sad, the lady in the tower;
> White, white, sitting at the casement window.
> Fair, fair, her red-powdered face;
> Small, small, she puts out her pale hand.
> Once she was a dancing-house girl,
> Now she is a wandering man's wife.
> The wandering man went, but did not return.
> It is hard alone to keep an empty bed.[27]

Li P'an-lung's imitation of the piece is as follows.

> Swaying, swaying, the visitor in the horse-drawn carriage;
> Clinging, clinging, the Yen (or is it a Chao?) woman.
> Sleek, sleek, she stands beside the reed pipe;
> Inviting, inviting, the words from her window.
> Round, round, her high bun jutting;

---

[26] [Adapted from the translation by Richard Wilhelm/Cary F. Baynes, *The I Ching or Book of Changes* (1950; 2d ed., 1961; rpt. New York: Pantheon Books, 1964), 1: 327.]

[27] [Translation by Arthur Waley, *One Hundred and Seventy Chinese Poems* (1918; rpt. London: Jonathan Cape, 1969), p. 24. The lineation and punctuation have been altered to highlight parallels with Li P'an-lung's imitation.]

Buoyant, buoyant, her waist sash puffed out.
Like floating clouds suddenly returning,
The wanderer is off roaming without destination.
Weather cold, brocade coverlets thin,
It is hard alone to keep an empty bed.

The latter version mostly traces over its model. In the following age such verse writing was to be strongly criticized as being a foolish undertaking.

Li P'an-lung's approach to writing did have its rationale, as clarified by statements made in the prefaces to two series of poems he modeled on late Han verse. In the one he says that it is precisely because a horse's reins are pulled as tight as possible that the horse will rush straight forward with increased vigor. And in the other he explains that it was his aim in such poetry to fill in the parts left unstated by the ancients. Li's friend, Wang Shih-chen, described the process when characterizing Li P'an-lung's verse: "As for those termed ancient writers, the expressions attained by them freely enter and leave the tip of Li P'an-lung's brush, and yet they leave no trace [of being other than his expression]. Also, expressions secreted by Heaven and Earth that had never issued from the ancients found creation in his breast, yet they were not different from ancient expression."[28]

Li P'an-lung died in 1570 at the age of fifty-six during the reign of the Lung-ch'ing emperor. He had left White-Snow Tower temporarily to serve again as a regional official. But upon the death of his mother he was overcome with grief and died; from this we know that Li was also a man of strong emotion.[29]

## Wang Shih-chen
## (1526–1590)

Wang Shih-chen's name is commonly linked with that of Li P'an-lung, the two being known as "Li and Wang" (in contrast with

[28] Although stated emphatically by Li P'an-lung and Wang Shih-chen, such arguments do not seem appropriate to literary composition. They may be of value as principles of performance for music, dance, and other performing arts, where artistic forms exist prior to being (re)enacted.

[29] A favorite food of Li P'an-lung was onion dumplings cooked by his beloved concubine, surnamed Ts'ai. Also, Li was good at hunting with a bow and arrow;

the Earlier Seven Masters, "Li and Ho"). In the latter half of the sixteenth century they initially shared the leadership of the Old Phraseology movement, which in effect made them the cultural arbiters of the age. But upon the death of Li P'an-lung, Wang Shih-chen alone assumed that role.

Like other major figures in the movement Wang Shih-chen was a man of strong passion. But the environment he was born and grew up in was quite different from that of both the Earlier Seven Masters leader, Li Meng-yang, and his own staunch friend, Li P'an-lung. Wang Shih-chen did not come from a poor family living in a backward, out-of-the-way locale. He was born in T'ai-ts'ang, Chekiang, adjacent to Soochow, the area that for more than two hundred and fifty years had been the center of townsman literature. In the preceding decades Soochow had produced two greats, Shen Chou and Wen Cheng-ming,[30] whose coterie included eccentric figures like Chu Yun-ming and T'ang Yin. But the Soochow tradition was, for the most part, an urbane and refined one, one that looked with skepticism upon the Old Phraseology movement that was produced in the new atmosphere of the north. It is true that Soochow had produced Hsu Chen-ch'ing, one of the Earlier Seven Masters. And the four famous Huang-fu brothers (including Huang-fu Fang) of Soochow and their cousin Huang Hsing-ts'eng were devotees of Li Meng-yang. But this did not alter the overall complexion of the Soochow literary tradition.

Moreover, inasmuch as Wang Shih-chen's father and grandfather had been Presented Scholars, the poet's antecedents were different from those of Li Meng-yang and Li P'an-lung. The father, Wang Yü,[31] earned a reputation as a famous military official by fighting Mongols in the north, Manchus in the northeast, and Japanese pirates in the southeast.[32] The son's highly emotional temperament is in part attributable to him. Yet his upbringing remained that of a well-to-do family.

---

Wang Shih-chen wrote "A Song on Seeing Li P'an-lung Shoot," which praises his friend's archery, the opening couplet of which reads: "Mr. Li draws a bow three-stone strong; / Shooting left, shooting right, of a bent none can resist."

[30] As a youth Wang Shih-chen even enjoyed the favor of Wen Cheng-ming.

[31] The name can also be read Wang Shu.

[32] [*Wo-k'ou,* or "Japanese pirates," in fact also included Koreans and a number of Chinese.]

Wang Shih-chen's passionate spirit accounts for the way he overcame (indeed, went counter to) the tradition of his native Soochow and became a leading figure in the Old Phraseology movement. Wang's biography is filled with his passionate doings. He became a Presented Scholar in 1547 at the age of twenty-one and served for several years in the Ministry of Justice. Yang Chi-sheng, a graduate of the metropolitan examinations the same year Wang passed (and hence a virtual classmate), was put in prison for having severely castigated the prime minister, Yen Sung. Wang sent food and clothing to the prisoner and even drafted a petition on behalf of his wife. After the petition proved to no avail and Yang was executed, Wang personally went to claim the body. All of this earned Yen Sung's hatred. By way of revenge a few years later Yen Sung had Wang Shih-chen's father put in prison, using the pretext of a military defeat by the latter. Abandoning his post in the Ministry of Justice, Wang Shih-chen, along with his younger brother Wang Shih-mou, came daily to the minister's gate to beg for clemency. In the end the father was executed. But Wang was successful during the reign of the next emperor in his vehement campaign to have his father's good name restored. Eventually, Wang Shih-chen returned to public life as a regional official.

Speaking of himself in his later years, Wang Shih-chen reminisced, "As a young man from Wu, I would discuss poetry with men of Soochow, but grew tired of it." Wang came instead to idolize literature of North China, particularly the writing of Li Meng-yang.[33] When he was fifteen, his tutor set him the task of writing a poem on the theme of a precious sword; the following couplet from the exercise reveals how much his writing was already in the Old Phraseology style.

> While youths dance drunkenly in Lo-yang streets,
> Generals fight bloodily on sandy wastes.

After Wang Shih-chen became a Presented Scholar and met Li P'an-lung, his poetry turned even more in this direction.

Wang Shih-chen and Li P'an-lung looked upon themselves as

---

[33] This is related in the preface Wang Shih-chen wrote to the *Li-shih shan-ts'ang chi* (Li Family Mountain-Library Collection).

the literary leaders of the age. The following is from a series of five-character old-style poems that Wang Shih-chen wrote for Li P'an-lung when the former was returning to his native area on a short leave. It well illustrates both the friendship and ambition of the two young men.

> Today, departing from you, my friend,
> I gaze back while heading for my native place.
> A native place is not without its pleasures,
> But how can my friend share them?
> The one departing feels ineffably sad;
> The one left behind paces back and forth.
> Flesh and bones, though tightly bound,
> Once severed forget one another.[34]
> It is only to liver and gall,
> Submitable to light, that our friendship can be compared.[35]
> Can one deny we are like the sun and moon,
> East and west raising the light?
> I truly know there is dear intimacy
> Only through openhearted feeling.
> Though I have tears of tenderness,
> How can they express what is in my heart?

A drunken Li P'an-lung once supposedly told Wang Shih-chen, everything that is outstanding in the world appears in pairs: "If there is a Confucius, there is bound to be a Tso Ch'iu-ming (the putative author of the *Tso chuan*, or *Tso Commentary [to the Spring and Autumn Annals]*)." But Wang Shih-chen did not reply, and there was a strange expression on his face.[36] Li P'an-lung hastily added: "I misspoke. If there is a Confucius, there is bound to be a Lao-tzu."

The letters written between Li P'an-lung and Wang Shih-chen are filled with expressions of praise for each other's writing as the finest of the age, even the finest of all time. This is also true of the

---

[34] "Flesh and bones" (i.e., brothers) can be separated.

[35] Liver and gall, being transparent, can be submitted to light. [Liver and gall also are colored by the same experiences and thus are more intimately related than "flesh and bones" brothers, whose relationship is more one of happenstance.]

[36] [Inasmuch as Tso Ch'iu-ming was considered Confucius's disciple and not his equal, Wang Shih-chen felt he was being called Li P'an-lung's disciple and not his equal.]

poems exchanged between the two. We have already seen a poem
Li P'an-lung wrote when Wang Shih-chen visited him at his post
in Shun-te.[37] The following, written in the same rhyme category
as Li's verse, is the poem Wang Shih-chen wrote on the occasion;
it is entitled "Upon Li P'an-lung's Invitation to Climb the Prefec-
tural Tower."

With cup of wine, having climbed the tower for a look,
You lean on the railing, tree leaves sadly desolate.
Inexhaustible, the heavenly winds blowing on this great mass;
Who would have thought Mt. Yueh's reflected hue dominates all Hsing-
        chou?[38]
In the sword box stars move, a double-dragon night;
Between clapper sounds it turns cold, a myriad-horse autumn.[39]
I would ask the secretaries on your staff,
How many are up to accompanying Li Ying on his rovings?

In the final couplet Li P'an-lung is likened to Li Ying of the Later
Han dynasty. The implied answer to Wang's question—the im-
port of which is, "How many are equal to Li Ying (i.e., equal to
you, Li P'an-lung) in writing ability?"—is, "I may be, but no one
else in your immediate circle is."

For twenty years after Li P'an-lung's death Wang Shih-chen
stood alone as the leading literary light of the age. In his later years
he became a high official of ministerial rank, serving in the second-
ary capital of Nanking rather than Peking. In addition to the col-
lections of belles lettres by him that have been handed down to
us—the *Yen-chou shan-jen ssu-pu kao*, or *Manuscripts in the Four
Categories by the Yen-chou Recluse* (in 174 chapters), and the sup-
plemented edition of the same work (*Hsu kao*, in 207 chapters)—
Wang Shih-chen also compiled works of history—the *Yen-shan-
t'ang pieh-chi*, or *Collected Writings from the Yen-Mountain Hall*,
and the *Yen-chou shih-liao*, or *Yen-chou Historical Materials*—as

---

[37] See p. 157.
[38] See n. 23 above.
[39] [This couplet might be paraphrased as follows:

In the box two dragon swords (i.e., two heroes—you and I) come to life on this
    starry night;
The night-watch clapper marks a growing chill, as for countless horses in
    autumn.]

well as writings on the arts—the *Wang-shih shu-yuan*, or *Mr. Wang's Calligraphy Garden*, and the *Wang-shih hua-yuan*, or *Mr. Wang's Painting Garden*. From these one can see that in terms of both intelligence and learning Wang Shih-chen was talented in areas that went beyond the scope of Li P'an-lung.

The most outstanding man of the age, Wang Shih-chen was highly influential, the world at his feet. Even Soochow and other areas in the south, where reservations about Old Phraseology were still the order of the day, proved no exception. Literary men of the time who showed Wang their allegiance were given his support; those who opposed him received contempt. He ranked his followers in groupings that orbited around himself, even terming his old comrades—Li P'an-lung, Hsu Chung-hsing, Liang Yu-yü, Wu Kuo-lun, and Tsung Ch'en—the Earlier Five Masters (*Ch'ien wu-tzu*). Other groupings included the Later Five Masters (*Hou wu-tzu*), Expanded Five Masters (*Kuang wu-tzu*), Supplementary Five Masters (*Hsu wu-tzu*), and Final Five Masters (*Mo wu-tzu*).

The lavish gardens he erected in his native T'ai-ts'ang were first given the Buddhist name Hsiao-chih lin, or Small-Scale Jetavana,[40] which was later changed to Yen-shan yuan, or Yen-Mountain Garden. Notwithstanding the repose suggested by such titles, throngs of visitors, including Taoist priests, Buddhist monks, and hosts of others, came daily to pay their respects and to seek Wang's instruction in letters. Thus, until 1590 when he died at the age of sixty-four,[41] Wang Shih-chen virtually monopolized the late sixteenth-century literary scene.[42]

On account of having followed his models to excess, Wang Shih-chen, like Li P'an-lung, wrote many poems that are too confined or constricted. But because Wang possessed greater breadth

---

[40] [Jetavana was the name of the favorite resort of Buddha; see William Edward Soothill and Lewis Hodous, *A Dictionary of Chinese Buddhist Terms* (1934; rpt. Taipei: Buddhist Culture Service, 1962), p. 310.]

[41] I.e., just prior to the time Hideyoshi invaded Korea (in 1592).

[42] Wang Shih-chen was a devotee of Wang Tao-chen (1558–1580), a Taoist priestess and daughter of the important official Wang Hsi-chueh (from the same home district as the poet). After the death of her fiancé, Wang Tao-chen led a religious life under the name T'an-yang tzu, or Cloud-Dynamic Master; dying young, she was said to have transformed herself into an immortal. Wang Shih-chen wrote a biography of her.

of talent than Li, his poems display considerably more suppleness and beauty. A few will be offered here by way of example.

The following is a five-character regulated verse entitled "On First Entering Soochow after the Disaster, Drinking Informally with My Younger Brother." It was written in 1552 at the age of twenty-seven, when Wang Shih-chen's home district of T'ai-ts'ang was invaded by Japanese pirates and his entire family fled to Soochow.

> Since both of us got caught in the disaster,
> I can scarcely believe you are again before my eyes.
> Though our lives are initially our own,
> Everything tends to depend on others.
> Surely Heaven's will does not back a pack of thieves!
> In times of trouble, loved ones become dearer.
> I cannot bear to recall the past;
> Even drunken words wound the spirit.

Wang Shih-chen wrote a seven-character old-style poem in memory of Sun I-yuan, a poet-recluse who died before Wang was born, having spent his years wandering. Sun's origins and social status being unclear, some claimed he was the illegitimate son of a previous emperor. In Wang's poem, entitled "Making a Libation at the Grave of Sun I-yuan," Sun is likened to Ting-ling Wei of the Later Han, who metamorphosed into a crane and returned to perch on the stone columns at his home. The opening couplet refers to Sun's uncertain origins.

> Now dead, he has no need of descendants;
> When alive, he could not need ancestors.
> Although he suddenly rose, towering above the ancients,
> Still he ended in a lonely heap of dust.
> For fifty years now, between Tao-ch'ang and Shan-yin,[43]

[43] [Sun I-yuan was buried in the Tao-ch'ang Hills, and Shan-yin was one of the regions where he wandered; both are in Chekiang. The line might also be rendered—understanding the time period stated to refer to Sun's forty-six-year life span (1484–1520) rather than the roughly fifty years since his death—"For fifty years, [he wandered] Tao-ch'ang and Shan-yin"—or alternatively (taking "shan-yin" in its concrete sense)—"Fifty years he passed in the shadow of Tao-ch'ang Hills."]

As a crane, how could he return to perch on stone columns?[44]
Look over at the lotus-flower palm on Mt. T'ai-hua;[45]
We should hear his pipes and song up there.

The following seven-character regulated verse, "Presented to Liang Ch'en-yü," was dedicated to the author of the *Wan-sha chi*, or *Story of Washing Silk*, a play that was highly popular in the late sixteenth century. Liang Ch'en-yü (1520–1580) was among the ranks of Old Phraseology poets.

Having inscribed your Han Pass stele, your hair starts turning gray;
A piece completed on Liang Garden, you sit even prouder.[46]
Your box holds more swords, sharp as autumn frost, than other heroes;
In high-class popular song, you are like famous men long past.[47]
Chiang-liang travelers copy out *Master of the Golden Tower*;
Women of Chien-yeh sing "Jade-Tree Flowers."[48]
Who says you return to a house bare but for the walls standing,
When a charming Wen-chün awaits to personally brew tea for you?

The final couplet alludes to Ssu-ma Hsiang-ju of the Former Han, about whose poverty it was said, "His house was so bare that the only things standing in it were the four walls." Liang Ch'en-yü is likened to that poet, whose wife was Wen-chün.

When Ch'i Chi-kuang, the famous general who had fought

---

[44] [In other words, like Ting-ling Wei, Sun I-yuan may have become an immortal but, unlike that metamorphosed crane, he cannot "return" to perch on stone columns because, given both his doubtful origins and his life as a wanderer, he has neither a legitimate nor fixed home to return to.]

[45] The summit of this peak in distant Shensi is in the shape of a lotus-flower palm.

[46] [Wang Shih-chen likens Liang Ch'en-yü to Han period figures who wrote pieces on the topics mentioned.]

[47] [In the complementary lines of this couplet Liang is said to be both martial and lettered. (The phrase "high-class" renders the term "spring snows," i.e., "[Warm] Spring" and "[White] Snows," ancient songs of the state of Ch'u, which were said to be properly elevated.)]

[48] [This couplet alludes to works of the past that were well received by the public at large; Liang's writing is implicitly being likened to them in flattering terms. The sixth-century *Chin-lou tzu* (Master of the Golden Tower), was by Emperor Yuan-ti of the Liang dynasty, the title being the emperor's literary name. Chiang-liang (in present-day Hupei), Emperor Yuan-ti's capital, was a place name associated with Six Dynasties ballads. "Jade Tree Flowers" is the truncated title of a ballad by the last emperor of the sixth-century Ch'en dynasty, whose capital Chien-yeh was the same city of Chiang-liang.]

Japanese pirates harassing the southeast coast of China,[49] paid a
visit to Yen-Mountain Garden, Wang Shih-chen composed the
following poem. It is the fifth in a series of ten seven-character
quatrains entitled "Upon Being Presented a Precious Sword by
General Ch'i."

> What on the ocean blue once cut through raging whales,
> At this banquet has become a parting gift for one unworthy.
> That its lotus has dulled and scales turned grey,[50]
> Is because a troubled world has gradually grown peaceful.[51]

The seven-character regulated-verse section of Wang Shih-
chen's *Yen-chou shan-jen ssu-pu kao* includes poems written in im-
itation of the style of Po Chü-i, whose poetry was shunned by Old
Phraseology adherents. Wang apologetically adds phrases like
"Scarcely Worth Preserving" and "In a Modified Style" to the titles
of such poems. The following is an example from a series entitled
"Trusting to My Pen, In a Miscellany of Styles."

> Flowers vie once, and they are fresh but once;
> Five times my gate has quietly closed, five times the season turned to
>    spring.[52]
> Gossamer threads afar in the wind, beyond the world's dust;[53]
> A yellowing leaf in the rain—my body in dreams.
> A healable sickness can scarcely be called a sickness;
> Poverty amenable to explanation is not poverty.[54]

---

[49] [Note the study by Ray Huang, *1557, A Year of No Significance: The Ming
Dynasty in Decline* (New Haven: Yale University Press, 1981); it includes a chapter
devoted to Ch'i Chi-kuang (pp. 156–88), as well as one each devoted to other
figures mentioned in this volume: the Wan-li emperor (pp. 1–41), Chang Chü-
cheng (pp. 75–103), and Li Chih (pp. 189–221).]

[50] [A "lotus" was said to blossom on swords tempered by the famous sword-
smith of antiquity, Ou Yeh (Ou, the Forger). Fish scales presumably were blade
markings.]

[51] [The poet is saying, the peaceful state of the world is thanks to you, general.]

[52] [The poem is about Wang Shih-chen's career; when his gate was closed, he
was in retreat.]

[53] [The poet's official career, which is likened to fragile and unreal gossamer
threads, is less real than dust.]

[54] [That is to say, a poverty that is not one's fault (or one that has resulted from
choice) is nothing to be ashamed of.]

Don't take lightly your rendezvous with Hsiang-p'ing;
He who is abandoning his official cap is sick of running about.[55]

It has been said that Wang Shih-chen in his later years had a change of literary taste. There are well-known anecdotes recounting that when his friend Liu Feng visited him on his deathbed, Wang was absorbed in reading poetry by the author who was most to Old Phraseology writers' distaste, Su Shih. But such stories are an exaggeration; from the *Yen-chou shan-jen ssu-pu kao* it is clear that Wang Shih-chen read Su Shih's poetry from an early age.

In his later years, Wang Shih-chen is also said to have reminisced as follows:

> What I enjoy is reading, writing, and wine. Wine leads me to improper conduct, but it helps when I feel depressed. Writing has been of use for my career, but in truth it has not been all that important. My days have been spent with wine, which has occasioned censure for my way of life. I gained a name for letters, but fame brought on the envy of others, and because of envy I met with setbacks. Seeing the setbacks and envy I encountered, Heaven took mercy on me, placing me beyond the cares of the world.[56]

## The Failures and Achievements of Old Phraseology

Old Phraseology dominated sixteenth-century China. But in the following century the movement met with severe criticism, and it has remained in bad repute ever since. The writings of most of its authors are now all but forgotten.

Even during its sixteenth-century heyday there were signs of an impending decline in the movement's reputation. At a time

[55] [Hsiang-p'ing is Hsiang Ch'ang, a recluse of Later Han times who wandered China's sacred peaks once his children were married. In the poem's final line, the one who is abandoning his official's hat is the poet, who is tired of "running about" (i.e., serving).]

[56] The citation is from the *Min shichi saishi den* (Biographies of the Seven Talented Masters of the Ming), compiled by Sen Seishi in 1750; I am not acquainted with the source he was drawing on. As will be elaborated in the section on "The Failures and Achievements of Old Phraseology" that follows, this was one of the works that emerged from the mid-Edo atmosphere of respect for Old Phraseology advocated by Ogyū Sorai.

when it was almost universally held that "Prose must follow the Ch'in and Han," Kuei Yu-kuang, now considered the finest prose stylist of the Ming, used "old-style prose" (*ku-wen*) of the T'ang and Sung dynasties as his model. When Kuei Yu-kuang criticized Wang Shih-chen for being a "pretentious mediocrity," Wang replied, "I may be pretentious, but I'm certainly not a mediocrity." Also, Hsu Wei and T'ang Hsien-tsu—the one a totally uninhibited literary figure, the other well known as a major playwright—expressed strong criticism of Wang Shih-chen. But these were only scattered attacks that did not affect the latter's overwhelming authority as arbiter of literary affairs.

As will be described in the next chapter, it was only in the seventeenth century that a large-scale reaction to Old Phraseology took place. It started with Yuan Hung-tao and other Kung-an School figures at the beginning of the century. There followed attacks by Chung Hsing, T'an Yuan-ch'un, and other Ching-ling School writers. And scathing criticisms by the great figure of the transition between the late Ming and early Ch'ing dynasties, Ch'ien Ch'ien-i, gave it the finishing blow. The movement's later reputation was set.

The major failures of the Old Phraseology movement, as noted by Ch'ien Ch'ien-i and others, can be summarized as follows. First, the advocacy of congruence between one's own writing and a literary model had the net effect of turning literature into simple imitation. The most flagrant examples are found in Li P'an-lung's verses imitative of early ballads and old-style poems. According to Old Phraseology, a writer was supposed to efface himself completely as a person living in the sixteenth century and to try to make his writing at one with, not just the diction and expression of Han and Wei verse and High T'ang poetry, but also their emotional content. This made for a forced mismatch of periods. Ch'ien Ch'ien-i criticized the result as being "a bogus bronze"; it was, he said, like "playing a part in someone else's clothes."

Second, Old Phraseology did not even succeed in producing good imitations or fakes. Since writers merely half digested the models they were emulating, imitation went only skin-deep, never getting to the essence. Thus the expansiveness of Tu Fu's poetry was crudely imitated, but its fine detail was disregarded. In reference to these imitations one should note that in Ming times scholarly mastery of the classical language was at its lowest level. Even when trying to imitate classical diction writers would include words and expressions not found in the models they were using, which made their imitations all the more odd. For example, a written character meaning "to beat" (*ta*) that Li P'an-lung occasionally uses in his prose is completely absent from the Ch'in and Han writing that served as his model. Such slips occurred not only in the specific words that are used, but also in the subject matter that is treated. The reader will recall the line cited earlier, "Rats from the wall chatter beside my bed," written by Li Meng-yang while in prison.[57] Although references to household rats can be found in earlier Chinese poetry, they seldom appear in the T'ang verse that was Li's putative model here; rather, they are frequently found in the poetry Old Phraseology advocates insisted should most be avoided, that of the Sung period, especially in poems by Su Shih. One could cite many such instances.

Third, the literary models that were selected were limited to literature of the past that was distinguished mostly for its intensity—namely, Ch'in and Han prose and High T'ang poetry—with the result that other potential models, ones outstanding for their fine detail and classical grace, were ignored.

Fourth, the models to be imitated were fixed and quite limited in range and number, which led to much monotonous repetition in Old Phraseology writing.

Fifth, because of the attempt to make writing congruent with classical models, the works that were produced poorly reflect sixteenth-century contemporary realities. This was not necessarily true of the *prose* of Old Phraseology authors. Although the prose writings of Li Meng-yang and Li P'an-lung, especially the accounts they wrote of their family background, are written in an odd, artificial-*Shih chi* style, they describe in fresh ways a stratum of society that had not received treatment in earlier traditional-style prose. But the situation was different as regards *poetry*. To try to make one's own writing at one, both in content and feeling,

[57] [See p. 143.]

with that of eighth-century verse (or that of the third century and earlier) was to rob poetry of its freedom and to divorce the writer from contemporary feelings and realities.[58] Two of the most celebrated incidents of the century, Li Meng-yang's incarcerations and Wang Shih-chen's campaign to restore his father's name, provide good examples; in the poetry of these famous figures it is difficult to find details about either circumstance, to say nothing of what feelings they had about them.

Old Phraseology is guilty of all of the above. Put simply, the movement presents a story of failed archaizing.

But there were accomplishments by Old Phraseology writers that cannot be overlooked. Basically these have to do with literary theory and literary criticism. First, there are the theories concerning the nature of poetry and the nature of literature that the movement engendered. For example, Li Meng-yang argued that poetry issues from "feeling" (*ch'ing*), that "rhythm" (*tiao*) is paramount to it, and that these must be accompanied by "color" (*se*, i.e., sense elements). Old Phraseology writers made Ch'in and Han prose and High T'ang poetry their sole literary models because they viewed these works as the ones that best met these criteria for what constitutes literature. It was foolish and rash the way they let themselves be too bound to their models, but the rationale behind their program still merits attention. They made assertions that had not been made, or at least had not been made clearly, by earlier literary critics. A good example is the importance Ho Ching-ming accorded the poetic expression of love.

The second achievement of the Old Phraseology movement lies in its elaboration of the view that literature is the most exalted human activity. It is not that such a view had never been expressed before. A similar point had been made in the third century,[59] one that influenced writers until the seventh or eighth century, or even until Sung period thinkers argued for the prime importance of

---

[58] Moreover, as noted in chap. 1, writers of the Sung and later dynasties were unlike poets of the T'ang and earlier periods in that they did not immerse themselves in sorrow. (Nor, apparently, did the environment prompt them to such immersion.) Much as Old Phraseology writers disliked Su Shih, they could not but be under his influence, being like him in this respect. Still, they insisted on making poetry of only the T'ang and earlier periods their model.

[59] [The author is here presumably referring to Ts'ao P'i.]

philosophy. The attitude of late Yuan and early Ming *wen-jen* had also been similarly oriented. But it was rare to find earlier figures as resolute as Old Phraseology writers in holding that literature is the supreme human undertaking. In the sixteenth century this view grew widespread among townsmen and formed an important part of the atmosphere of the age.[60]

The third contribution of the Old Phraseology movement is found in its evaluation of past literature. Notwithstanding the fact that the movement's writers naively bound themselves hand and foot to literary models, their commendations of "the Ch'in and Han for prose" and "the High T'ang for poetry" were, in fact, an appropriate reordering of literary history. It is objectively the case that High T'ang poetry is the soundest or among the soundest poetry in the Chinese tradition—an opinion confirmed by all modern histories of Chinese literature. Such a view of High T'ang verse can be traced back to the *Ts'ang-lang shih-hua*, or *Poetry Talks by Ts'ang-lang*, by Yen Yü of the Southern Sung, and to the *T'ang-shih p'in-hui*, or *A Graded Anthology of T'ang Poetry*, by Kao Ping of the early Ming. But the Earlier and Later Seven Masters gave it its final form. Moreover, their high praise for the poetry of the Han and Wei dynasties also brought about a rediscovery of that long-forgotten body of literature. Fang Wei-na's (d. 1572) large-scale anthology of pre-T'ang poetry, the *Ku-shih chi*, or *Record of Ancient Poetry*, developed out of this milieu and has remained a major contribution. Moreover, several critical works on poetry by Old Phraseology writers are of value and are still read today. These include Wang Shih-chen's *I-yuan chih-yen*, or *Goblet Words from the Garden of Art*, Hsieh Chen's *Ssu-ming shih-hua*, or *Poetry Talks by Ssu-ming*, and the *Shih sou*, or *Thicket of Poetry*, by one of Wang Shih-chen's disciples, Hu Ying-lin.[61]

In addition to these achievements, there were other important effects the movement had. One should point out the great service rendered by Old Phraseology in making the *Shih chi*, or *Records of the Historian*, a classic that for the past few centuries all must read. Yet prior to its being advocated as the sole model for prose writing

---

[60] One might say it formed a necessary developmental stage in civilization.

[61] Hu Ying-lin (1551–1602) was among the Final Five Masters (*Mo wu-tzu*) grouping of Wang Shih-chen's disciples.

by Old Phraseology theorists, Ssu-ma Ch'ien's work had not even been readily available. K'ang Hai, one of the Earlier Seven Masters, stated in the preface to his newly compiled edition of the work that, because a complete edition of the *Shih chi* had not been in circulation since the Chung-t'ung reign period (1260–1264) of the Yuan, the work could only be read in fragments in anthologies. He tells of devoting more than ten years' effort to assembling missing chapters so as to make the work available to the world. Modern readers accustomed to thinking of the *Shih chi* as a standard work may find this hard to imagine, but such was the case before the Old Phraseology movement.

The flourishing of sixteenth-century drama and vernacular fiction should be viewed as an indirect success of the Old Phraseology movement, inasmuch as the one occurred in tandem with the other. The sixteenth century was a great age for drama[62] and, as previously noted, dramatists like K'ang Hai and Wang Chiu-ssu were Old Phraseology poets. The period provides a good example of how a flourishing of the traditional literary forms spilled over and helped give rise to a similar development in fiction. Even though there is no basis for it in fact, the theory current at the time, that the anonymous author of the famous novel *Chin p'ing mei* was Wang Shih-chen, illustrates how people of the period perceived that the flourishing of Old Phraseology writing and the flourishing of fiction were interrelated.

The Old Phraseology movement also has great significance for the social history of the period. As noted at the beginning of this chapter, notwithstanding the pretentiousness it was dressed up in, the movement in fact offered quite a simple approach to writing. It easily satisfied the desire of ordinary townsmen to achieve what they thought was a high level of writing, with the result (as illustrated by the variety of guests who would call on Wang Shih-chen) that more and more townsmen participated in writing poems. In turn, the view that literature is the supreme human activity came to permeate townsman thinking.

[62] As given detailed study by Aoki Masaru in his *Shina kinsei gikyoku shi* (A History of Chinese Drama of the Later Premodern Dynasties) (Tokyo: Kōbundō, 1930). [Chinese translation by Wang Ku-lu, *Chung-kuo chin-shih hsi-ch'ü shih* (Peking: Tso-chia, 1958).]

Old Phraseology played an important role in influencing the development of Edo-period Confucianism in Japan. Ogyū Sorai's (1666–1728) approach to learning developed in reaction to the emphasis on a severe seriousness found in both the speculative Neo-Confucianism of the Sung dynasty and its Japanese heirs; what Sorai advocated in its stead was a tolerant magnanimity. He made philology the starting point for elucidating the early philosophical texts he used for such advocacy. The approach was prompted by his having read the works of Li P'an-lung and Wang Shih-chen. In his own words, it was through "Heaven's indulgent spirit" that their writings provided the revelation. Specifically, Sorai took and applied to philosophical study the approach to writing of Li P'an-lung and Wang Shih-chen—that of trying to reproduce ancient literature by making one's own writing identical with the linguistic world of the ancients. Sorai hoped to grasp the *Analects* and other writings as they really were, by entering into their linguistic universe.[63] The approach was to dominate Japanese Confucianism and led to the National Learning (*kokugaku*) of Motoori Norinaga (1730–1801).

Ogyū Sorai and his followers were also the literary as well as philosophical heirs of Old Phraseology. This is reflected in both their understanding and appreciation of Chinese literature and in their own writings in Chinese. In 1724 Sorai's disciple, Hattori Nankaku (1683–1759), reprinted the *T'ang-shih hsuan*, or *T'ang Poetry Selections*—called the *Tōshi sen* in Japanese—an anthology of verse purportedly by Li P'an-lung. Even though a century and a half had passed since the appearance of the original work in China, the reprint became a best-seller in Japan. The work consists of the section on T'ang poetry in Li P'an-lung's *Ku-chin shih shan*, or *Old and New Poems Excised*. Although nominally an anthology of verse from the entire dynasty, the work contains poems only from the Early and High T'ang periods; Middle and Late T'ang poets like Po Chü-i are not represented. And within the confines of the periods that are represented, there is a marked preference for only those poems that are martial or full of energy—a reflection of the

[63] For more about this, see my "Nihon no shinjō" ("The Heart of Japan"), 1958; reprinted in *Yoshikawa Kōjirō zenshū*, 17: 102–4.

kind of poetry the compiler was advocating. If one considers that even today the *Tōshi sen* serves as a point of departure for many Japanese in their appreciation of Chinese poetry, the influence of the Old Phraseology movement can be seen, if only in an indirect way, still to be operative.[64]

[64] I might add that in my own anthologies of T'ang poetry—the *Shin Tōshi sen* (New Selection of T'ang Poetry), 1952, and *Shin Tōshi sen zokuhen* (New Selection of T'ang Poetry: A Continuation), 1954—the criteria for inclusion are different from those of Li P'an-lung; reprinted in *Yoshikawa Kōjirō zenshū*, 11: 45–163, and 228–369, respectively.

# Chapter 8

# THE LATE MING,
# 1600–1650

## Townsman Poetry Reaches the Saturation Point

The first half of the seventeenth century marks the final decades of the Ming dynasty. When the century began, the longest-ruling Ming sovereign, the Wan-li emperor, was already in the twenty-eighth year of a reign that was to last an additional twenty years. His tenure was followed by the seven-year one of the T'ien-ch'i emperor (r. 1620–1627). Finally, the Ch'ung-chen emperor's seventeen-year span brought the dynasty to an end in 1644. The political history of the period, from the late years of the preceding century until the dynasty's fall, is one of incessant feuding between bureaucratic groups. Factional feuds, often involving the support of townsmen, were frequently related to secret struggles at court.

Embroiled in factional dissension, China suffered both internally from revolts that broke out among the peasantry and externally from the force of Manchu arms (accompanied by effective use of psychological warfare) under the leadership of the Aisin Gioro clansman Nurhaci (d. 1626). Manchus were able to take power by reaping the benefit of Chinese internal strife. Establishing a new dynasty they called the Ch'ing (or "pure"), Nurhaci's descendants were to rule a unifed China until 1911.

Surprisingly, there was little sense of urgency among Ming subjects that a crisis impended until the Ch'ung-chen emperor committed suicide in 1644.[1] Indeed over the first half of the seventeenth century, the huge growth in townsman poetry that had been brought about by the Old Phraseology movement of the previous century continued unabated. If anything, poetry writing further swelled, reaching what might be called the saturation point.

Late Ming poets were not only officials and wealthy men of local influence who chose not to become bureaucrats. Many also came from poor precincts. The final chapters of Ch'ien Ch'ien-i's *Lieh-ch'ao shih-chi*, or *Poetry Collection of Successive Reigns*, include a considerable number of poems by such writers. For example, there was Ch'en Ang (fl. 1573) from Miao-t'ien in Fukien, who styled himself Po-yun hsien-sheng, or Gentleman of the White Clouds. After fleeing from invading Japanese pirates and spending some time unsettled, he ended up on the banks of the Ch'in-huai River in Nanking, where he supported himself by telling fortunes, selling straw sandals, and writing poems and prose compositions for others. Fortune-telling was also the livelihood of a poet from Soochow, Yuan Ching-hsiu (dates uncertain). Others in Ch'ien Ch'ien-i's anthology include T'ung P'ei (fl. 1573) from Lung-yu in Chekiang who, like his father before him, was a bookseller and T'ang Ju-hsun (fl. 1624), a blind man living in a poor district of Sung-chiang.

As an example of the fairly respectable level of poetry they wrote, I will cite a poem by Ch'en Ang. A five-character regulated verse entitled "The City Breached, I Take My Wife and Flee to Hsien-yu Temple in the Hu Range," the poem was written while the poet was on the run from invading Japanese pirates.

> Amid death and disorder, barely alive,
> To whom can we turn in hunger and cold?
> In the morning we fled, hearing the dead crying;
> At night we scurry away, Hsien-yu Temple in sight.
> There is a path, but the winds are frightful;
> Not a single mountain where birds will stay.

[1] The suicide occurred on the nineteenth day of the third month (April 24), 1644.

My good wife demands of heaven—
"When will the robbers let up?"

Among such townsman poets were those who, dissatisfied
with their straitened circumstances, traveled widely with no fixed
destination, trying to sell their writings to high officials and the
wealthy. At the time the term for such men was *shan-jen*, or "hill
men."[2] From contemporary works like Shen Te-fu's (1578–1642)
*Yeh-huo pien*, or *Information Gathered Unofficially*, one can gather
how prevalent the phenomenon was and what a problem it posed.

Townsmen of the time (including *shan-jen*) formed literary
groups. Some of these groups became satellite organizations of
political factions. The most prominent examples are the Tung-lin
Party (*Tung-lin tang*), which evolved from a Confucian study
group into a huge political organization, and the Restoration So-
ciety (*Fu she*) touched on below.

Drama and vernacular fiction continued to flourish over the
first half of the seventeenth century. Books appeared having elab-
orate illustrations, and narratives of the period included ones that
were erotic; both were manifestations of townsman wealth and
leisure.

The main poetic trend in this milieu was one of reaction to
Old Phraseology. Although townsmen had been swept up in that
movement (which presented an aristocratic surface appeal that
was, in fact, simple and straightforward), many came to tire of its
confining strictures and sought a freer approach to writing. The
ever increasing quantity of poetry that was being produced also
brought about a change in poetic quality. At the same time there
were groups that continued to act as heirs to Old Phraseology.
Thus, in parallel with the political disarray of the time, the literary
world was divided into competing camps. Yet the general trend
ran counter to Old Phraseology.

As noted at the end of the last chapter, even during the move-
ment's sixteenth-century heyday a few voices critical of Old
Phraseology could be heard. Specifically, there were criticisms by
Kuei Yu-kuang (1506–1571) of Kiangsu, Hsu Wei (1521–1593)
of Chekiang, and T'ang Hsien-tsu (1550–1617) of Kiangsi. The
three were later to be highly praised as prophets by Ch'ien Ch'ien-

---

[2] [The term includes the meaning "recluse."]

i, the seventeenth-century arch-antagonist of Old Phraseology. Yet they had spoken merely as isolated critics. It was only with the appearance of the Kung-an School in the late sixteenth and early seventeenth centuries that a fully developed anti-Old Phraseology movement emerged.

None of the three sixteenth-century critics of Old Phraseology was an outstanding poet. Kuei Yu-kuang, although a great prose writer, did not have a similar talent for poetry. Hsu Wei's verse was not as good as his painting and calligraphy.[3] And even though T'ang Hsien-tsu, the author of the *Mu-tan-t'ing huan-hun chi*, or *Story of the Return of the Soul to Peony Pavilion*,[4] was proud of his poetry, it was not of the caliber of his plays.[5]

The only poetic example I will offer of writing by the three is a poem of particular interest to Japanese. It is a seven-character quatrain Hsu Wei wrote about a Japanese pirate.

> The barbarian woman, out of fear of demons, has tattooed her body red;
> When her husband left, he tenderly gave her a seamless shift.[6]
> This morning as he meets his end in China,
> She still climbs Mt. Aso to gaze at ocean sails.

According to Hsu Wei's own appended commentary, "In their land [i.e., Japan] Mt. Aso (A-su shan) is the highest peak."

---

[3] Hsu Wei served as secretary to Hu Tsung-hsien, a general who fought Japanese pirate-invaders; he is described as having been eccentric in behavior. ["When, in 1565, Hu Tsung-hsien lost his high post and was thrown into prison, Hsu [Wei] became terrified, fearing that he too might be implicated. He attempted suicide and confesses, in an unusually frank 'obituary,' that he was pretending madness. In this mood anything could upset him. His wife aroused his suspicions. Perhaps it was his own fault, for he had destroyed his testicles. In any event, he beat her to death, and consequently was imprisoned (1566)." Liang I-cheng and L. Carrington Goodrich, "Hsü Wei," in *Dictionary of Ming Biography*, p. 610.]

[4] [Translated into English by Cyril Birch, *The Peony Pavilion* (Bloomington: Indiana University Press, 1980), and into German by Vincenz Hundhausen, *Die Rückkehr der Seele: Ein romantisches Drama in deutscher Sprache* (Zurich and Leipzig, 1937).] The work is one of four plays included in the *Yü-ming-t'ang ssu-meng*, or *Four Dreams in Jade-Tea Hall*, by T'ang Hsien-tsu.

[5] Kuei Yu-kuang was older than both Li P'an-lung and Wang Shih-chen; Hsu Wei was younger than Li, but older than Wang; and T'ang Hsien-tsu was younger than both Li and Wang.

[6] [Perhaps a kind of symbolic chastity belt.]

# The Kung-an School

The Kung-an School (*Kung-an p'ai*) of the late Ming dynasty comprised a group of poets centered around three brothers who came from the small port of Kung-an on the Yangtze River in Hupei: Yuan Tsung-tao (1560–1600), Yuan Hung-tao (1568–1610), and Yuan Chung-tao (1570–1623).[7] Also known as the Three Yuans of Kung-an (*Kung-an san-Yuan*), the trio all became Presented Scholars. They denounced the Old Phraseology movement for engaging in pointless imitation and argued instead for prose and poetry free in feeling and expression. The two poets toward whom Old Phraseology writers held the greatest aversion, Po Chü-i and Su Shih, were the very writers whom Kung-an School adherents praised the highest. In fact the eldest of the Yuan brothers, Yuan Tsung-tao, named his library Po-Su chai, or Po and Su Studio, and his literary corpus was titled the *Po-Su-chai chi*, or *Collected Writings from the Po and Su Studio*.

The most famous of the Kung-an School brothers was the middle one, Yuan Hung-tao. His poetry, characterized by freedom and clarity, marked a major change from Old Phraseology writing. Because it had these qualities it lent itself well to reflecting current realities. By way of example I will offer a five-character old-style poem written while Yuan Hung-tao was serving in Peking; it is entitled "Second Month, Twenty-First Day—Walking in the Moonlight at Ch'ung-kuo Temple."[8]

> The moon's cold light penetrates the sangharama,[9]
> Lighting up the inscription on the gate.
> Walking in moonlight throughout the city,

[7] [For studies, see Hung Ming-shui, "Yüan Hung-tao and the Late Ming Literary Movement," Unpublished Ph.D. dissertation, University of Wisconsin, 1974; Jonathan Chaves, *Pilgrim of the Clouds: Poems and Essays by Yüan Hung-tao and His Brothers* (New York: Weatherhill, 1978); Martine Vallette-Hémery, *Yuan Hongdao (1568–1610): Théorie et pratique littéraires* (Paris: Collège de France, Institut des Hautes Etudes Chinoises, 1982); idem, *Nuages et pierres: Yüan Hongdao (Hung-tao)* (Paris: Publications Orientalistes de France, 1982); and Chou Chih-p'ing, *Yüan Hung-tao and the Kung-an School* (Cambridge: Cambridge University Press, 1988).

[8] [It was at this temple in the western part of the capital that the Yuan brothers organized a literary coterie named the P'u-t'ao she, or Grape Society.]

[9] [I.e., a monastery.]

Nowhere is there a white to compare with this.
Recluse monks shut all the doors,
Hiding from the moon as from visitors.
On empty steps, reflected coiling branches—
Old in appearance, they are hard as rock.
Cold penetrates the body, like a flute echoing in frost;
Even wine cannot warm the heart.
I am wrapped in layers of felt,
Footsteps now gone from capital streets.
Though a watchman with wooden clapper makes his rounds,
Used to seeing him, I feel little pity.
But oh! How I do feel sorry for those in desert wastes,
Upon whom, on such long nights, these bright cold rays shine.

Yuan Hung-tao, as befitted a friend of the idiosyncratic thinker Li Chih, also wrote poems freely expressive of singular ideas. For example, there is the following old-style verse entitled "A 'Little by Little' Poem, Written on the Wall in Jest."

The bright moon little by little higher;
Green hills little by little lower.
Flower branches little by little redden,
Spring colors little by little fade.
While my salary little by little increases,
My teeth little by little decrease.
As my concubines little by little multiply,
Their faces little by little waste away.
Of lowly position when in one's prime,
Youth is not the time for pleasure.[10]
Lady Luck and Lady Disaster,
Never more than a step apart.[11]
Heaven and Earth have their defects,
The human world all awry.
"Where can one find perfect happiness?"
Bowing my head, I would ask an immortal's instruction.[12]

Regulated verses by Yuan Hung-tao are sometimes written in an excessively bantering style that slips into vulgar humor. Note

[10] In other words, by the time someone has the time and money to devote to pleasure, he is already old.

[11] These two female gods, called "Meritorious" and "Swarthy" in the original, appear in the *Ta-pan nieh-p'an ching* (Mahaparinirvana sutra), chap. 11.

[12] [Cf. the translation by Chaves, *Pilgrim of the Clouds*, p. 39, which also appears in idem, *Later Chinese Poetry*, p. 345.]

the final couplet in the following, entitled "Late Spring, Together with Mr. Hsieh, Mr. Wang, and My Younger Brother, On an Excursion North of the City Walls—Viewing the Ponds of Various Temples, We Arrive at a Waterside Pavilion beside Te-sheng Bridge and Await the Moon."

This inept one at last enjoys a break from office;
Who, no matter where, would not let out a smile?
Now in layers, now spread out—waters in the breeze;
Half tipsy, half drunk—mountains in the haze.
Where boards have fallen in the imperial waterway, golden fish appear;
Whence petals fluttered from palace trees, young swallows return.
Pale greens and light browns—foliage all about—
Surely this envelops us better than a beautiful woman.[13]

The poetic style advocated by Yuan Hung-tao and his brothers immediately proved popular as an alternative to Old Phraseology. The fact that Yuan Hung-tao served for a period as District Magistrate in Soochow also doubtless helped attract a large number of townsman followers from that region.[14] The poet died toward the beginning of the seventeenth century, in 1610.

[13] [The final couplet is open to a more muted interpretation than that of the author: "Pale greens and light browns, everywhere to be had; / They (in the form of catkins, petals, and the like) stick to us even better than a courtesan's coiffure"—that is, better than her hair sticks to her and/or her customers.]

[14] The writings of Yuan Hung-tao were transmitted to Japan early by a Ming refugee, Ch'en Yuan-yun (1568–1671). They became favorite reading of the early Edo monk Gensei (1623–1668) of Fukakusa in Kyoto. In a letter Gensei wrote to Ch'en he relates:

> A few days ago I looked in town for the *Yuan Chung-lang chi* (Collected Writings of Yuan Hung-tao) and found it. His *yueh-fu* ballads are superb; I can scarcely add more. His "Kuang *Chuang*" ("Expanding on *Chuang-tzu*") reveals profound familiarity with its subject. And from the flair with which he tells his *P'ing-shih* (Story of the [Flower Arrangement] Vase),* one can envision the character of the man. Also, when he speaks of the Buddhist Dharma in his letters, his insights are absolutely correct. I have been enjoying the work immensely. It is thanks to word from you that I learned such a collection exists. And that I now have a copy and can read it is indeed your "gift" to me.

\* [*"Yüan Hung-tao's monograph on flower arrangement, P'ing-shih, 1 ch., included in his collected works, is indicative of his outlook on life and mode of living. It made its way to Japan probably in the 18th century and was then reprinted there, and resulted in the initiation of a sect. The Kōdōryū [Hung-tao School] of flower arrangement in Japan is said to be currently in its twenty-fourth (teacher-disciple) succession. The style of this*

Yuan Chung-tao, the youngest of the Kung-an brothers, lived later into the century, dying in 1623. The following, from a series of five-character old-style poems entitled "Expressing My Soul," serves to represent his work.

> Along the great embankment, pendant willows—
> How luxuriantly hangs their fresh green!
> Once the north wind comes,
> Decayed, they turn into old trees.
> The four seasons press on in succession;
> How quickly passes the luster of time.
> In life, value matching your temperament;
> What's the point forcing oneself?
> If it's pleasure, give vent to pleasure—
> With women and song, take desire to the limit!
> If it's solitude, then give over to solitude—
> With disheveled hair enter empty valleys!
> What's to be gained, pursuing this transient world,
> Being hesitant or dull witted about it?

The poet is in effect saying, be it with pleasure or retreat from the world, take things to the limit! In advocating such a course Yuan Chung-tao displays the spirit of a man of the Ming.

## The Ching-ling School

During the period roughly from 1620 to 1630[15] the Ching-ling School (*Ching-ling p'ai*) was in vogue. Ching-ling was another name for T'ien-men prefecture in Hupei, near the Kung-an of the Kung-an School. Two of Ching-ling's native sons, Chung Hsing (1574–1624) and T'an Yuan-ch'un (1586–1631), were the school's principal advocates. The poetic style of the group was basically a variation of that propounded by the Kung-an School. Both were alike in opposing Old Phraseology and in advocating a poetry that was unconstrained. But whereas Kung-an writers took

---

school is simple and natural, using mainly three, and sometimes five, stems of three height levels." C. N. Tay, "Yüan Hung-tao," in Dictionary of Ming Biography, p. 1637. Parts of the treatise are translated (and the remainder summarized) by Lin Yutang, The Importance of Living (New York: John Day, 1937), pp. 310–16.]

[15] I.e., from the last year of the Wan-li emperor's reign, through the time of the T'ien-ch'i emperor, until the beginning of the Ch'ung-chen emperor's rule.

delight in simple expression, Ching-ling authors were partial to strange diction and odd formulations. They also enjoyed a peculiar kind of quiescence they termed "profundity and detachment" (*shen-yu ku-ch'iao*), of the sort illustrated in the following five-character old-style poem by Chung Hsing entitled "The Mountain and the Moon."

> What has the mountain to do with the moon?
> Gazing silently, I suddenly understand.
> A lone trail of mist emerges from beyond,
> Then becomes one with the cold void.
> Wherever pure light builds up,
> Excess cold is fully exhausted.
> All sentiments gravitate to the night—
> Beneath these rays, activity and repose.

The following is a poem Chung Hsing wrote while traveling down the Yangtze from Wu-ch'ang to take the civil-service examinations in Nanking. It is the seventh in a series of twelve seven-character regulated verses entitled "River Travel, In a Breezy Style."

Village mists, town trees, ever in the distance—
Unfolding, they reveal blue rivulets and faint green.
The wind with us to White Fish, we scramble to market;
When the river passes Yellow Swan, multitudinous grow the pebbles.
Lost in thought about my family, with a start I realize we have parted;
Enjoying my first visit to this land, it seems like a return.
Of late here in the South, with the fresh flooding,
Rice plants and shrimp won't be as fat as in years past.

T'an Yuan-ch'un also took delight in novel conceits prone to the eccentric. The following seven-character old-style poem, "Summer Night, In Imitation of an Ancient Sentiment," is a case in point.

The Wu woman affixes a flower pattern to woven silk-gauze,
To be donned by singing girls of the South.
At night, loath to let the fragrant breeze pass,
She cuts and sews—cuts gauze to make bed curtains.[16]

---

[16] [This first half of the poem describes a seamstress, the second half (that follows) a singsong girl naked in bed.]

A bright moon, pure white, shines through gauze curtains;
Gauze flowers, one after the other, form shadows on fragrant skin.
My lover comes and flatters me my skin has blossomed;
Taking a wrap, I cover my body, the flowers now on the wrap.

The Ching-ling School, like its Kung-an counterpart, held sway for a period. Its advocates, Chung Hsing and T'an Yuan-ch'un, also made poetic anthologies. As a reaction against Li P'an-lung's *Ku-chin shih shan*, or *Old and New Poems Excised*, they produced a volume of pre-T'ang verse, the fifteen-chapter *Ku-shih kuei*, or *Ancient Poetry: A Return*, and a volume of T'ang verse, the thirty-six-chapter *T'ang-shih kuei*, or *T'ang Poetry: A Return*, both of which circulated widely.[17]

Although he was not a Ching-ling School adherent, I would like to add a short discussion here of Wang Yen-hung (d. 1642), a poet from Chin-t'an in Kiangsu. Wang wrote poems in a "boudoir style" mostly imitative of Li Shang-yin and Han Wo of the late T'ang.[18] The following five-character quatrain, written in 1618 (at about the time that Nurhaci was occupying Fu-shun), is offered by way of example; it is titled "On an Occasion."

My drunken pallor lessens in the fresh air,
The aroma of tea stronger after rain.[19]
Book in hand, I examine your makeup,
As we both face a burnerful of incense.

## The Transition to Ch'ing Dynasty Poetry

The Kung-an School and Ching-ling School had a temporary vogue, but their influence was short-lived. The movements were well received by townsmen because they offered a freedom that overcame the constrictions of Old Phraseology. But inasmuch as the poetry of the two schools tended toward the expression of

[17] These works came to be read in Japan in late Edo times as part of a reaction to Ogyū Sorai's earlier advocacy of Old Phraseology.

[18] Wang Yen-hung authored the *I-yü chi* (Doubtful Rain-Clouds Collection). The work was favorite reading for the modern Japanese writer well known for his erotic interests, Nagai Kafū (1879–1959).

[19] [The tea's aroma presumably is stronger because rainwater has been used to brew it.]

minor themes using language lacking in gravity, in the final analysis it must be judged insubstantial. Offering a direction different from the virtual cul-de-sac of Old Phraseology, the schools themselves proved dead ends.

There again emerged a desire for serious poetry; it became stronger as awareness grew that a crisis was at hand. The first poet of seriousness to appear was Ch'ien Ch'ien-i (1582–1664). Not only was he a poet; as one of the leaders of the largest political group of the time, the Tung-lin Party, he was also a political figure.[20] His reputation in these two roles dominated the late Ming until the fall of the dynasty. Then, in betrayal of the expectations of others, he hastily rendered allegiance to the new Ch'ing dynasty. Notwithstanding this, Ch'ien Ch'ien-i's intense criticism was such as to effect a change of direction in the poetic world of the time away from Old Phraseology.

In the meantime the Restoration Society, which counted Chang P'u a member, and the Seeds (i.e., Incipient Awareness) Society (*Chi she*),[21] which included Ch'en Tzu-lung, each made the revamping of Old Phraseology part of its program. The Restoration Society was a particularly large organization, holding an assembly at Tiger Hill near Soochow in 1633 with more than two thousand in attendance. Serious poets like Wu Wei-yeh (1609–1671) and Ku Yen-wu (1613–1682) emerged from its ranks. But the most substantive poetry of these writers was to ap-

---

[20] [For background to discussion in this section, see Charles O. Hucker, "The Tung-lin Movement of the Late Ming Period," in *Chinese Thought and Institutions*, ed. John K. Fairbank (Chicago: University of Chicago Press, 1957), pp. 132–62; Jerry Dennerline, "The Tung-lin Party in Action: From Loyal Opposition to Loyalism," chap. 2, *The Chia-ting Loyalists: Confucian Leadership and Social Change in Seventeenth-Century China* (New Haven: Yale University Press, 1981), pp. 43–68; and William S. Atwell, "From Education to Politics: The Fu She," in *The Unfolding of Neo-Confucianism*, eds. Wm. Theodore de Bary and the Conference on Seventeenth-Century Chinese Thought (New York: Columbia University Press, 1975), pp. 333–67.]

[21] [The term "seeds" comes from the *I ching* (Classic of Change). "To know the seeds, that is divine indeed. In his association with those above him, the superior man does not flatter. In his association with those beneath him, he is not arrogant. For he knows the seeds. The seeds are the first imperceptible beginning of movement, the first trace of good fortune (or misfortune) that shows itself. The superior man perceives the seeds and immediately takes action. He does not wait even a whole day." Wilhelm/Baynes, *The I ching*, 1: 367.]

pear only after they experienced the fall of the dynasty and the advent of Manchu rule.

Such writing signals the inception of a poetry that was to take a course different from what we have witnessed over the Ming period. It marks the beginning of the last of traditional Chinese literature. The overall history of Ming poetry can be viewed as a process that led to the emergence of Ch'ing verse. Given the time and opportunity, I hope to discuss the later development more fully in an outline of Ch'ing dynasty poetry.[22]

An extended final word is in order concerning Ch'ien Ch'ien-i's *Lieh-ch'ao shih-chi*, or *Poetry Collection of Successive Reigns*. The work stands out qualitatively and quantitatively as an anthology of Ming dynasty poetry. Modeling his work on Yuan Hao-wen's *Chung-chou chi*, or *Anthology of the Heartland*, Ch'ien Ch'ien-i put his wide learning to excellent use by undertaking to produce a history of the Ming dynasty through its poetry. But whereas Yuan Hao-wen had to treat the poetry of only one hundred years of a lesser dynasty, Ch'ien Ch'ien-i confronted the task of ordering 276 years of poetry from the imperial Ming. The sections that comprise the anthology can be summarized roughly as follows:

> *Ch'ien-chi*   2 chaps. Poetry by emperors and members of the imperial family
> *Chia ch'ien-chi*   11 chaps. Poetry of the sixteen-year period from the time the Founder Emperor took up arms until the dynasty was founded (1352–1368)
> *Chia-chi*   22 chaps. 2 reigns, 34 years. Poems of the Hung-wu and Chien-wen reign periods (1368–1402)
> *I-chi*   8 chaps. 5 reigns, 62 years. Poems of the Yung-lo through T'ien-shun reign periods (1403–1465)
> *Ping-chi*   16 chaps. 3 reigns, 57 years. Poems of the Ch'eng-hua through Cheng-te reign periods (1465–1522)
> *Ting-chi*   16 chaps. 6 reigns, 122 years. Poems of the Chia-ching through Ch'ung-chen reign periods (1522–1644)
> *Jun-chi*   6 chaps. Poems by Buddhist priests, Taoist adepts, women, eunuchs, foreigners, etc.

[22] [See chap. 1, n. 1.]

The *Lieh-ch'ao shih-chi* is a work that reflects great breadth and energy. It includes approximately two thousand short biographies that Ch'ien Ch'ien-i appended to the poem selections of individual entrants. These later came into circulation as a volume entitled the *Lieh-ch'ao shih-chi hsiao-chuan*, or *Short Biographies from the Poetry Collection of Successive Reigns*. Yet an understanding of the development of Ming poetry can only come from wide reading in the poems of the collection proper; it is not enough just to read the biographies. The treatment of Ming poetry I have presented in this volume results in part from extensive reading in Ch'ien Ch'ien-i's work.

It is a defect of the *Lieh-ch'ao shih-chi* that Ch'ien Ch'ien-i was unduly averse to Old Phraseology. Chu I-tsun (1629–1709) sought to redress the imbalance by compiling the *Ming-shih tsung*, or *A Ming Poetry Compendium*, an anthology of the work of more than thirty-four hundred poets. But because Chu I-tsun took pains to display complete impartiality in his selection and comments, the work is comparatively colorless.

# *Afterword*

## William S. Atwell

"*Wen shih pu fen chia*, 'Literature and History do not divide their patrimony,' says an old Chinese academic maxim, or more simply, literature and history are inseparable. The wisdom, indeed the necessity, of observing this is widely recognized but inadequately followed." So wrote the historian Frederick W. Mote in the introduction to his elegant biography of the poet Kao Ch'i (1336–1374), which was published by Princeton University Press in 1962. In that path-breaking work Mote demonstrated just how important a careful study of poets and their poetry could be to an understanding of the intellectual, cultural, and political worlds of late imperial China. As he wrote of Kao Ch'i: "Through him we are enabled to see much of his time and his place, his society and his civilization. In his poetry we find a marvelously sensitive record of what the great and small affairs of his daily life, as well as some of the larger issues of his time, meant to a man like him. This discovery may bring us closer to the meaning of his life, and of his times."

In 1963, a year after *The Poet Kao Ch'i, 1336–1374* appeared, Mote's words were echoed by one of this century's foremost students of traditional Chinese literature, Yoshikawa Kōjirō: "For authors of the Chin, Yuan, Ming, and Ch'ing dynasties, as for those of preceding periods, it was poetry and nonfiction prose that formed the heart of Chinese writing. It is to these literary forms, and especially to poetry, that one must look for their most serious expression of feeling." In reading this and many other passages in John Timothy Wixted's careful and very welcome translation of Yoshikawa's *Gen Min shi gaisetsu*, I was struck by how infrequently recent historians of China in the West (as opposed to Professor Wixted and his fellow students of Chinese literature) have followed Professor Mote's advice and made extensive use of poetry in their research. Nor, with few exceptions, have they paid much attention to Professor Yoshikawa's magnificent contributions to the study of traditional Chinese civilization.

There are perhaps two main reasons for this. First, few Western historians of China today possess Mote's or Yoshikawa's linguistic abilities. For many, then, reading classical Chinese prose is difficult enough; attempting to make sophisticated historical use of traditional poetry, much of which is filled with complex historical and classical allusions, often seems to be merely asking for trouble. Second, the recent emphasis on social and economic history both in East Asia and the West has meant that many historians have turned their attention away from China's so-called scholar-elite (including its great and not-so-great poets) to other groups in society (merchants, peddlers, handicraft workers, "managerial landlords," "proto-bankers," heterodox religious groups, and so on) that previously had been unrepresented or at least underrepresented in the historical literature.

Generally speaking, this development was and is no bad thing. At their best, social and economic historians of China in recent years have provided important new perspectives on premodern Chinese society and laid solid foundations on which to build research in many other fields, including Chinese literature. Nevertheless, there is always a danger the pendulum will swing too far. Interest in history or society "from the bottom up" should not lead to the assumption that the ideas and activities of China's old "scholar-elite" are uninteresting or unimportant to our understanding of traditional Chinese civilization. There can be few other civilizations in which a social and political elite has had such a profound impact on so many levels of society and aspects of culture. As Professors Mote and Yoshikawa suggest, therefore, a comprehensive study of late imperial China demands an appreciation for, and an understanding of, that period's poetry. For those who read Japanese, Chinese,[1] and now English, there is perhaps no better way to begin than with this study which, after twenty-five years, is still the best, indeed the only, concise introduction to its subject in any language.

This is not to say that *Five Hundred Years of Chinese Poetry, 1150–1650* should be read solely for its historical rather than its literary insights. To the contrary, although he was a brilliant and deeply learned student of Chinese literature, as a historian Yoshikawa Kōjirō sometimes left a good deal to be desired. For example, throughout this book which, it should be emphasized, was intended not for specialists but rather for the educated *general* reader in Japan, Yoshikawa argues that many of the most important poets of the Chin, Yuan, and Ming dynasties were *shimin* (*shih-min* in Chinese), a term which Professor Wixted translates, quite reasonably, as "townsmen." Thus we read statements like the following:

> Although the system of inheriting position by birth existed to some degree through T'ang times, it had disappeared by the Sung. The officials of later

---

[1] As Professor Wixted indicates in the Translator's Preface, there is a Chinese translation of *Gen Min shi gaisetsu* by Cheng Ch'ing-mao.

dynasties were ordinary townsmen who gained their position in government not through family status but by individual ability. As a result, their lives were never completely cut off . . . from the lives of ordinary townsmen. This being the case, officials of townsman origins frequently became the leaders of townsman poetry, which in turn helped stimulate a further increase in the number of townsman poets.

Here Yoshikawa clearly is drawing on the important work of Naitō Konan and perhaps that of Miyazaki Ichisada and others, but at times his use of the term *shimin* is so vague as to render it almost meaningless. For example, is it really useful to argue that Chu Hsi's version of Neo-Confucianism became "the philosophy of life for the townsmen of the [late imperial] period," that Su Shih (1037–1101), Yang Wei-chen (1296–1370), and Wang Shih-chen (1526–1590) all had "townsman origins," or that Kao Ch'i's brilliant and original work "marks the culmination of a century and a half of the tradition of townsman poetry"? That urban developments in China during the late imperial period were of great importance both culturally and economically cannot be denied, but one wonders to what extent Yoshikawa's deep interest in what might be called the "townsman culture" (*chōnin no bunka*) of Tokugawa Japan (1603–1867), an interest that is revealed (among other places) in the footnotes to this work, colored his understanding of Chinese social, intellectual, and cultural history. To what extent, in other words, did Yoshikawa see Soochow or Sung-chiang during the Yuan and Ming periods as the precursor to eighteenth-century Kyoto or Osaka?

Nor are Yoshikawa's comments on Chinese political history always sufficiently detailed or convincing. For example, is it possible to accept Yoshikawa's confident assertion that, except for the T'u-mu Incident of 1449 and the *wo-k'ou* raids of the 1550s, the "internal peace [of fifteenth- and sixteenth-century China] was scarcely disturbed"? Similarly, given the vast amount of reform literature that was produced in China during the 1620s and 1630s, some of it by writers discussed by Yoshikawa, does it make sense for him to say that "there was little sense of urgency among Ming subjects that a crisis impended until the Ch'ung-chen emperor committed suicide"?

In Professor Yoshikawa's defense, it must be reiterated that he was a student of Chinese literature; he was not particularly interested in political history. A case in point is his disappointing and hurried sweep through the last fifty years of Ming poetry, a period during which many of the period's finest poets were deeply involved in political and even military activities. For some reason Yoshikawa does not seem to want to explore this last fact in any depth. For this and other reasons, then, it probably would be advisable for those who are not familiar with the history of late imperial China to read *Five Hundred Years of Chinese Poetry, 1150–1650* in conjunction with other works that would help to provide a more realistic and detailed political context. In addition to the works mentioned by Professor Wixted in his supplementary notes to the text, the following books might be useful in this regard: John W. Dardess, *Confucianism and Autocracy: Professional Elites in the Founding of the Ming Dynasty* (Berkeley: University of California Press, 1983); idem, *Conquerors and Confucians: Aspects of Political Change in Late Yuan China* (New York: Columbia University Press, 1973); William Theodore de Bary, ed., *Self and Society in Ming Thought* (New York: Columbia University Press, 1970); idem et al., eds., *The Unfolding of Neo-Confucianism* (New York: Columbia University Press, 1975); Edward L. Dreyer, *Early Ming China* (Stanford: Stanford University Press, 1982); Edward L. Farmer, *Early Ming Government: The Evolution of Dual Capitals* (Cambridge, Mass.: Harvard University Press, 1976); Charles O. Hucker, *The Censorial System of Ming China* (Stanford: Stanford University Press, 1966); idem, ed., *Chinese Government in Ming Times: Seven Studies* (New York: Columbia University Press, 1969); idem, *The Ming Dynasty: Its Origins and Evolving Institutions* (Ann Arbor: Center for Chinese Studies, University of Michigan, 1978); Willard J. Peterson, *Bitter Gourd: Fang I-chih and the Impetus for Intellectual Change* (New Haven: Yale University Press, 1979); and Frederic Wakeman, Jr., *The Great Enterprise: The Manchu Reconstruction of Imperial Order in Seventeenth-Century China* (Berkeley: University of California Press, 1985). Aside from the *Dictionary of Ming Biography, 1368–1644* edited by L. Carrington Goodrich and Fang Chaoying, which Professor Wixted has noted and which contains biographies of many of the poets discussed by Yoshikawa, probably the single most useful Western-language reference work for much of the period covered here will be F. W. Mote and Denis Twitchett, eds., *The Cambridge History of China, Volume 7: The Ming Dynasty, 1368–1644, Part 1* (Cambridge: Cambridge University Press, 1988).

Given some of the shortcomings of *Five Hundred Years of Chinese Poetry, 1150–1650* mentioned above, how will those who are not students of Chinese literature benefit by reading it? First of all, they will encounter many wonderful poems (in excellent translations by Professor Wixted) by some of the most important intellectual and political leaders of the period. Different readers will have their own favorites, but I was particularly taken with Yuan Hao-wen's "With Chang Hung-lueh, Court Attendant, Discussing Literature," which is translated on pp. 40–41, with Liu Chi's poem on the striking contrasts between rural and urban life in fourteenth-century Chiang-nan on p. 116, and with Yang Hsun-chi's revealing poem on his struggle to become educated on p. 131. As the authors of these verses no doubt intended and would have hoped, all three of their poems (and many others in the book) have both historical *and* literary value.

I would also call the reader's attention to Professor Yoshikawa's account of the formation of "poetry clubs" or "societies" (*shih she* or *yin-shih she*) and the compilation of poetry manuals in China during the late thirteenth and early fourteenth centuries (see chapter 3, "Poetry of Ordinary Townsmen," and chapter 4, "Two Developments Come to Fruition" and "Yang Wei-chen"). For those who have been concerned, as this writer has, with the literary, educational, political, and even the social activities of late Ming "scholarly societies" (*wen she*) such as the Restoration Society (*Fu she*) and the Seeds (i.e., Incipient Awareness) Society (*Chi she*), there is much of historical and comparative interest here.

Nor should students of Ming history overlook Professor Yoshikawa's important discussion of the so-called Old Phraseology (*Ku-wen-tz'u*) movement in chapter 7. Although it can (and undoubtedly will) be argued that Yoshikawa has overstated the importance of that "movement" for Ming literary history (here one again wonders how much his interest in Japanese developments, and particularly in the literary ideas of Ogyū Sorai [1666–1728], has affected his views), Old Phraseology proponents did have enormous influence in the late Ming cultural world. Moreover, although Yoshikawa characteristically does not emphasize the point, that influence extended to the realm of political thought. For example, important figures in late Ming "statecraft" (*ching-shih*) scholarship such as Chang P'u (1602–1641) and Ch'en Tzu-lung (1608–1647), both of whom are mentioned briefly in chapter 8, championed Old Phraseology in part because they believed that many of their contemporaries had come to rely too heavily on easy-to-read but often inaccurate commentaries on the classics and other early works. Chang, Ch'en, and their friends saw this as unfortunate, not because they were devoted to deciphering obscure ancient texts for their own sake, but because they believed that many of those texts (but not necessarily the commentaries) contained practical information that could be used to solve contemporary problems.

As in other scholarly fields, then, a comprehensive understanding of late Ming political thought demands an appreciation of Ming literature and a familiarity with Chinese literary theory. And although Yoshikawa Kōjirō undoubtedly would not approve of all the ways his *Five Hundred Years of Chinese Poetry, 1150–1650* is likely to be put to use by historians and others, he too would have applauded the idea that in traditional

China at least, literature and history were inseparable. Indeed, as he wrote in the opening chapter of this work:

> Poetry was a literary form having an ancient tradition, and the writing of poetry carried with it a consciousness of being the guardian of tradition. But at the same time poetry was also the literary form that expressed most faithfully both the new emotions springing up spontaneously from within the people over succeeding ages and their reactions to new realities they were daily confronting.

# Index

**DATE DUE**

|  |  |  |  |
|--|--|--|--|
|  |  |  |  |
|  |  |  |  |
|  |  |  |  |
|  |  |  |  |
|  |  |  |  |
|  |  |  |  |
|  |  |  |  |
|  |  |  |  |
|  |  |  |  |
|  |  |  |  |